THE
ARIAN WITNESS

THE ARIAN WITNESS:

OR

THE TESTIMONY OF ARIAN SCRIPTURES IN CORROBORATION OF BIBLICAL HISTORY AND THE RUDIMENTS OF

CHRISTIAN DOCTRINE.

INCLUDING DISSERTATIONS ON THE ORIGINAL HOME AND EARLY ADVENTURES OF

INDO-ARIANS,

BY THE

REV. K. M. BANERJEA

GYAN

Published by

Gyan Publishing House
5, Ansari Road
Daryaganj, New Delhi-110002
Phone: 011-47034999, 9811692060
E-mail: books@gyanbooks.com

Distribution Network
gyanbooks.com
India, USA, Canada, UK, Australia, France

ISBN: 978-81-212-7931-4 (PB)
First Published, 1875

2nd Impression 2023

Printed at: Gyan Press, Delhi.

THE ARIAN WITNESS
Author: K. M. BANERJEA

THE

ARIAN WITNESS:

OR

THE TESTIMONY OF ARIAN SCRIPTURES IN CORROBORATION OF BIBLICAL HISTORY AND THE RUDIMENTS

OF

CHRISTIAN DOCTRINE.

INCLUDING DISSERTATIONS ON THE ORIGINAL HOME AND EARLY ADVENTURES OF

INDO-ARIANS,

BY THE

REV. K. M. BANERJEA,

MEMBER OF THE BOARD OF EXAMINERS, (LATE COLLEGE OF FORT WILLIAM,)
HONORARY EXAMINING CHAPLAIN OF THE LORD BISHOP OF CALCUTTA,
HONORARY MEMBER OF THE ROYAL ASIATIC SOCIETY OF LONDON.

CALCUTTA:

THACKER, SPINK & CO.

LONDON:—TRÜBNER AND CO., 57 AND 59, LUDGATE HILL,

1875.

He appears there as the fiercest of the goddess's enemies, receiving his death wounds at her hands. In the Rig Veda, however, the gods themselves are, all of them, termed and accosted as *asuras*, and one of them, introduced at the moment as the Creator of the Universe, is called the *all-knowing and wise Asura.* And yet the same Veda elsewhere gives an opposite picture of the character indicated by the term, corresponding to the modern ideal of a demon and an ogre, and the very same individuals are sometimes represented as *asuras*, and again lauded as *destroyers of asuras*.

The commentator Sáyanácharia felt no difficulty in interpreting the term, where it occurred in the demoniacal sense. In truth, it required no elaborate interpretation *there*. In that sense the word would be familiar even to a child. But the commentator's ingenuity was severely taxed when he had to interpret "asura" as a term applicable to the gods. He had to fabricate novel derivations and etymologies, too often revolting to common sense. In one case "Agni" was found burdened with the title "Ásura," (आसुर, a patronymic from Asura) and the commentator, deriving it from *Asura*, interpreted it as a *destroyer of asuras*, the relation, he said, was in that place that of a *destroyer and his victim!* The grammatical logic, here propounded, might have justified the application of the surname "Bonapartist" to the hero of Waterloo, by whom Napoleon was ruined.

Elsewhere, again, the commentator adopted a derivation of the term (as applicable to *gods*) which the cautious Professor Wilson himself called, "an unusual sense of the word," adding, however, "but it would scarcely be decorous *to call Varuna an Asura.*"[1] An unusual derivation might be excused in the case of an extraordinary term, *hapax legomenon.* But "asura" is is a term constantly to be found in the Rig Veda, and *oftener* in a divine than a diabolical sense. Here then was the difficulty. Unless we allowed the interpretation of the Rig Veda to receive light from sources outside the limits of India, we must accept an unpleasant position between the two horns of a dilemma. We must either submit to unnatural derivations and unusual interpretations *as a rule,* or confound the Indo-Arian gods with the Indo-Arian demons.

For himself, the author fails to understand why scholars who had themselves broached or admitted the foreign origin of Indo-Arians, on the other side of the Indus, should be shy of allowing Indo-Arian documents or legends to be interpreted with trans-Indus

---

[1] Wilson's translation of the Rig Veda, vol. i. p. 64.

light. Would it have been fair criticism in England to restrict the interpretation of an old Anglo-Saxon document to ideals purely Druidical and insular, to the jealous exclusion of all light from the continent of Europe? In the case of the word Asura, we find that Varuna, held for the moment as the framer of the heavens and earth, is called "the all-knowing Asura." Is it fair criticism to fall back on "the unusual sense of the word" suggested by Sáyana to the exclusion of the obvious inference that the title appears as a translation of the Iranian term "Ahura-Mazda," applied to the Supreme Being, with which Indo-Arians must have been familiar before they crossed the Indus? The interpretation of the Iranian title is, according to Parsee doctors, "the wise Lord."[a] This itself supplies a clue to the meaning of Asura as generally applied to the gods in the Rig Veda. And in the case of Agni, the patronymic "Ásura" was obviously owing to his being so called (Ahurine) in the Zend Avesta, as the son of Ahura Mazda. The Rig Veda itself seems to recognize this filiation by representing Agni as *the son of Power*.

But this is only a solution of a part of the problem. The same term is again used in an opposite sense.

---

[a] See p. 116 *infra*.

And this reflection suggested the question of the origin of the Iranian word "ahura" for *lord*. "Assur" is often found in the Holy Scriptures in the ethnical sense of *Assyrian*. Here the author was led to consult the Cuneiform inscriptions for confirmation of that idea. The Inscriptions fully explained the difficulty. "Assur" or "Asur" was there found both as an ethnic term, expressive of the Assyrian nation and country, and also as a term of dignity and sanctity applicable to princes and gods. On the one hand it was used as a term of distinction for kings, generals, and towns,[3] and on the other it was the title of the "great deities." It was in the first ethnic sense that the Rig Veda execrated it as the title of a hated nation after the Arian settlement in India, but in the second sense of dignity and sanctity both Iranians and Indo-Arians had of old alike

---

[3] Many kings and chief officers had the term "Assur" prefixed or affixed to their names as a symbol of dignity. In the list of kings given at the end of Mr. George Smith's *Assyrian discoveries* (p. 445) there are numbers of namee with that prefix or affix, such as Assur-Zakiresir, Ninip-tugul-assuri, Assur-nadin-ahi, Assur-nirari, Assur-bel-nisinu, &c. Tiglathpileser II. says of an officer, "My general Assur-dain-ani." Also; "A palace, a seat of my royalty within it I placed, Kar-Assur its name I called." Again, "In Ulluba, a city I built, Assur-basa its name I called. Smith's *Assyrian discoveries*, pp. 267, 271, 272. The last mentioned name is a curious linguistic proof of relations between Assyrians and Indo-Arians. It is a pure Sanscrit term.—Assur-basa (আসুর বাস) *the residence of Asuras.*

attached it to their respective deities, though the Indians afterwards gradually dropped its use in the sacred sense, and applied it exclusively to the abhorrent idea of ungodly ogres and demons. The Rig Veda as their earliest record continues a witness of both senses, but the later Vedas and all subsequent *sastras* give exclusively the odious sense of evil spirits, hostile to gods and Brahmins, and inimical to their long-cherished institution of Sacrificial ceremonies.

The light thus thrown on the solution of a long debated question stimulated the author to make further inquiry into the Cuneiform records of Assyria. If the "Asuras" were Assyrians, then some further light might naturally be expected from the same source on events with which *Asuras* were connected. The suggestion received curious confirmation from "Sanda," long known in Indian tradition as the *guru* of Asuras. The Rig Veda recognizes the same name in a sense which might be applicable to a *guru* as well as a god. Now Sanda is found to have been an Assyrian god, or the man-bull. And Sanda in Sanscrit also means a bull.[4]

The Cuneiform Inscriptions, again, disclosed ano-

---

[4] See p. 75, *infra*.

ther name Anu, as among the gods of Assyria. Anu is also found as a Vedic character, whom a Pouranic Legend describes as the parent of Mlecchas or aliens. We also find the A'navas, sons or followers of Anu, engaged in action with other characters that are referable to Assyrian regions. These facts raised a presumption that the Anu of the Veda was identical with the Anu of the Inscriptions. This remark is applicable to another individual named "Turvasu," a brother of Anu. Indian records styled him the father of "Yavanas," who were also aliens from Brahminical society. The Inscriptions supply us with a king Tubusu[5] and a town Tarvazu.[6]

The story of the Asura Vritra slain by Indra is a further link which connects Assyrian with Indian legends. In the Rig Veda that arch enemy of the Arians is identified with the Serpent Ahi and styled a Dása (destroyer). Vritra seems therefore identical with "the snake Dahaka" of the Zend Avesta. And it was in Bawri (Babylon) that "the snake Dahaka," alias Vritra, appears before Ardvi-sura (a sacred character of the Zend Avesta) and asks as a boon that he might destroy the whole of Ariana. Vritra was therefore an Assyrian combatant, by overthrowing whom Indra entitled himself to the thanks

---

[5] See p. 73 *infra*. [6] *Smith's Assyrian Discoveries*, p. 255.

of the Iranians (who worshipped him as Verethraghna) as well as of the Indo-Arians.

The author must here acknowledge and correct a mistake incautiously committed in the *Introductory Essay* prefixed to his edition of a small portion of the Rig Veda published a few months ago. Adverting to "Kustaspi" of the Cuneiform Inscriptions, as possibly the same character as the Vistaspa of the Zend Avesta and Ishtaswa of the Rig Veda, he took Kustaspi to be a contemporary of Tiglath-pileser I. This was a mistake. The name of Kustaspi occurs in the Inscriptions of Tiglath-pileser II. The synchronism attempted to be made out between the senior Tiglath-pileser and the Rig Veda does of course lose its ground as far as it was based on the error now corrected. But the synchronism itself does not absolutely fail. Its second ground founded on the story of "Sambara the son Kulitara" remains firm.

Nor is the theory of Zoroasterian teaching, having proceeded from Assyria, nullified by the failure of the ground about Kustaspi of the Cuneiform Inscriptions. It is expressly said in the Zend Avesta that Ardisura received in Bawri or Babylon the supplications of both friends and foes, complying with the former but rejecting the latter. And the very name *Ahura* Mazda was derived from "Asur", the Assyrian term for god or lord.

With reference to the theological part of the book, the author is content to leave it to speak for itself. He has hitherto abstained from a hortatory tone. A clergyman may be excused for one word of advice on taking leave of his readers. The Vedas persistently proclaim a mysterious fact—*the Lord of the creation offered himself a sacrifice for the benefit of gods*, or those who were once mortal, such as we are, but had since been promoted to celestial regions. The same Lord, "the giver of self," also initiated the rites of Sacrifice, which is a "reflection" of Himself. Can the intelligent Hindu, so acute, so quick in all other respects, fail to see how the most ancient and revered of his national records thus acknowledge and bear testimony to the fundamental principles of the Faith of which the Sovereign of the empire is herself by her royal title "the Defender?" Is it too much to say that where the persuasions of our primitive ancestors thus concur with the rudiments of that Faith, piety to God, and loyalty to the Crown, allegiance to Truth, and Reverence for our Fathers, all combine to stimulate inquiry into the mystery suggested by the self-sacrifice of Prajapati, "whose shadow, whose death is immortality itself?"

Ballygunge, 15*th December*, 1875.

CONTENTS.

CHAPTER III.

CHAPTER IV.

CHAPTER V.

Page

CHAPTER VI.

CHAPTER VII.

CHAPTER VIII.

THE ARIAN WITNESS.

INTRODUCTION.

The Christian scheme of salvation is thus epitomized by St. Paul: "Now therefore ye are no more strangers and foreigners, but fellow-citizens with the saints, and of the household of God; and are built upon the foundation of the Apostles and Prophets, Jesus Christ himself being the chief corner stone." (Ephes. ii. 19, 20). This household is a "kingdom," and it is a "kingdom prepared from the foundation of the world." (Matthew xxv. 34). It has also a roll or register in which all its members are noted down, the roll being otherwise called "the book of life of the Lamb slain from the foundation of the world." (Rev. xiii. 8). And this discloses that inscrutable ruling of our Creator and Supreme Governor that "without shedding of blood is no remission." (Heb. ix. 22.)

This rule or law is above human logic. Into the policy of Heavenly jurisprudence, it would be a presumption to pry. The finite can never grasp the Infinite, or examine it like a *berry in the hand.*[1] Once satisfied, that it is God's will and God's decree, and

[1] हस्तामलक An Indian idiom.

that it meets a human difficulty and solves a spiritual problem, man's duty is to accept the solution.

To inquire into the *fact* of His decree and His declaration is only the exercise of a prerogative which has been vested in the human mind by the Author of our being. It is both a privilege and a duty, to examine the evidence of the fact, but the fact being found, and the decree being authenticated, that "the LORD has laid on him the iniquity of us all," and that "with his stripes we are healed," we must remember that a decree is intended for obedience and guidance, not for wrangling and disputation.

Such is the Christian scheme. It has for its cornerstone the Sacrifice of the Lamb slain from the foundation of the world. It involves the inscrutable law of Infinite Wisdom and Heavenly Counsel that without shedding of blood there is no remission. It was available for human salvation from the moment that it had become necessary for it. The principles of Adam's religion, in the primitive age, were thus the same as ours, now in the fulness of time. Reference was made to it on the Fall of our first parents, and the introduction of sin. The seed of the woman (Gen. iii. 15) was no other than the Lamb slain from the foundation of the world. His sacrifice, though accomplished in time, was commemorated and typified from the beginning. The primeval institution of Sacrifices is evident from the practice of Abel, who "by faith offered a more excellent sacrifice than Cain, by which he obtained witness that he was righteous, God testifying of his gifts: and by it, he, being dead, yet speaketh." (Heb. xi. 4). The same was again typified in the offerings which Noah presented on the altar he had builded, and they met with the same result of God's acceptance, for we are told, "the Lord smelt a sweet savour" (Gen. viii. 21). The identical practice under a similar persuasion we notice in the time of Job, who offered burnt-offerings "continually," saying, "It may be that my sons have sinned and cursed God in their hearts." (Job i. 5). These are indisputable facts. They manifest the way in which pious souls betook themselves to "the Lamb of God which taketh away the sin of the world."[2] They indicate the hopes which inspired those "that looked for redemption in Israel."[3]

We may fairly presume from these recorded instances of Abel's, Noah's, and Job's offerings that they were consequent on the institution of such sacrifices from the beginning under divine direction, at once commemorative, and prefigurative, of the great Sacrifice of "the Lamb slain from the foundation of the world." Noah was not many generations distant from Adam, and he could have introduced and kept up in the postdiluvian world what he knew to have been ordained before the deluge. Speaking now from the Christian point of view, we can reasonably conclude that the sacrifices, acceptably offered by the patriarchs we have named, were typical of the Great Sacrifice accomplished on Mount Calvary which they foreshadowed. For "other foundation can no man lay than that is

---

[2] John i. 29. [3] Luke ii. 38.

laid, which is Jesus Christ."[4] Nor is it possible "that the blood of bulls and of goats should take away sins,"[5] in any age or country. It was, to use and adapt a Vedic expression, only a *fore-shadowing of the truly Saving Sacrifice.*[6]

Assuming, then, that the offering of Sacrifices was a recognized institution from the very days of Noah in the post-diluvian world, it might be reasonably expected that the practice would not immediately die away. If Noah and Job knew what they were about, and performed the offerings with the solemnity of religious ceremonies, each would instruct his own children and grand children in what he would necessarily consider as the first and most important duty of the human race. The practice would thus be transmitted to their posterity as a binding divine institution. The institution would, doubtless, be maintained with the tenacity with which men usually keep up practices derived from their immediate superiors and forefathers, and never allow any to fall into desuetude without valid reasons. They would indeed be cherished as heir-looms out of respect for their parents, and nothing short of a mental or social revolution could account for their entire extinction. Such a revolution, again, might be expected to be a fact as notorious as that which originally caused the initiation of the practice which it overturned.

---

[4] 1 Cor. iii. 11.

[5] Heb. x. 4.

[6] यज्ञो वा अवति तस्य वा छाया क्रियते। *Tándia Mahá Bráhmana, vol. i, p.* 332 *in Bibliotheca Indica.*

The institution we are speaking of would *as a fact* be therefore capable of proof or disproof from the history of Noah's descendants, by which we mean the history of mankind. The perpetuation of the practice would be corroborative of the institution and of the principles which originated it, while its entire neglect, without a valid cause, would tend to damage the presumption of its divine origin. If the practice were found in vogue among mankind for countless generations, and never fallen into oblivion without such a counter movement as we have suggested, the fact would add no small weight to the reasons for which we have presumed its divine original. If, on the contrary, the practice were wholly lost sight of after the days of Noah, such an abrupt discontinuance must weaken those reasons.

We must here add that it is only the overt acts, the offerings and ceremonies, which, if true, we would expect to find in the history of mankind. The theology, or the doctrine involved, might be insensibly perverted, or even die away altogether, through ignorance or mental imbecility. In our own country, and before our own sight, we find many instances of the maintenance of festivals, epochs, and ceremonies, combined with total forgetfulness of the principles on which they were founded. We find the last day of Choitra still kept up as a festival, and publicly advertized as a holiday, under the name of the *Choit sankránti.* Probably not one in a thousand is aware of the meaning involved in the term—or of the fact of the sun's entrance into Aries, and the consequent contact of the ecliptic and the equator on that day, many centuries ago. The precession of the equinox has long antiquated the congruity of the festival on the day it is held, but it still continues as an inviolate practice, valuable to the historian, only as an unerring clue to the date when the present Indian Calendar was first formed.

We find again an era prevailing in Bengal observed in all business transactions in the vernacular, and respected even in courts of justice. The present is the year 1282 of that era, but there seems to be no authentic record of the event which initiated it. The era is still kept up, though the history of its origin has been forgotten. We can only guess that it is the continuance, on the principle of the Indian Calendar, of the *Hegira* which was probably imposed on Bengal, centuries ago, by some of the earlier Mahometan rulers, but the *solar* principle of the Indian calendar being essentially different from the Mahometan lunar principle, the Bengalee *san* has long ceased to be identical with the Hegira, though, perhaps, coincident with it at some point in its past course.

Tradition may keep up a practice or festival involving overt acts, but it is not adequate for the perpetuation of the doctrine or idea which originated the practice. The perpetuation of a ceremony by imitating one's father's practice, patent to the eye, is easier than the psychological process of rightly comprehending and correctly teaching the dogma or sentiment which initiated the ceremony.

But while ignorance or misconception of the doctrine or event involved in, or supposed to be commemorated by, a practice, perpetuated as a visible ceremony, detracts nothing from the corroborative evidence we have mentioned before, and is therefore no disproof of that doctrine, its actual transmission, along with the practice, even in a distorted form, adds considerable strength to that evidence. The institution of sacrifices was, as we have already asserted, typical of Him who "was once offered to bear the sins of many."[7] The continued prevalence of the practice among the families of men would itself be corroborative evidence of the original institution, and there could be no detraction from it, even if it appeared anywhere that it was maintained in ignorance of the doctrine it was intended to commemorate. For people might have perpetuated the visible ceremony without comprehending its psychological cause. But if we find in any place that, along with the perpetuation of the practice, there was a traditional teaching that the ceremony had the mysterious power of abolishing sin and depriving death of its terrors, the fact would add still greater force to our argument.

With these preliminary observations I now proceed to state the object aimed at in this Essay. It is, to borrow an expression from Milton:

> "That to the height of this great argument
> I may assert eternal Providence
> And justify the ways of God to men."

Men have not been wanting, to assail, as far as they could, the integrity of God's Truth, and es-

[7] Heb. ix. 28.

pecially that portion of it, which is indeed its chief corner-stone, the Sacrifice *of the Lamb of God which taketh away the sin of the world.* Their weapons of aggression have only been "theories, imperfect in their parts, and too often with hasty generalizations, but those settled results in which the body of philosophers agree," far from contradicting Scripture, "often confirm and illustrate the statements of the Inspired Volume."[8] The direct evidences, on which all teaching of God's Revelation rests, are in themselves quite sufficient for giving an intelligent "reason for the faith" that is in us, as against high-sounding cavils. The palpable and unmistakeable tendency of infidelity, especially in a mixed community such as is found in India, to overturn the moral basis on which society is founded, and by virtue whereof it maintains its sacred institutions for the public weal, is also sufficient in itself to serve as a beacon and warning, which can only endear the doctrine of the Cross to all lovers of purity and order, and impel them to cling to their "Rock" of defence with greater tenacity than ever before. It is to corroborate the above evidence, and to strengthen the preventive force of the above beacon, that the present work is undertaken.

We shall not anticipate our "Arian Witness" here, but we shall give a brief abstract of what we expect him to say when produced before the bar of a Truth-loving conscience. While we look for many things in his evidence calculated to moderate the infidelity of

[8] Pratt's Scripture and Science not at variance, p. 371.

the times, generally, his voice will be entitled to especial deference among those in our own country who profess a religious veneration for antiquity and the *old paths*, and make a parade of their *Sanátan Dharma.* He will depose to the non-existence of caste in the primitive state of Brahminism, when the very idea of the present religious or social distinctions would have been stigmatized as revolutionary—as a sort of "*nova res.*" He will tell us that the "Lord, or rather the *Preserver*, of the Creation"[9] offered himself a Sacrifice for the welfare of souls, that were born as "mortals," but had attained to immortality in heaven by religious exercises duly performed on the earth, somewhat corresponding to our idea of "the spirits of just men made perfect."[10] We shall hear from him that "Sacrifice" was the authorized means for the remission of sins—that it was the way by which "Devas," who were originally but "men," had passed to celestial bliss, and that it still continues the beaten track for the same goal. The idea of the seed of the woman bruising the serpent's head was also known to him with more or less of distinctness. He knew of "the great Dragon" "that old serpent, called the Devil and Satan"[11] whose subjugation and destruction has always been the great struggle of life with God-fearing men. He will strikingly confirm the Mosaic account of the Creation, and will likewise speak of various traditions

---

[9] प्रजापति Sayana almost invariably derives पति from पा *to preserve*, and interprets it accordingly.

[10] Heb. xii. 23.

[11] Rev. xii. 9.

tending to corroborate some of the very points in Sacred history on which men in modern times have most frequently made shipwreck of their faith.

We look to our Witness also for the disproof of an idea often broached against Hindoo Christians that they are rebels against the *sanátana dharma* of the country, and apostates from the faith that has animated the Hindoo mind, and the rule of life that has governed Hindoo practice, from time immemorial. This essay aspires likewise to the patriotic honor of proving that while all Hindoos who have been instructed in Western literature, science, and history have departed from the faith derived from their immediate forefathers, Hindoo Christians can alone have the satisfaction of knowing that the fundamental principles of the Gospel were recognized, and acknowledged, both in theory and practice, by their primitive ancestors, the Brahminical Arians of India, and that if the authors of the Vedas could by any possibility now return to the world, they would at once recognize the Indian Christians, far more complacently as their own descendants, than any other body of educated natives. It may indeed be confidently asserted that such of our countrymen as have imbibed, along with the history and science of Europe, the sentiments of western infidelity, can, from the ancient Arian point of view, be described in no better light than those who were stigmatized in olden days as revilers of the Vedas,[12] neglecters of sacri-

[12] वेदनिन्दकाः So Manu calls contemners of the Veda. It must be remembered that "Veda," as an abstract term, often stands for *the Word* or *Revelation*. This will be discussed in the sequel.

fices,[13] and as men of no religion whatsoever. Resuscitated Rishis (if the idea of the possibility can be conceived for argument's sake) would find "the orthodox" Hindoo himself the greatest foe to the system they had bequeathed to their descendants.[14] We do not say this censoriously. We only speak in self-defence, because WE are often singled out and proscribed as

---

[13] Neglecters or opposers of sacrifice are considered outlaws and traitors, and are classed with persons that do not deserve the name of men:

> धनोरधि विषुणक्ते व्यायन्नयज्वानः सनकाः प्रेतिमीयुः
> पराचिच्छीर्षा ववृजुस्त इन्द्रायज्वानो यज्वभिः स्पर्धमानाः
> प्र यद्दिवो हरिवः स्थातरुग्र निरव्रताँ अधमो रोदस्योः ।
> अन्यव्रतममानुषमयज्वानमदेवयुं
> अव स्वः सखा दुधुवीत पर्वतः सुघ्नाय दस्युं पर्वतः

Rig Veda, I. 33, 4, 5 viii. 70. 11.

The Vedas are full of such denunciations in numerous places.

[14] The learned and highly accomplished author of the Antiquities of Orissa, deservedly honoured as an authority by all orthodox Hindoos, himself remarks:

"At a time when the rituals of the Vedic worship deluged the country with the blood of thousands of animals slaughtered in the name of God, the universal benevolence of Sakya appealed to the feeling of the people with a force and directness of purpose, which proved irresistible. No man, who had seen a dozen heads of cattle killed by spikes driven into their chests, the usual mode of sacrifice at the time, could for a moment deny the superiority of a religion which preached mercy for all created beings, and absolutely prohibited slaughter of every kind. But the Brahmins were not slow in perceiving their weak points; they soon dropped the sacrifices of the Vedas; inculcated universal love and kindness even in the words of their rivals; &c."—*Antiquities of Orissa, by Baboo Rájendra Lála Mitra.*

"*outlaws,*" *and rebels* against Brahminism. If we are so, we seem to be in good company.

In presenting the corroborative testimony of the Arian family to Biblical facts and principles, we shall labour in the first place to manifest the competence of our witness to speak on those subjects from his familiarity with the times and places to which they relate. We hope to show that from his age and original settlement, he would naturally know something of all facts and principles which were likely to be known in Palestine and its neighbourhood.

It will be no argument against us to refer to the Arian's want of consistency in his evidence. We do not profess to produce his testimony as that of a friendly witness. We do not set him up as a select witness for ourselves, remarkable for his consistency or harmony of principles. Much less do we attach to him any. authority. Our sole argument is, that his statements and ideas, whatever they be, may have to be accounted for as *facts*, and that, howsoever they may be accounted for, they will be found corroborative of the principles and events which underlie the gospel dispensation.

THE ARIAN WITNESS.

CHAPTER I.

The original settlement of the Arians—the Caspians and Kasiapas.

In presenting our contemplated *Arian Evidence,* we shall follow the well-known Indian method of inquiring into a Witness's *name, pedigree, home, age,* and his relation to the subject on which his testimony is proposed to be recorded. The first four questions in our present case, we shall consolidate into one—the question of the Witness's *original settlement,* which will itself involve the discussion of the other points. This will probably detain us somewhat longer than might be anticipated at first sight. Many eminent scholars have fixed his primitive seat in the vicinity of the Hindoo Kush. With this conclusion we have never been satisfied. To us it seems there is a mixture of an anachronism and a *non-sequitur* lurking in their argument. The name "Airyana Vaejo" of the Zend Avesta they refer to Manu's "Ariavarta." The one, according to its own authorized interpreters, is an *un-*

geographical place,[1] the other is definitely placed between the Vindhya and Himalayan ranges. But, irrespective of the confusion of sites involved in this reference, Manu lived more than a thousand years *after* the Arians' entrance into India. He must have contemplated his ancestors' *Indian* residence, when he named it "Ariavarta." If he had any idea of their emigration from the other side of the Indus, he could not have identified the Indian Ariavarta with their home in Central Asia. *Ariavarta* or *Ariadesa*, is a term which was unknown before the age of Manu. The Rig Veda is altogether ignorant of it.

We shall therefore have to re-open the whole question and review every point connected with it. This will necessarily postpone for awhile the principal inquiry indicated by the title we have chosen for our work, but we hope this prolonged investigation

---

[1] Bunsen (cited by Bleeck vol i, p. 9) thus annotates on "Airyana Vaejo."

"The name of the first country is Airyanem Vaejo. By this is to be understood the original Arian home, the paradise of the Iranians. The ruler of this happy land was King Jima, the renowned Jemshid of Iranian legend. Ahura-Mazda and Zarathustra here adore the celestial source of water, the Ardvî çûrâ anâhitâ (It. 5, 17, 104). Here Zarathustra prays to the Drvâçpâ (the patroness of horses, It. 9, 25) and to Ashi (17, 245). Thus Airyana Vaêjô becomes altogether a mythical country, the seat of gods and heroes where there is neither sickness nor death, frost nor heat, as is the case in the realm of Jima. In the chapter before us, however, we may still discover the historical background."

We do not deny there may be a "historical background," but this we shall discuss in a future chapter.

of the preliminary question will not be irrelevant as far as our main object is concerned, and our undertaking will perhaps in the end escape the charge of a *misnomer*.

Strabo cites Eratosthenes who gives the boundaries of Ariana to be the river Indus in the East, "the great sea" in the South, the Paropamisus and the further mountain range up to "the Caspian gates" in the North, and the same line in the West which separates Parthia from Media, Karmania from Paraetacene and Persia. Strabo himself, however, appears somewhat indistinct. Considering that India, which, long before his time, had become the most important of Arian countries, was ignored in the East, and that Media which, as we shall see afterwards, was the original seat of the Arian family, was excluded in the West, the word Ariana used by the geographer must have been meant distinctively for Irania or "*Iran*," though Persia itself seems to have been put out of the enclosure. Aria, as noticed by Arrian, was of itself not so extensive, and there must have been some confusion in the terminal lines given. On the whole we believe that the Greek geographer intended to give the Iranian territory of the time under the name of Ariana.

The omission of India will not, however, affect the present inquiry after the *original* home of the Arians, which must, in any case, have been outside the limits of India. The boundaries given by Eratosthenes may be regarded as the limits of the Iranian influence, as the author conceived it, in his own age. Media had probably then ceased to be reckoned Arian, and the immigration to India was evidently unnoticed and unthought of by Greek writers.

Before proceeding further, we feel it right to make a few observations suggested by the "Caspian gates" as among the boundaries of the Ariana of Eratosthenes. The Caspii, though living on the borders of Ariana, and otherwise an insignificant people, were, however, an integral portion of the Arian Family. In their primitive state, they could scarcely have been absolutely an unimportant nation, when they gave the name, with almost universal assent, to the great inland sea of Asia. Herodotus groups them twice in the satrapies of Darius, once with the Pausicæ, the Pantimathi, and the Daritæ in the eleventh,[2] and again with the Sacans in the fifteenth.[3] Some learned critics were puzzled at this double grouping, and had suspected the correctness of the reading in reference to the latter satrapy. The Caspii of the eleventh group they had no difficulty in referring to the people after whom the Caspian Sea was called. Those of the fifteenth satrapy, however, they conjectured to have been either the Casii or the Caspeiri, albeit both were people far too remote from the Persian empire, and from the nation with whom they were classed in the 15th satrapy, to justify the probability of the conjecture. Prof. Rawlinson considers the more Eastern Caspii as the original branch of the Arian stock, and the Westerns, who had given the name to the sea, as a colony from the Easterns. To

---

[2] Herod. iii. 92.   [3] Herod. iii. 93.

us, however, the reverse appears probable, as we shall afterwards see in due course.

That the Caspii were of the Arian stock appears from their very name. According to Pott (Etymologische Forschungen) that name is "derived from the Old Persian *'u* (which is the Sanskrit *su*, the Zend *hu*, and the Greek εὐ) "good," and *aςpa*, a "horse." Prof. Rawlinson, who cites the above in a note,[4] expresses a doubt whether in such a case a χ instead of a κ should not have been the initial of Caspii.

A χ might doubtless have been reasonably expected under the circumstances, for the κ, like the Latin *c*, is most frequently found to correspond to the Sanskrit palatial sibilant श ; but examples are not wanting of its answering to the dental sibilant स also. The word κήρυξ is derived from γῆρυς for "voice," which in Sanskrit is स्वर, and the word is often used in the Rig Veda in a *heraldic* sense, as in I. xviii. 1. And the Latin, *com* or *con* constantly stands for the Sanskrit *sam* or *san*.[5]

The substitution of a non-aspirated consonant for its corresponding aspirate is also frequently noticed among dialectic peculiarities in Greek, and therefore the absence of the aspirate in the word Caspii cannot vitiate the above etymology. We shall see presently that an aspirate *was* introduced in the name by certain parties.

---

[4] Rawlinson's Herod. iii., p. 447.

[5] As *completus* and सम्पूर्णः *contactus* and संस्पर्शः

A curious story, found in the Rig Veda, gives further confirmation to the above etymology, and points to a closer connexion of the Caspii with the Indian Arians. There is a certain similarity of sound between Caspia and Kasiapa, which by a *metathesis* may be considered as identical vocables. There is an Indian myth which makes Kasiapa, a progenitor of huge noxious animals[6], singularly corresponding to the classical myth about the Caspian Sea producing similar specimens of animal monstrosity. This, however, is a single coincidence of myths on which alone no historical reliance can be placed. But there is also an Indian Pauranic legend that Kasiapa was *the father of the sun*, and among synonyms of the solar luminary is a patronymic signifying a "son of Kasiapa."[7]

This patronymic is still used in ceremonial obeisances to the sun.[8] Now the Rig Veda relates an anecdote of a king, who was also *a father of the sun*, and his name

---

[6] Rajah Radhakant's *Sabda Kalpa druma*, summarizes various legends, and makes Kasiapa father of serpents by his wife Krodhavasá, of wild beasts by Saramá, of aquatic monsters by Timi, of nágas by Kadru. Diodorus Siculus attributes a similar prolific power to the Caspian Sea. "In that sea are said to be produced many serpents of immense size and fishes of all kinds widely differing in color from those of our country," xvii. 75.

[7] काश्यपस्य अपत्यमिति काश्यपेयः सूर्यः । काश्यपेयः सप्ताश्वो मिहिरः खग इति शब्दरत्नावली *Sabda-sakti-mahárnava.*

[8] जवाकुसुमसंकाशं काश्यपेयं महाद्युतिं ।
ध्वान्तारिं सर्वपापघ्नं प्रणतोस्मि दिवाकरं ॥

"I make obeisance to the maker of day, the great luminary, brilliant like the Hibiscus, the son of Kasiapa, the enemy of darkness, and the destroyer of all sin."

is, according to Pott, etymologically identical with Caspa. The Pauranic legend and the Vedic story may be fairly supposed to refer to the same individual as "father of the sun," and we shall now show how this consideration tends to confirm that etymology, and to connect Kasiapa with the Caspians.

The 15th mantra of the Rig Veda, I. 61, reads thus:

अस्मा इदु त्यदनुदाय्येषामेको यद्वव्ने भूरेरीशानः ।
प्रैतशं सूर्य्ये पस्पृधानं सौवश्व्ये सुष्विमावदिन्द्रः ॥

Rosen thus translates it:

"Illi utique istud compositum est horum *sacrificantium carmen*, quod *ille* elegit, unus multae *opulentiae* dominus: Etasam, cum Súrya, Suasvae filio, dimicantem, libamina parantem, adjuvit Indras."

Sayana's commentary on the same is to the following effect:

"The second hemistich refers to the following story. There was a king named Suaswa. He was desirous of having a son, and worshipped the sun with a view thereto. The sun himself became his son. With him a great Rishi named Etasa had a fight. That is here spoken of. This Indra, defying the sun who was the son of Suaswa, protected the Rishi of that name (Etasa), eminent for his libations of the soma."[9]

The word "Suaswa," the name of the above king,

---

[9] उत्तरार्द्धस्येयमाख्यायिका । स्वश्वो नाम कश्चिद्राजा । स च पुत्रकामः सूर्यमुपासांचक्रे । तस्य च सूर्य एव पुत्रो बभूव । तेन सहैतशनाम्न ऋषेर्युद्धं जातमिति तदेतदिहोच्यते । अयमिन्द्रः सौवश्व्ये स्वश्वपुत्रे पस्पृधानं स्पर्धमानं सुष्विं सोमानामभिषोतारमेतत्संज्ञकमृषिं प्रावत् प्रारक्षत ।

father of the sun, is compounded of "su," *good*, and "aswa," *horse*. The Zend *sp* is always represented in the Sanskrit by *sw*, as *vispa* and *viswa*, and "aspa" itself is well known to be synonymous with "aswa." "Su-aswa" is therefore equivalent to "Suaspa," and by eliminating the *u* and substituting *C* for *S* in Romanizing the name "Suaspa, father of the sun," we get "Caspa," or the same that Pott's Etymology gives us. If we add to this the legend of Kasiapa already mentioned, the two characters may be fairly identified, and we can need no further apology for connecting the Caspii, or if we may Arianize the word, the *Caspas*, with our ancient Rishi Kasiapa.

We may make bold to add that the Puranas appear to identify Kasiapa, still more circumstantially, with the Vedic character "Suaspa" or Kaspa. They relate the same story with reference to Kasiapa[10] which

---

10 तमुवाच हरिः प्रीतः कश्यपं धूतकल्मषं ।
वरं वरय भद्रं ते वरार्होऽसि मतो मम ॥
तच्छ्रुत्वा वचनं तस्य मारीचः कश्यपोऽब्रवीत् ।
पुत्रत्वं गच्छ भगवन्नदित्या मम चानघ ॥
भ्राता भव यवीयांस्त्वं शक्रस्यासुरसूदन ।
विरोचनस्य बलवान् बलिः पुत्रो महासुरः ॥
अवध्यः सर्वलोकानां सदेवासुररक्षसां ।
भविष्यति स शक्रश्च स्वराज्याच्चारयिष्यति ॥
त्रैलोक्येऽपहृते तेन विमुखे च शचीपतौ ।
अदित्याम् द्वादशादित्यः सम्भविष्यामि कश्यपात् ॥
मन्वन्तरे तु सम्प्राप्ते तथा वैवस्वते द्विजाः ।
वामनः कश्यपाद्विष्णुरादित्यां सम्बभूव ह ॥
त्रिभिः क्रमैरिमं लोकं जित्वा येन महात्मना ।
पुरन्दराय त्रैलोक्यं दत्तं निहतकण्टकं ॥

"Then Hari, gratified, spake to Kasiapa, whose taint of sin had been purged away: 'Ask a boon.' Hearing these words of his,

Sáyana relates about Suaspa—Vishnu being only substituted for the sun. This story, again, is connected with the subjugation of Bali, an "Asura" or Iranian, perhaps Assyrian, by means of three strides, thus extending Kasiapa's connection to the very neighbourhood of Caspia, where conflicts may be easily conceived to have taken place between "the devas," who were chiefs of the future emigrants to India, and "the Asuras" i. e. Iranian, or, more probably, Assyrian followers of Ahura Mazda.

It must be remembered that the Vedic word Bali is different from the ordinary Sanskrit "Balin," or Balí with a long *í*. And as the individual, indicated by it in the Satapatha Brahmana, is called an Asura, the mind is involuntarily led to the quarter where both those vocables are found like household

---

Kasiapa, son of Marichi, replied: Sinless lord, become the son of Aditi and myself. Slayer of the Asuras, become the younger brother of Indra." *Ramayana* (*Muir's Sanskrit Texts*, vol. iv. p. 116.

(Vishnu says to Narada) "The great Asura Bali, the strong son of Virochana, shall be indestructible by all beings, including gods, Asuras, and Raxasas. He shall oust Sakra (Indra) from his kingdom. When the three worlds have been taken by Bali, and the lord of Sachi (Indra) has been put to flight, I shall be born as the twelve Adityas, the son of Kasiapa and Aditi." *Mahábhárata Sántiparva.*

"So when the Vaiwasvata manvantara was arrived, Vishnu was born as a dwarf, the son of Aditi and Kasiapa. By this great being after he had conquered these worlds by three paces, the three worlds were given to Purandara (Indra), their enemy being destroyed." *Vishnu Purana* iii. *Wilson's translation* (Muir's Sanskrit texts, vol. iv. p. 118).

words. Barring pronouns and particles, no two words occur so often in the Cuneiform Inscriptions, as "Assur biliya," or "Assur bil-ya," *Assur my lord.*[11] "Bili" comes evidently from *Bel*, which is found in the Inscriptions in the varying senses of a *god*, a *king*, a *lord*. "Bali" may be easily compared with either, and clearly appears to be an Assyrian prince.

The "three strides" of Vishnu are noticed in the Rig Veda, in language which clearly points to the place whence the Arians commenced their migratory march to India, perhaps under the guidance of Vishnu himself. The Hymnist deprecates a return *to the quarter of the world from whence Vishnu made his start with his three strides.* "May the gods save us," says he, "from that place of the earth from whence Vishnu made his start! Thrice did he take a step."[12]

We thus find that an important branch of the Arian stock, noticed in the Vedas, and connected with, if not descended from, a patriarch of great Indian celebrity, lived on the south-western coasts of the great inland sea of Asia, called after their own name. The myth about Kasiapa or Caspa, being father of the sun, probably meant nothing more than that he had originated or patronized the worship, or peculiar glorification, of the solar luminary in Asia. Perhaps this was also the secret of the Indian *solar* dynasty of yore.

---

[11] Norris's Assyrian Dictionary pp. 20, 40, 45, 85, 95, 96, 138, 151, 154, 301, 424, 541, 589, 620, 695, 703.

[12] अतो देवा अवंतु नो यतो विष्णुर्विचक्रमे । पृथिव्याः सप्तधामभिः ॥
इदं विष्णुर्विचक्रमे त्रेधा निदधे पदं । समूढमस्य पांसुरे ॥

Rig Veda I. 1, 22.

There is in the book of Ezra a curious reference to the place "Casiphia," which the Vulgate and the Syriac versions had evidently identified with Caspia, each reading it *Chasphia.* "And I gathered them together to the river that runneth to Ahava; and there abode we in tents three days: ... And I sent them with commandment unto Iddo, the chief at the place Casiphia, and I told them what they should say unto Iddo, and to his brethren the Nethinims, at the place Casiphia, that they should bring unto us ministers for the house of our God." (Ezra viii. 15, 17.)

Many eminent authors have followed the same identification, but later scholars of equal or even greater weight have rejected that idea, because Caspia is not in the direct route from Babylon to Jerusalem. They have not, however, found any other place or river corresponding to those mentioned in Ezra. We do not know whether Ahava can be the same as the river Azaba of the Cuneiform inscriptions. (*Norris* p. 22.)

The argument for rejecting the identification suggested by the Vulgate and the Syriac versions is (1) that Ezra must have taken the direct route from Babylon to Jerusalem, and (2) that as he had reached Ahava in only nine days from Babylon (vii. 9, viii. 15, 31,) his halting stage must have been too far from Caspia to allow a deputation to have travelled to and fro within three days. There is doubtless great force in this argument, but we are still not quite satisfied that it is conclusive as against the above versions.

In the first place there is no absolute necessity for holding that Ezra went straightway to Jerusalem without any detour for picking up stragglers or persons who may have, by eluding the vigilance of guards, escaped from captivity, to places which might have been known to their own countrymen, though of course unknown to the officers of Babylon. The time that Ezra took in his journey to Jerusalem would probably allow such detours. The question of a journey from Babylon to Ahava, and of a deputation from thence to Caspia and back, within three days, is undoubtedly beset with almost insuperable difficulties. Ezra, however, was not in want of money and other resources for quick journeys, and we are not satisfied that in the mouth of a Jew the word Babylon could never have a wider sense than the hundred-gated city itself, especially as the record of the decree of Cyrus, which Artaxerxes renewed and which Ezra was going to enforce, was "found at Achmetha (Ecbatana) in the palace that is in the province of the Medes." (Ezra vi. 2). A "province of Babylon" is also mentioned in vii. 16.

But whether Casiphia stood for Caspia or not, whether its situation was nearer to Babylon than to the Caspian mountains, it is clear that the Vulgate and the Syriac identified it with Caspia, reading it Chasphia. This confirms Pott's etymology and supplies the desideratum of an aspirate felt by Professor Rawlinson. Supposing, however, that the identification is wrong, and that there was another place called "Casiphia" within a moderate distance from Babylon, the word thereby assimilates with our Kasiapa still more closely, and in either case we find two other expressions in the Scriptural narrative corroborative of our view of

Arian connexion, south-west of the Caspian. These are the original Hebrew words, (1) for "ministers," and (2) for the name of the chief himself, "Iddo." They seem to be both connected with Arian vocables. The word for "ministers," is *musharathim*. Radically it is "sharath," the "mu" and the "im" being respectively the verbal prefix, and the plural affix, of the Hebrew grammar. Now "sharath" is the same as the Zend "zarath" (the initial element in Zoroaster's own name), and the Sanskrit "jarata" or "jarita," constantly used in the sense of *a minister of the choral service* at the Altar.[15] The Septuagint renders Musharathim ᾄδοντας or "singers" for the house of God, and the Arabic version, (to use the words of its Latin translator) *lectores ad domum Dei nostri*. The Vulgate and the Syriac both render it "ministers." And the name for the chief "Iddo" is a remarkable expression here. The name itself, as represented in the Roman character, is not uncommon in Hebrew. But it is generally spelt with an initial *Ain*—once with a *Yod*, and once with a *Yod* followed by an *Ain*—and thrice with a terminal *Alif*.[16] In the instance before us, however, it is spelt without any *Ain* or *Yod*.

---

[15] Professor Max Muller's Index to the Rig Veda gives the following references to passages where "jarita" occurs in the Nom. Sing. alone, to say nothing of its other cases and numbers: I. 38, 5; 46, 12; 63, 2; 165, 14; III. 52, 5; IV. 17, 9; V. 36, 3; 4; 43, 1; VIII. 44, 28; X. 6, 1; 100, 6; 11; 142, 1. All these we have verified for ourselves.

[16] 1 Kings iv. 14; 1 Chron. vi. 6; 2 Chron. xxvii. 21; Zec. i. 1, 7; Ezra v. 1; vi. 14.

Its initial is only an *Alif* with a *hiruck*, representing a simple vocal *i*, without any guttural or semivowel, and being exactly equivalent to the Sanskrit *i*. And "Iddo," thus spelt, stands probably for "Indo," on the same principle on which "Hoddu" stands indisputably for "Hondu" (Esther i. 1). Now "Indo" is certainly an Arian and a Brahminical name, whether we compare it with "Indu" (moon) or "Indra," in which (according to the *Satapatha Bráhmana)* the *r* is an *arbitrary* interpolation.[17] "This breath which is in the midst is Indra. He by his might kindled these breaths in the midst: inasmuch as he kindled them, he is the kindler *(Indha)*. They call Indha "Indra" imperceptibly [*paroksham*]: for the gods love that which is imperceptible. *(Dr. Muir's translation, Sanskrit Texts, vol.* iv., *p.* 20.)

We have already seen that the name "Suaswa" (Zendice *Suaspa* or rather *Huaspa*) etymologically corresponds with "Caspa." We must now add that the same character is celebrated in the Khordah-Avesta in the following terms: "The Fravashi of the pure *Hvaspa* praise we."[18] And the same vocable is also in the Rig Veda constantly used as an adjective, or attributive, in the sense of *connected with*, or *possessed of good horses*, and applied to gods, Rishis, men, and things.

---

[17] स योऽयं मध्ये प्राण एष एवेन्द्रः। तान् एष प्राणान् मध्यत इन्द्रियेणैन्ध यदैन्धः तस्मादिन्धः। इन्धो ह वै तं इन्द्र इत्याचक्षते परोक्षं। परोक्षकामा हि देवाः।

[18] Bleeck iii. 97.

We often find in its pages *well-horsed chariots*, *well-horsed* men, *well-horsed* Indra, *well-horsed* Rishis, *well-horsed* Agni.[19] We also find pious men praying for *well-horsed* sons.[20] Sometimes, again, the word is "Suaswia" corresponding exactly with *Caspia*, in the same or a similar sense. We have *suaswia wealth*, *suaswia Indra*, *suaswia boons*.[21] In one place we actually have "suaswia sindhu" or *Caspia Sea*.[22] Sayana makes it a "river rich in horses," but the word "sindhu" also stands for a *sea*.[23] Its present signification is

---

[19] Rig V. iv. 45 Speaking of the chariot of the Aswins, the hymnist says : रथः स्वश्वो अजरो यो अस्ति । "It is well-horsed and undecaying." R. V. 117-2 यो वामश्विना मनसो जवीयान्रथः स्वश्वो विश आजिगाति । "The car that is swifter than thought and *well-horsed* &c."

Rig V. i. 84-6 न किः स्वश्वः "No one, O Indra, is *well-horsed* like thee" मां नरः स्वश्वा वाजयन्तः Rig Veda iv. 42. 5 "Let *well-horsed heroes* eager for a fight follow me."

Rig V. iv. 29-2 स्वश्वो यो अभीरुर्मन्यमानः "Indra who is *well-horsed*, fearless &c." R. V. v. 33. 3 रश्मीं देव यमसे स्वश्वः "O lord Indra, *well-horsed* thyself, thou tightenest the reins."

Rig V. v. 65-2 स्वश्वासः "We (Rishis, sons of Atri) being *well-horsed*."

Rig V. iv. 2. 4 स्वश्वो अग्ने "O Agni, thou being *well-horsed*, &c."

[20] Rig V. vi. 33-1 सौवश्व्यं यो वनवत्स्वश्वो वृत्रा समत्सु सासहदमित्रान् O Indra give us such a son "as, being *horsed* himself, may overcome a troop of horses and overthrow all adverse opponents."

[21] Rig V. ii. 1-5 त्वमाशुहेमा ररिषे स्वश्व्यं "thou shalt grant well-horsed boons."

[22] Rig V. x. 75-8 स्वश्वा सिन्धुः सुरथा सुवासा "the Suaswa Sindhu &c.

[23] Rig V. x. 43-7 आपो न सिन्धुमभि यत् समक्षरन्त्सोमास इन्द्रं कुल्या इव ह्रदं.

"When the soma liquors flow into Indra like waters into the sea or canals into a lake &c."

almost exclusively a *sea* or *ocean*. Its primary meaning in the Veda is *flowing water*, and, as it applies to a river, because it is a stream, so it is applicable to a sea because of its tidal rise under the influence of the moon.[24] "Suaswa sindhu" may therefore stand for the Caspian sea, or a river of the name of Sindon which falls into the Caspian.[25]

---

[24] Rig V. ix. 86-19 सोम.. आपा सिन्धुनां "The moon is the cause of the flowing of waters."

[25] The presence of "Sindicus" and some other maritime places bearing similar names beyond the Caspian and on the Euxine has been noticed by historians. Bean gives in his Classical Atlas a river "Sindone" falling into the Caspian. The Assyrian inscriptions also inform us of a city Hindanu on the banks of the Euphrates, Norris's Assyrian Dictionary, pp. 345 and 434. We likewise read of a Hayanu, son of Gabbar, who was chief of "Hindan" near the Euphrates. Ibid, p. 417.

CHAPTER II.

Arians' Original Settlement, Vedic Testimony, Assyrian Inscriptions.

Proceeding now with our inquiry into the primitive seat of the Arian family, the *pratna okas* as the Rig Veda calls it, the first difficulty which stares us in the face is the obscurity in which its early history is enveloped. The Brahmins and the Iranians were for a long period the only guardians of Arian honor and dignity in Asia. Both were, doubtless, races up to any effort requiring intellectual vigour and activity. But History or Chronology had never been a favourite study with either. The one considered it undignified to write anything but verse and poetry, and the other disdained to instruct posterity except through the puzzles of Cuneiform Inscriptions. History was thus left to the tender mercies of Poetry and Sculpture. And each of these chroniclers of events had on it shackles, hard to be borne, in the discharge of its office, so far as it related to the instruction of posterity. Poetry was bound by the dictum which declared its very life to consist in "rasa," which means *flavour*. Unless facts are themselves *flavorous* or *sensational*, the historian-poet must be between two fires. He must supply both *truth* and *flavour*, or he must forfeit his character for the consolidated office. But departures from truth cannot be quickly discovered. Like travellers' tales they may pass muster for the moment. Even where ground is found for suspicion, the process of detection is tardy. Want of flavour on the other hand is perceived *instanter*. It is a *sensation*, and the operation follows immediately on the presentation of the object. The conviction of the offender becomes simultaneous with the commission of the offence. The historian-poet, like most other men, provides against the evil of the moment, and leaves his character for truthfulness to the contingencies and chances of the future. He seasons a small modicum of *truth* with a liberal dose of *spicy* inventions.

And as to the Cuneiform inscriptions, they can only give detached lessons—isolated bits of facts—and these again may remain veiled for ages, secure from the prying looks of posterity, like "gems of purest ray," and pearls of the highest value, which repose undisturbed in "the dark unfathomed caves of oceans." Posterity's fruition of them must be dependent on sheer chance or lucky venture.

To add to the misfortunes of Archæology, the Brahmins, as descendants of Arian emigrants, had from the beginning so isolated themselves from "Ariana," as to have lost all sympathy for their cousins in Asia, in a very short space of time. They did indeed for some time recognize them as *quasi-brothers*, *(Bhratrivya)*, but they soon turned that endearing vocable into a term of reproach, and it became subsequently a word for an enemy.[1]

Consanguinity or any connection with Asiatic Arians or Iranians was in the end altogether ignored. It is difficult to form a clear conception of the causes which induced such an unaccountable estrangement. There are no formal records on the subject. Neither the Brahmins nor the Iranians have given any consecutive narratives of their quarrel. They had no Thucydides on either side to chronicle their differences, or to preserve a record of their eventful conflicts from the oblivious effects of time. It is only from glimpses of light which incidently shoot forth through the pages of the Vedas and the Zend Avesta that we are able to form any idea on the subject. Comparing the notes of these two sets of authorities, the respective sacred books of the two branches of Asia's great family, we are led to the inference that both parties originally recognized the same objects of worship, viz. the Sun,

---

[1] भ्रातृव्यः This word literally means a quasi-brother, a step-brother. a brother-in-law, or a first cousin, just as *pritrivya* means a quasi-father, an uncle. The following passage shows how this word was used in the Vedas: एतया वै देवा असुरानत्यक्रामन्नति पाप्मानं भ्रातृव्यं क्रामति य एतया स्तुते। *Tándya-mahá-Bráhamana* vol. i. p. 105. The commentator says: एतया द्वसप्तया विष्टुत्या खलु देवाः पूर्वं असुरानत्यक्रामन् अतिक्रान्तवन्तः तिरस्कृतवन्त इत्यर्थः। तस्मादन्योऽपि यो यजमान एतया स्तुते सोऽपि पाप्मानं पापरूपं भ्रातृव्यं शत्रुं अतिक्रामति अतिक्रान्तो भवति। The following is a consolidated translation of the Vedic verse and its commentary. "By this sacrificial hymn the devas had, aforetime, overcome the Asuras (Assyrians?) Therefore whatever other sacrificer makes worships by means of the same, he also overcomes that incarnation of sin, the Bhratrivya, a (quasi-brother) i. e. the enemy.

Fire and the elements of Nature. What the exact import of that worship was we cannot confidently declare, but whatever the theological character of their adoration might have been, neither condemned the other for it—both allowed and practised it. Both also theoretically allowed the primitive institution of Sacrifices, though, probably, they differed widely as to the mode of conducting them.

The distinctive feature of the Zoroastrian doctrine of *two* eternal principles of Good and Evil respectively, appears in the Sacred Records of both. "Ahura-mazda," which in the Zend Avesta was often abbreviated into the simple initial "Ahura," and "Anghro mainyus," were also acknowledged in the Rig Veda. Varuna, to whom the same sort of creative agency is attributed which the Vendidad ascribed to "Ormuzd," is, in the 24th Súkta of the first Mandal, addressed as the *eminently wise* "Asura" (Zendice Ahura), and Anghro-mainyus, the principle of Evil, appears in the same Hymn under the style of "Nir-riti," which is synonymous with his Zendic appellation. "Nir-riti" literally means *un-righteous*, and is, according to Sayana, equivalent to "Pápa-devatá" or the *deity of sin.*[2] But notwithstanding all these coincidences of faith, it appears that the two parties could not agree on the *mode* of conducting their sacrifices. The seceding party, which emigrated to India, seems to have been

---

[2] उरुं हि राजा वरुणश्चकार सूर्याय पन्थामन्वेतवा।

बाधस्व दूरे निर्ऋतिं पराचैः कृतं चिदेनः प्रमुमुग्ध्यस्मत्।

क्षयन्नस्मभ्यमसुर प्रचेता राजन्नेनांसि शिश्रथः कृतानि।

opposed to the teaching of Zoroaster, as it was maintained by his successors, and hurled defiance against those who contemplated its forcible imposition on their belief or practice.

The seceders were, however, as zealous Fire-worshippers at the time of the separation, as the general bulk of the Arians whom they left behind in Central Asia, and who were subsequently stigmatized by the Mahometans as *Gebers* and *Atash-parasts.* The Vedas declare that Fire was as much an object of adoration with "modern" Rishis (*i. e.* probably, the post-immigration separatists) as with the "ancients" before the separation.[3]

Indeed the Iranian and Indian branches vied with each other in doing honor to Agni. Both claimed him as their own divine herald or *convener.* The one honoured him as the son of the supreme Ahura-mazdao,[4] the other as *their elected divine herald conversant with all things.*[5] Both contended also for the monopoly of the

---

[3] अग्निः पूर्वेभिर्ऋषिभिरीड्यो नूतनैरुत । R. V. I. 1, 2.

[4] The Fire, the son of Ahura Mazda, we praise, the pure lord of purity, Bleeck ii. 22. "Messenger of Ahura Mazda is Naryo Çanha," (a name of Fire). Vendidad Farg. xix. 112.

[5] अग्निं दूतं वृणीमहे होतारं विश्ववेदसं ।

"We elect Agni, our herald and convener, conversant with all things." Rig. Ved. i. 12.1.

अस्माकमस्तु केवलः

"May he be *only ours.*" i. 1310.

Agni was also honoured on the one hand by the Rig. Veda as "the navel of the earth" नाभिरग्निः पृथिव्याः i. 59-2, and on the other hand by the Zend Avesta as "the navel of the Kings." Bleeck iii. 146.

Sun as their especial object of adoration.[6] The same rivalry may be inferred with reference to Indra,[7] whom the Iranians also worshipped under the title of Verethraghna. But the Indian branch, it would seem, declined to acknowledge a common *guru* or spiritual

---

[6] देवासुराः संयत्ता आसन्। त आदित्ये व्यायच्छन्त। तं देवाः समजयन्।

"The Devas and Asuras were fighting. They were disputing about A'ditya. [Each party claiming this divinity for itself, so the commentator explains it.] The devas won him." *Taittiriya Brahmana.*

देवाश्च वा असुराश्चादित्ये व्यायच्छन्त देवा अभ्यजयन।

"The Devas and Asuras disputed about Aditya. The Devas won him." *Tandya Mahá Bráhmana*, p. 275.

[7] Indra is so well known as the prevailing god of the Vedas that we need not cite more than one sentence in which the authors express their desire of monopolizing him. "May he be ours only" अस्माकमस्तु केवलः Rig. Veda i. 7. 10.

And in the Zend, a whole "Yasht" with 63 paragraphs is devoted to the glorification of Verethraghana. A few sentences will suffice here: "Who among the heavenly Yazatas is the best armed? Then answered Ahura Mazda, "Verethraghna, created by Ahura, O holy Zarathrustra."

"Vĕrĕthraghna, created by Ahura, praise we; the worker of manhood, the worker of death, the worker of continuance; who stands of himself, averts by himself. To him offered the pure Zarathustra, in the mind of Vĕrĕthraghna, in the speech of Vĕrĕthraghna, in the act of Vĕrĕthraghna, in the saying of Vĕrĕthraghna, in the answers of Vĕrĕthraghna.

"To him gave Vĕrĕthraghna, created by Ahura, the fountain of right, strength of arms, health of the whole body, thriving of the whole body and strength of sight as Karô-maçyô possesses it, who is under the water, who in Rañha, the far-to-step-over, deep, a thousand men (deep), has (each) water-drop of the size of a hair (always) in mind." *Bleeck* iii. 106.

preceptor. The Brahmins recognized the seniority of some "Asura guru" or Iranian preceptor, but they refused to submit to the doctrine of Zoroaster.

The seniority which the Indians accorded to the preceptors of the Asuras appears from the very second verse of the Rig Veda, already cited. "Agni was an object of laudation with the ancient Rishis and is so with the moderns too." The "ancients" could be no other than the pre-emigration sages. Sáyana says in his commentary on the passage in question: "This Agni was an object of laudation or praise with the ancients, namely, with Bhrigu, Angiras, and other Rishis."[8] Now Bhrigu was by universal Indian tradition reputed the father of Sukra, *preceptor of Asuras*, who was otherwise described by the patronymics "Usana" and "Bhargava," the honorific "Kavi" (sage), and the stellar distinction "Venas"—he being still held in Indian astronomy as the regent of Venus. The Vedic Usana is doubtless connected with the Zendic patriarch "Us," thus noticed in the Yaçna XXIX. "This one is known to me here, who alone heard our precepts: Zarathustra, the Holy, he asks from Us, Mazda and Asha, assistance for announcing, I will make him skilful of speech." (Bleeck ii. p. 84) He is called Kavi Usa in the Bahram Yast. It is probably he that is also extolled in the Khordah-Avesta under the names of Uçi-nemo and Uçnáka. "The Fravashi of the pure Uçi-nemo and *Uçnáka* praise we" (Bleeck iii. 96). And in the word "Bhar-

[8] अयमग्निः पुरातनैर्भृग्वङ्गिरःप्रभृतिभिर्ऋषिभिरपि स्तुत्यः। *Sáyana.*

gava," easily contracted into "Bhargao," we may detect the first element of the word "Farg-ard," the name given to the Chapters of the Vendidad. "Farg" must have the same relation to "Farg-ard" that "Visp" has to "Visp-erd," and "Farg" may be easily identified with "Bhargao." In the absence, as far as we know, of a better derivation of "Fargard," we cannot help referring it to "Bhargao," the "guru" of the Asuras.

But from some cause which we cannot divine at this distance of time, the Indian Arians refused to submit to the doctrine of Zoroaster's teachership, which was sought to be imposed on them, probably by force of arms.

We cannot say with any confidence or precision who Zoroaster's patron, bearing the name "Vistaspa" in the Zend Avesta, was. It appears that he was a zealous promoter of his prophetical protege's doctrine. The Persians identify this Vistaspa (whom they call Gustaspa), the patron of Zoroaster, with Hystaspes, the father of king Darius. It is true enough that Darius himself spells his father's name "Vishtaspa" in the cuneiform inscriptions of Behistan.[9] But our difficulty in accepting this tradition consists in the mention of the same name in the Rig Veda. To suppose that the Rig Veda was written *after* the age of Darius Hystaspes would be preposterous. We are therefore driven to the conclusion that the Vistaspa of the Zenda Avesta, the promoter of the Zoroaste-

---

[9] Rawlinson's Herodotus, vol. ii, p. 490.

rian doctrine, must have been a more ancient character, different from the father of Darius. And if Gustaspa be another form of the name of Vistaspa, the Assyrian inscriptions would favour the idea of a more ancient character of that name. We have a "Kustaspi," a *chief of Comukha who paid tribute to Tiglathpileser.*[10] This would be in the 8th century before Christ. If such a name there was, some two hundred years anterior to Darius, there can be no difficulty in supposing the existence of a third person of the same name, still more ancient, who might correspond with the age of the Rig Vedas, and with the character noticed in the Zend Avesta. As a promoter of the Zoroasterian doctrine, he would doubtless, after the fashion of Oriental princes, and, even of Occidental princes too a few centuries ago, seek to impose it on the populace by means of the sword. But the seceding Arians hurled defiance at him and refused submission. "What can Ishtaswa", said they, "What can Ishtarasmi, rulers of the world as they are, do against our protecting men ?"[11] That Ishtaswa was the same as the Vistaspa of the Zend Avasta, no one will dispute, especially as we learn from Dr. Hyde that the name was sometimes written with a *ya* (يستاسپ) instead of a *wau.*

Whatever the actual points of difference may have been, the parties became very much embittered against each other. The Brahmins reviled the "Asuras," or

---

[10] Norris' Assyrian Dictionary, p. 628.

[11] किमिष्टाश्व इष्टरश्मिरेत ईशानासस्तरुष ऋञ्जते नॄन्। Rig. Veda i. 122.13.

chiefs of the Iranians, and the Iranians railed at "the devas" or chiefs of the Brahmins. Doubtless the Indian branch was the most intellectual of the Asiatic Arian stock, while those whom the separatists left behind were, on the other hand, conspicuous for courage and physical strength. The Iranians warned their followers against the guerilla warfare of the devas. The Indians were always betraying signs of anxiety and panic at the superior strength of their adversaries, and were, as fugitives, longing for a settled habitation and dwelling.

The Zend Avesta calls upon its followers to stand fast to their faith, and beware of sudden attacks from the Devas. "Every one, both men and women, ought to-day to choose his creed (between the Devas and the Ahura religion). Ye offspring of renowned ancestors, awake to agree with us (*i. e.* to approve of my lore, to be delivered to you at this moment)."

"You cannot belong to both of them: One of the Devas, against whom we are fighting, might overtake you, when in deliberation (what faith you are to embrace) whispering you to choose the naught mind."[12]

The Indians, on the other hand, as the Rig Veda itself shows, were invoking their chiefs not to leave them in the lurch, but join them in *this land of divine sacrifices*.[13] Indra was especially accosted to abandon

---

[12] Haug's Essays, p. 142.

[13] स नः पावक दीदिवोऽग्ने देवाँ इहा वह। Rig. V. i. 12. 10. On this Sayana says इह, देवयजनदेशे।

"O thou illuminating purifier bring the Devas here [to this land of the worship of Devas.]"

their "pristine habitation," and come to the multitude of sacrificers awaiting his commands, and looking for his protection, with the same feeling of allegiance and affection with which, in former days and in their original settlement, they had called him father."[14] His followers appear at times to have been somewhat uneasy about his perseverance and firmness, and offered *to provision him themselves*. They besought him to give up parley *with other people, passing them over*. They were constantly praying that Agni might be able "to conduct the Devas here," and that Indra, as he had killed the Asura Vritra of yore (probably an Assyrian character, real or imaginary) for which he was honoured in the Zend Avesta as "Verethraghna," would likewise arm himself against all "Vritras," or foes of Devas, and overcome their tricks by counter strategies.

नराशंसमिह प्रियमस्मिन्यज्ञ उपह्वये । Ibid I. 13. 3.

Again says Sayana इह, देवयजनदेशे ।

"I invite the beloved Narásansa (Fire) to this sacrifice here [in this land of the worship of Devas]."

[14] अनु प्रत्नस्यौकसो हुवे तुविप्रतिं नरं ।
यं ते पूर्वं पिता हुवे ॥ Rig Veda I. 30. 9.
तं त्वा वाजेषु वाजिनं वाजयामः शतक्रतो । R. V. I. 4. 9.
मा नो अति ख्य आगहि ॥ Ibid I. 4. 3.
मायभिरिन्द्र मायिनं त्वं शुष्णमवातिरः । Ibid I. 11. 7.

"I call back our heroic man (Indra) from our pristine home whom i. e., thee (O Indra) in days of yore I used to accost our father and protector."

"We provision thee, the warrior, in war."

"Do not parley with others, passing over us. Come to us."

"O Indra, thou killedst Sushna, the crafty (Asura) by (counter) stratagems."

How long the encounter lasted, it is impossible to say, but it appears that when they settled down in their respective localities of Central Asia and India, the Iranians found sufficient occupation in martial conflicts with their immediate neighbours and with nations more to the West, while the Brahmins kept themselves resolutely within the confines of India, and solemnly prohibited even tours and pleasure excursions beyond the Indus. Their jealousy of any further intercourse with their trans-Indus brethren was parallel, in history, only with that of Jeroboam for any inter-communication between the ten revolted tribes and the two that continued faithful to the house of David. Like the Jews and Samaritans, the Brahmins and Iranians excluded each other from all social relations, so that even a cup of cold water would neither be offered nor accepted between themselves.

The Brahmins were desirous of considering themselves as dead to the Iranians, and the Iranians to themselves. Hence they formally recorded nothing about the ancient exploits or adventures of their forefathers in Central Asia. They seem even to have abstained from teaching their children the former history of their own race, which they were manifestly desirous of obliterating from human memory.

But notwithstanding the efforts of the Indian Arians to isolate themselves within the well defined and almost inaccessible boundaries of their new habitation, they could not, as lovers of learning, be so Vandalic as to destroy records. Nor could they obliterate, from the tablets of their own memory, the hymns and odes which they had delighted to sing and chant as religious exercises. True it is, that they were anxious to ignore all trans-Indus events, and to put on the appearance of "autochthones" in India. But learning and letters prove dangerous accompaniments when the object is to suppress information. You cannot conceal live coals within your handkerchief, nor can the refulgence of Saraswati be so completely secreted as that no streaks of light should at all escape. The Arians had too much intellectual activity to drop at once into a state of mental stagnation. Nor was the time of a forced emigration from one's "pristine home," replete with a thousand pleasing associations, favourable for active intellects to remain dormant and torpid, or to submit, without a struggle or murmur, to a coerced banishment from the land of their birth. The authors of the Vedas could not under such circumstances cease from thinking, cogitating, chanting, and reciting. And they would necessarily think, cogitate, chant, and recite those things in which they had taken pleasure since their infancy. The human mind loves to dwell on past ideas, imbibed with a mother's milk. It cannot dismiss them summarily. The Indian Arians were no exception to this rule. We find accordingly that at the very time when their sense of injury was the strongest against their brethren in Ariana, when they seem to have renounced their allegiance to the representatives of Ahura Mazda, they involuntarily gave utterance to expressions and ideas, once dear to them, which, notwithstanding all efforts, they could not forget or ignore. The word Asura (or Ahura Sanscritized) which became in a very short time a vocable for wicked spirits, and was practically identified in India with Anghro-Mainyus, expressive of the fulness of evil combined with lawless strength, still retained a solemn reverence which their minds could not renounce by a sudden revulsion. They knew that "Asura" did not mean an evil spirit, that it was a title of distinction corresponding to the idea of a "lord," and applied equally to gods and heroes. It was applied to one that was lately their common divinity, "Ahura Mazda," or the *great Asura*. They were now desirous of profaning the term against their inmost conviction. They knew that the term was connected with their own ideas of sanctity and dignity, and that it implied nothing unholy or unmanly. And they were spell-bound by their own minds. An old writer had given the epithet of *philalethes*[15] to the human soul. It is a *lover of truth*, and although a false tongue will often give utterance to an untruth, yet the mind can never turn such a traitor to itself, as to *think* that to be true which it knows to be false. And what a man decidedly *thinks* to be right and true, will often escape his lips in spite of himself. We find a striking illustration of this in the Indian Arian's case. He had been driven from home by differences with his Central Asiatic brethren. He was under a bitter sense of unmerited injury and wrong, suffered at their hands. He had determined to cut them altogether, with all their principles, ceremonies, and religious terminology. And yet we

---

15 Simplicius in his commentary on Aristotle *de Anima*.

find him involuntarily applying to his own Devas and leaders, in his exile, the very term of respect and reverence to which he was accustomed in Ariana. Indra, his highest object of reverence, is himself invoked as "Asura."[16] "Thou, O Indra, art king, do thou and all the gods protect men. Do thou, O Asura, save us." Varuna also is similarly addressed: "Remaining with us, do thou, O illustrious and eminently wise Asura, absolve the sins we have committed."[17] The exiles wished for the protection of Varuna. They wished him "to remain" with them in their new habitation, and they involuntarily accosted him with the time-honoured title, which they were impelled to believe would be most acceptable to him. We also find the Maruts, Mitra, Twastri, Prajápati, Agni, Váyu, Saraswatí, Pusha, Savitri, Parjania, similarly accosted or spoken of as *Asuras*.[18] Mitra and Varuna, again, frequently linked in the Veda as *gods in the dual*, are also sometimes linked as *asuraw*.[19] The term

---

[16] त्वं राजेन्द्र ये च देवा रक्षा नॄन् पाह्यसुर त्वमस्मान् । Rig Veda I. 174-1. The term "Asura" is also applied to Indra in I. 54. 3, viii. 90. 6, x. 55. 4; 96. 11; 99; 2, 12; 105, 11.

[17] अव ते हेळो वरुण नमोभिरव यज्ञेभिरीमहे हविर्भिः ।
क्षयन्नस्मभ्यमसुर प्रचेता राजन्नेनांसि शिश्रथः कृतानि ॥ Rig Veda I. 24, 14. Varuna is also called Asura in ii. 27. 10; 28. 7. iv. 53. 1.

[18] The Maruts are called Asuras in i. 64. 2 Twastri in i. 110. 3. Prajapati in x. 10. 2. Agni in v. 12-1; 15. 1; 27. 1 Sarasvati in vii. 96. 1 असुर्यायै सरस्वत्यै । Vayu in v. 42. 1 Pusha in v. 51. 11. Savitri in v. 49. 2. Parjania in v. 63. 3, 7; 83. 6.

[19] इमा वां मित्रावरुणा सुवृक्तिमिषं न कृण्वे असुरा नवीयः । Rig Veda vii. 36. 2.
ता हि देवानामसुरा तावर्या ता नः क्षितीः करतमूर्जयन्तीः । vii. 65. 2.

Asura is also solemnly applied to the Creator of the Heavens and the earth, and the Supreme Governor of all worlds. We have already cited a passage to that effect, and we shall add another here still more remarkable. "The all-knowing Asura established the Heavens and fixed the limits of the earth. He sat as the supreme Ruler of all worlds. These were the works of Varuna."[20] Notwithstanding the rider about Varuna, the author's mind here was evidently contemplating the Zoroastrian divinity Ahura Mazda. The "all-knowing Asura" may be considered as a translation of "Ahura Mazda" itself, the last word is doubtless the Zend vocable for the Sanscrit "Mahat." In the Zend "zota" for Sanscrit "hota," "Azis" for "Ahi," "Azem" for "Aham," "zemaka" for "hemaka," "zer" for "hiran," *(gold)*, we detect the rule of the Sanscrit *h* being transliterated by *z* in the Zend. And therefore "mazd" is the same as *mahat*. But the same word appears to represent "magus" also, which

---

महान्ता मित्रावरुणा सम्राजा देवावसुरा । viii. 25, 4.

The titles "Asuras among Devas," "Devas and Asuras," and as in i. 131. 1. v. 41. 3. "Celestial Asuras" were like the adjective Asura in the sense of strong as in v. 12. 1; 27. 1, perhaps artistically used to break the fall of the term "Asura" from a *sacred* to a *diabolical* sense.

[20] Rig Veda viii. 42. 1 अस्तभ्नाद्द्यामसुरो विश्ववेदा अमिमीत वरिमाणं पृथिव्याः ।

आसीदद्विश्वा भुवनानि सम्राड्विश्वेत्तानि वरुणस्य व्रतानि ॥ Again in x. 177, 1 the word Asura is applied to the Supreme Being *by whose "máyá" or mysterious influence the wise obtain a mental vision of the sun as if the luminary were actually within their hearts :* पतङ्गमक्तमसुरस्य मायया हृदा पश्यन्ति मनसा विपश्चितः ।

signifies knowledge and wisdom. "Mazda" accordingly stands both for greatness and knowledge, and Ahura Mazda is aptly represented here by "the all-knowing Asura, who sat as the supreme ruler of all worlds."

These considerations tend to prove that the Arian ancestors of the Brahmins migrated to India from regions where Zoroaster's doctrine was the rule of human faith. The Vedic hymns we have already cited, themselves show that the minds of their authors were so saturated with the principles of that system, that at the very time, and in the very records, in which they contemplated the foundation of another and a different body of divinity, ideas and sentiments found utterance, positively at variance with their main object. We have in the same Veda the sacrificial ministers and hymnists themselves called Asuras,[21] and the very hymnists again invoking the destruction of Asuras.[22] We have almost all the Vedic gods worshipped, honoured and prayed unto under that title, and yet we find the same gods meditating the slaughter of Asuras, and complacently described as having accomplished their purpose.[23] The identical *mandala* of the Rig Veda

---

[21] Rig V. i. 108. 6 यदब्रवं प्रथमं वां वृणानोऽयं सोमो असुरैर्नो विहव्यः। ... "This soma has been offered by our priests (Asuras)."

[22] ii. 30. 4 बृहस्पते तपुषाश्नेव विध्य वृकद्वरसो असुरस्य वीरान्। "Pierce, O Brihaspati, with thy burning thunderbolt the sons of the Asura covering the gate."

[23] x. 53. 4 तदद्य वाचः प्रथमं मसीय येनासुराँ अभि देवा असाम। "I shall now recite that principal formula by which the gods and myself may overthrow the Asuras."

which attributed the creation of the heavens and earth to the "all-knowing Asura," denied the divinity of the Asuras; and posted them as impious Rakshasas.[24] The very chief god of the Veda, the hope and refuge of the Arian emigrants, Indra himself, is, in numerous hymns, worshipped and accosted as an Asura, and, again, in other hymns, is complimented as the "destroyer of Vritras, Dasyus, enemies and Asuras," his dazzling brilliance being fixed in the air as the solar luminary.[25] This tissue of inconsistencies shows a strange mental conflict among the Arians when they separated from their brethren in Central Asia.

One psychological explanation of that mental phe-

---

x. 157. 4 हत्वाय देवा असुरान्यदायन्देवा देवत्वमभिरक्षमाणाः । "When the gods returned after slaughtering the Asuras, then they maintained their position as gods."

[24] viii. 96. 9 अनायुधासो असुरा अदेवाश्चक्रेण ताँ अप वप ऋजीषिन् । "Therefore, O consumer of the soma, mow down the unarmed ungodly Asuras by means of thy discus."

viii. 97. 1 या इंद्र भुज आभर स्वर्वाँ असुरेभ्यः । "Enthroned in heaven all the wealth you have got, (you have obtained by killing) the Asuras (or mighty Rakshasas)" so Sayana interprets it.

[25] x. 170, 2 विभ्राड्बृहत्सुभृतं वाजसातमं धर्मन्दिवो धरुणे सत्यमर्पितं ।
अमित्रहा वृत्रहा दस्युहंतमं ज्योतिर्जज्ञे असुरहा सपत्नहा ॥

"A great super-excellent light which giveth satisfying food was produced and placed in the upholder of the firmament (the sun) which was itself indestructible but was the destroyer of foes, the destroyer of Vritra, the exterminator of Dasyus, the destroyer of Asuras, the destroyer of enemies."

vi. 22. 4 कस्ते भागः किं वयो दुध्र खिद्वः पुरुहूत पुरूवसोऽसुरघ्नः ।
"O Indra, thou destroyer of Asuras, the scourge of thy foes, thou that art invoked by many and largely endowed with wealth. What share in sacrifice, what food is appropriated to thee."

nomenon may, however, be collected from the Vedas and the Zend Avesta themselves. Indra had evidently left an impression on the Iranian mind, scarcely fainter than his stamp on the emigrant Arian. In the Zend Avesta, he is at the same time both worshipped as an archangel, as *the best armed among the Yazatas*, and also condemned as a Deva. He was worshipped as the Destroyer of Vritra, and repudiated as a demon. We have already given a concise specimen of the encomiums passed on him in the "Bahram Yasht," composed especially in commemoration of the triumphs of "Verethraghna," or slayer of Vritra. And yet every true Zoroasterian had to protest against him by saying, "I combat Indra." (*Bleeck's Zend Avesta* i, 93.) In the Indian Scriptures, however, Vritra is himself called an Asura,—an ungodly demon, who met at the hands of Indra a well-merited destruction. This "Asura" could not have been an Iranian chief, opposed exclusively to the seceding Arians. He must have been a common enemy of the whole Arian family of Asia, or both branches would not have chanted songs of congratulation on his death. His title or surname of Asura was probably an ethnic designation, and it naturally leads to the inference that he was an Assyrian. Conflicts between Assyrians and Arians are conceivable in themselves, and have actually been recorded both in History *and the Zend Avesta.* An Assyrian expedition against Arian regions under Ninus is mentioned by Justin and Diodorus, and the Zend itself represents "the snake Daháka," asking a boon from Ardvi-sura in the region of Bawri (Babylon), that he might desolate "the seven Karesvares" or the whole of Ariana. The Rig Veda appears to identify "the snake Daháka" with Vritra, describing him as a "snake," and a "Dása," which is synonymous with "Daháka," each having the same meaning as the "Abaddon" or "Apollyon" of the Apocalypse.[26] Asura itself, as an ethnic appellative, naturally points to Assyria.

Vritra is said to have restrained *the waters*, and Indra to have released the same by destroying him. The native commentator Sáyana construes it as an allegory, expressive of a liberal shower of rain, by

---

[26] The Aban Yasht says: "To her offered the Snake Daháka with three jaws, in the region of Bawri, a hundred male horses, a thousand cows, ten thousand small cattle. Then prayed he her for this favor: Grant me, O good, most profitable Ardví-çúra, spotless, that I may make the seven Karesvares empty of men." Bleeck iii. 34. And the Rig Veda thus describes the fall of Vritra:

अहन्नहिं पर्वते शिश्रियाणं त्वष्टास्मै वज्रं स्वर्यं ततक्ष ।

* * *

अपादहस्तो अपृतन्यदिन्द्रमास्य वज्रमधि सानौ जघान ।
वृष्णो वध्रिः प्रतिमानं बुभूषन् पुरुत्रा वृत्रो अशयद्व्यस्तः ॥

* * *

दासपत्नीरहिगोपा अतिष्ठन्निरुद्धा आपः पणिनेव गावः । Rig Veda I. 32, 2, 7, 11.

"He (Indra) struck the serpent reposing in the mountain. Twastri made for him a brilliant thunderbolt. Without feet and hands he had challenged Indra, who discharged his thunderbolt at his head like the summit of a mountain.

Like an impotent person affecting the appearance of a vigorous man, he dropped, crippled in many a limb. The waters guarded by the Destoyer (Dása), the serpent, had remained shut up like the cows by Panis."

the action of thunder and lightning on the clouds. This would be no explanation, however, of the encomiums lavished on Verethraghna in the Zend Avesta, and the frequent doxologies in the Rig Veda to the honor and glory of Vritrahá. It is possible that Vritra might have attempted against an Arian town (but foiled by Indra) what Cyrus afterwards successfully accomplished against Babylon, by turning the waters of the Euphrates into an artificial channel and causing a ford for his army to effect the capture of the city.

But whether the story be a veritable narrative, or an allegory, the consentient ideas of the Iranian and Indian Arians on the subject become a great fact, on which may be fairly based any psychological considerations, explanatory of their notion of "Ahura" or "Asura." Can it be doubted that when the Arians from the plains or table lands of Central Asia gave utterance to the word "Ahura" or "Asura," in the palmy days of the Assyrian empire, that they would thereby mean either a native of Assyria, or a recognized prince, chief, or noble of that empire? In other words, the vocable "Asura" passing the Arian's lips must, at the time and place just mentioned, have stood for the identical ideas which the Cuneiform Inscriptions disclose.

Now Asura, we have seen, is found as a household word in the Inscriptions. We have already referred to some of the numerous places where it occurs in the sense of "Asur, my lord." We shall now add that the different senses in which the word "Assur" is used in

7

the Inscriptions correspond almost exactly with the various senses which it has in the Rig Veda, barring only the denunciatory notions, subsequently occasioned in India by the schism between the Iranians and Indians.

In the Inscriptions the word indicates, in the first place, a god, a great god, and the king of the gods, thus:

"In honour of Assur, king of gods and of the gods of Assyria all of them, in goodness of health (and) joy of heart, may tribute much, (and) plenty stored, in it for ever accumulate."[27]

"In that day I elevated the hearts of the great gods, of Assur and the sun-god, &c."[28]

"In honour of Assur (and) Istar, great deities, my lords."[29]

"The power of Assur, of Istar, and of the great gods, &c."[30]

"Assur and Istar his prayers shall hear."[31]

"Assur and Istar thy prayers shall hear."[32]

The use of Asura in this same sense in the Rig Veda we have already noticed, and as those divinities

---

[27] Norris's Assyrian Dictionary, pp. 405 and 462, "Ina kibid Assur sar ili u ili Assur-ki kali-sunu, &c.,

[28] "Ina yomme suma adlul labbut ili rabi sa Assur u Samas, &c." *Ibid* p. 643.

[29] "Ina kibid Assur Istar ili rabbi bili-a." *Ibid*, p. 486.

[30] "Danan Assur Istar va ili rabi bili-ya." Ibid, p. 255.

[31] "Asur va Istar iqribi-*su* isimmu." *Ibid*, p. 192.

[32] "Asur " " iqribi-*ka* " Ibid, p. 504.

had wives, so the Assur divinities of the Cuneiform Inscriptions had also THEIR ladies.

"Before Ninkit, mother of the great gods, chosen wife of Assur."[33]

"Ninkit (?) wife of Bel (?), mother of the great gods."[34]

"For the sake of the temple of ...... the great exalted wife of Assur my Lord."[35]

"The great goddess wife of Bel."[36]

We cannot readily see why there should have been some hesitation in translating the two last Inscriptions as they stand in the original. In the former we have "bit Ninkit hirte ...... Asur" *the house of Ninkit wife of Asur*, and in the latter (albeit marked with a query) "Ninkit hirti Bel," *Ninkit the wife of Bel*. The hesitation was probably owing to two names being given as husbands of Ninkit. But it appears "Bel" and "Asur" were names or surnames of the same divine individual, and therefore we need not blush at the idea of an act of *polyandria* committed by Ninkit.

We have made numerous references to passages containing the words "Assur my Lord" in a divine sense. We shall here add a few other citations on the signification, attached to the term, of a prince, a nobleman, and an Assyrian.

---

[33] "Mahar Ninkit ummi ili rabi hirtu naramti Assur" *Norris's Assyrian Dictionary*, p. 455.

[34] "Ninkit hirti Bel um ili rabi." *Ibid* 454.

[35] "Ana vatuhut bit Ninkit hirte rabte namaddi Asur bil-ya." *Ibid* 301.

[36] "Ninkit (?) hirti Bel." *Ibid* p. 146.

"The decrees of Assur, the lord (and) prince, my Lord."

"The mighty weapons which Assur the lord furnished me."

"To the capture of Muzur, Assur the Lord urged me."[37]

"Assur" appears almost invariably with a double *s* in the English translation, but it frequently occurs in the original with a single horizontal arrow, and is Romanized with a single *s*. Such is the case with the passage last cited, notwithstanding the double *s* in the English version. Four more examples, where the originals have but one *s*, will suffice here :—

"Mighty son of Assur-dayan."

"By the high power of Assur my Lord."

"Whom Assur ...... to the government of the land of Assyria (*Mat Asur*) vigorously proclaimed him."

"He has subdued the enemies of Assur."[38]

Assur or Asur stood also for the Assyrian empire and its capital.

"Who Padi their king, holding the creed and service of Assyria, had expelled," (p. 18).

"The men of Assyria," (p. 73).

"Plantations in Assyria I established." (*Mat Asur*, p. 388).

"Buildings in the extent of all Assyria, I caused construct, (*ina naphar Asur gabbi l'usarkis*, p. 392)."

---

[37] Ibid, pp. 704, 568, 616. "Ana kasad Muzri *Asur* bilu, &c."

[38] Ibid, pp. 578, 579, 185. "Aplu kenu sa *Asur*-dayan." "Ina emuqi zirate sa *Asur* bili-ya." "Sa *Asur*. . . , ana saptu mat *Asur* kinis ibbu-su." "Usanqitu gini *Asur*."

The double *s* was doubtless owing to a *dagesh* in the original Hebrew word "Asshur,"[39] one of the sons of Shem, and used to represent Assyria, but the Assyrians themselves as they changed the *sh* into *s*, so they were not particularly tenacious of the double *s* either. In the Phonetic form, the god "Assur" has commonly two horizontal arrows, but it often appears with a single arrow representing a single *s*.[40] And we find that in the derivatives from the original "Assur," the double *s* is altogether dispensed with, as, "asarid" *eminent*, "asariduta" *eminence*, "asariddan" *chief*, "asurite" *chief*, "asarrite" *lofty*, "Telasurri" proper name of a country.[41]

We may therefore venture to identify the "Assur" or "Asur" of the Cuneiform inscriptions with the "Asura" of the Vedas. And this identification may account for the seeming inconsistencies in the Vedas in using that term in opposite senses. The seceding Arians, while still in Central Asia, may have reluctantly submitted to the introduction of the vocable "Asura," indicating gods and princes, and also honoured their own divinities and chiefs, with that title, and yet they may have ethnologically looked upon the term as hateful. We believe Ahura Mazda himself was so called, out of respect, real or pretended, for the paramount power in the palmy days of the Assyrian empire. One fact seems to be a conclusive proof of this.

---

[39] Gen. x. 22; Psalm xxxiii. 8.

[40] Norris's Assyrian Dictionary, p. 55.

[41] Ibid, pp. 57, 58.

The Zend Avesta says that Vistasp "brought forth the firm placed, bound (Law) from the Hunus" (Bleeck, iii. p. 92). Now Babylon, or at least a portion of it, was called Suanna, and the "Hunus" or *Sunus* were probably people inhabiting that place. "Dwelling within Suanna (Babylon)" *Norris*, p. 419. "Festivals of Suanna (Babylon)" p. 587.

And thus Indra may have been worshipped as a divinity under the title of Asura, and at the same time his exploits in destroying hostile Asuras, whether Assyrian or Iranian, may have been celebrated triumphantly in hymns and songs. The ovation accorded to the slayer of Vritra, both in the Vedas and the Zend Avesta, was probably owing to that person having been an Assyrian and a common enemy before the Indian immigration. And this appears still more evident from the overthrow of that Asura being reckoned as among the "ancient" exploits of Indra, previous to the Arian settlement in India."[42]

As far as our inquiry after the primitive home of the Arians, which is indeed the subject of this chapter, is concerned, we are thus led to look for it in the Westward of Asia—in the direction of "the land of Asur," from which was derived one of the most prevailing terms in the Rig Veda, and which still continues to haunt the Indian mind with visions of ogres and goblins. It is something to have arrived at the origin of this formidable term, which is annually symbolized, in the group of figures representing Durga

---

[42] इंद्रस्य नु वीर्याणि प्रवोचं यानि चकार प्रथमानि वज्री R. V. I. 32. 1..

and her companions, by the grinning ogre, receiving his death stroke, under the feet of the giant-killing goddess.

Nor have we been rambling like truants, forgetful of our business. We have been brought as far as the vicinity of Assyria in quest of the primitive home of the Arian family. And yet our rambles are not yet done with. We have more evidence from the Rig Veda in store throwing still clearer light on what we have advanced, and leading to the same direction in our detective course. We must now introduce the story of Saramá, the Panis, and the cows.

This is the most striking of all Vedic allusions to Central or rather Western Asian events. The narrative is thus epitomized by Sáyana by way of introduction to Rig Veda x. 108:[13] "The Panis, Asura officers of the Asura Vala, had stolen certain cows belonging to Brihaspati, the spiritual preceptor of Indra, and secreted them in a cavern. Indra, moved by Brihaspati, deputed the divine bitch, by name Saramá, to track the cows. She having crossed a great river reached the capital or palace of Vala, and saw the cows secured in a secret recess. Then the Panis, having heard of the dog's approach, entered into a conversation with a view to gain her over." The Hymn in question is accordingly a dialogue between the Panis

---

[13] ऐन्द्रपुरोहितस्य बृहस्पतेर्गोषु वलनाम्नोऽसुरस्य भटैः पणिनामकैरसुरैरपहृत्य गुहायां निहितासु सतीषु बृहस्पतिप्रेरितेनेन्द्रेण गवामन्वेषणाय सरमा नाम देवशुनी प्रेषिता। सा च महतीं नदीमुत्तीर्य वलपुरं प्राप्य गुप्तस्थाने नीतास्ता गा ददर्श। अथ तस्मिन्नन्तरे पणय इदं शुनागमनमवगच्छन्त एनां मित्रीकर्तुं संवादमकुर्वन्।

and Saramá, who are in the technical terminology of the Vedas, alternately the "Rishi" and "Devatá" of the several verses. In the first and every other odd verse as far as the 9th, the Panis are the "Rishi" or speaker, and Saramá the Devata or the person addressed. In the second and all other even verses the case is just the reverse; and in the eleventh or final verse Saramá is allowed the utterance of the last words. Whatever the nature of this narrative be, the Asuras, Panis, and the dog Saramá seem to have been household words with the Indian Arians. The story is alluded to in some forty or fifty hymns of the Rig Veda interspersed in all the Mandals thereof. The "lofty stronghold" (as it is called in i. 6, 5) was, according to the above description, close to a "great river," and the *Asuras*, who were officers or soldiers of Vala, were named Panis. Classical mythology supplies a clue to the identification of the characters and scenery described in the narrative. We have Belus or Bel as a representative surname of all the Belides or successors of Belus. Vala may be compared with Belus, the names being almost identical, without the classical termination in Belus. Panis may be fairly referred to Phineus,[44] a son of Belus, who had *his* representatives, again, in the Phinides.[45] The "stronghold" or capital of Vala may then legitimately stand for Babel, or Borsippa, the "great river," said to have been crossed by Sarama, being the Euphrates. The

---

[44] See Dr. Smith's Dictionary, and Classical Mythological, under the name Phineus.

[45] *φινειδης, ὁ απο τοῦ φινεως.*—*Suidas.*

Vedic references to such a capital of Vala, close to a "great river," with the Asuras, "Panayas,"[46] (perhaps brothers or cousins) advance us many a good step in determining the original home of the Arian family. Babel was at one time near enough to them, in their estimation, to enable its soldiers or princes to capture and carry off the cattle of Indra's *guru*—near enough also for them to depute a spy, who, Ulysses-like, being, by his cunning and sagacity, the very image of a "Laconian dog," might track the lost animals, as the king of Ithaca had done so successfully in *the Ajax* of Sophocles.[47]

After the ridicule which some scholars have passed on the story of Panis and the cows, it is not without some diffidence that we are noticing it here. But notwithstanding the ridicule, eminent critics have not disdained to treat it as a sort of nucleus for the story of the siege and destruction of Troy. The word "Vilu" (Rig V. I. 6, 5) has been identified with Ιλιος, and the dog Saramá has been dignified with the rank of no less a person than the beauteous queen of Sparta, whose name, in various forms, is still owned by numberless ladies in Europe, and for whom a

---

[46] "Panayas" is plural of "Panis," and must mean his descendants or successors, as the "Raghus," Yadus, and "Kurus," stand respectively for the successors and representatives of Raghu, Yadu, and Kuru.

[47] . . . . εὖ δέ σ' εκφέρει
κυνὸς Λακαίνης ὥς τις εὔρινος βάσις.

great fortress and a great nation had fallen victims to the vengeful rage of the Argives. The elevation of "Sarama" to "Helena," by the rule which allowed changes of *s* into *h*, and *r* into *l*, and classed all *nasals* in the same group, so that *m* might at pleasure pass for *n*, is perhaps an infliction of the Indian Nemesis on those, who, on the other hand, had seriously broached a diametrically opposite theory—the theory of the siege and destruction of Troy having been the nucleus of the oldest epic of India, the *Rámáyana.* But we have no pet theory of our own on the subject, and, however adverse our prejudices of early education may be against the conversion, into mythological vapour, of either Hector and Achilles on the one hand, or Ráma and Rávana on the other, we shall be delighted with the spectacle of a good archæological fight between the extinguishers of Troy, who would invest Homer with a knowledge of the Rig Veda, and the abolishers of Lanká who would turn Valmíki into an adept in Homeric Greek.

It is also not a small puzzle to see, at the same time, the *nucleus* of the Trojan story itself evaporated into a—*nothing.* We cannot say we are able, however willing, to follow the eminent editor of the Rig Veda Sanhita—to whom we are under no common obligations, and, but for whose unrivalled editorial feat, these pages themselves would perhaps never have seen the light—in holding *the cows* stolen by Panis to be nothing more than "the cows of the morning, the dawns, or the days themselves, which are represented as rescued at the end of each night by the power of Indra, or some similar solar gods."[48] Our difficulty in accepting this summary resolution of Saramá, Vala, Panis and the cows, into a *morning vapour*, arises from the very pages of the great work edited by Professor Max Müller. Allusions to the story are found throughout the Rig Veda. Every *mandala*, every division, has to say something on it. And although in certain instances, the story is illustrated by the similitude of a morning cloud, dissipating at sunrise, yet it is treated even there as a substantive narrative, ornamented by an example, but never as a type of the example itself. The names of Vala and Panis, with their antagonists, Indra and Brihaspati, aided by their dog Saramá (or some detective, allegorized as such) which recognized the lowing of the cows, and tracked them to a recess in the fortress, appear so constantly as the heroes of a veritable narrative, that although it may have been coloured with many myths and figures, yet there can be no absurdity in supposing some fact or facts underlying it.

But it is not our present purpose to uphold the narrative of Saramá and the Panis as a historical fact. Our business now is with the *fact of such a conception* in the minds of our Vedic writers. They speak of a *divine bitch* deputed by Indra, Brihaspati, and Angiras, to track some cattle, the property of Brihaspati and Angiras, which had been stolen and carried off by an Asura named Panis (or certain Asuras called

[48] Max Müller's Rig-Veda-Sanhita translated and explained, p. 31.

Panayas, plural of "Panis") to the capital or stronghold of Vala, also an Asura, by the side of a "great river." Saramá crosses the river and tracks the cattle in a cave appertaining to the same stronghold, which in one place (I. 6, 5) is indicated by the adjective "Vilu," and is also described as a high land or mountain. Indra attacks the stronghold and rescues the cattle. The story is recounted as among the *former* feats of Indra, by which he had entitled himself to the thanks of the Arian family for ever.

Now we find from other sources that there was an ancient king, or deified hero, named Belus, that he had, on an eminence on the banks of the river Euphrates, a fortified palace,[49] which was called "Babel," or "Borsippa," and sometimes "Babilu,"[50] in the original Assyrian tongue. Belus had a son named Phineus, who was a character of sufficient importance to have given occasion for a patronymic by which his descendants were known in after ages, as the Rághavas from Raghu in our country. Belus or Bel was also a representative character, and might stand as an epithet for any of his successors. We find also that the word "Assur" or "Asur" (sometimes, as we have already

---

[49] "In his palace which is Babylon joyfully I passed." Norris's Assyrian Dict., p. 409. "The walls of the fortress of Babel, its defence of war, I raised." *Ibid*, p. 500. "To Babylon the fortress of Bel." *Ibid*, p. 642. "The house of Birbir, the lofty citadel of Bel." *Ibid*, pp. 31, 119.

[50] "Ina Babilu-ki." *In Babylon. Ibid*, p. 543. "Sar Babilu-ki," *king of Babylon. Ibid*, p. 506. The second syllable of this term curiously corresponds with the Vedic "Vilu," the "lofty" fortress.

seen, there was only one sibilant) was a term expressive of dignity, and indeed of divinity, highly extolled among the descendants, successors, or followers of Belus.

The derivatives of "Assur" again bear testimony to the dignity attached to the idea of the original term. We have "asaritti" for *eminent*, lofty; "asariddan" and "asurite" for *chief.* The phrase "asariddan malki" stands for *chief of kings.* There is likewise a term "sar" (without the initial *a*) which is the ordinary word for "king." As "ina kibiti el sar apzu" *in honor of the god, king of waters.* We further learn from the same source that it was nothing unusual with the Assyrians, or descendants of Belus, to carry off spoils and captives to Babylon or Assyria. The kings themselves boastfully recorded, by means of indelible inscriptions, the carnage and other outrages they committed on their enemies—the numbers they impaled and crucified from time to time, and their plunder of cities and towns. Thus: "chief bow-men, assistants, drivers of four-wheeled chariots, common bow-men, headmen, cattle and sheep with conductors many, I carried off to Assyria."[51] Again, "sheep, which not numbered, from among them I carried off."[52] "Goats and young, their property, not to be counted I carried off."[53] "Sheep many, plunder much, I plundered."[54] Once more; "horses, camels,

[51] *Norris's Assyr. Dict.*, p. 695.

[52] *Ibid*, p. 190.

[53] *Ibid*, p. 191.

[54] *Ibid*, p. 278.

bullocks, which at the approach of battle, had fled; my hands captured." "With 120 heads of cattle and sheep (which) he brought I received."[55]

If now we compare the Indian narrative with the records of Cuneiform inscriptions, there can scarcely remain a doubt that the Vala of the Rig Veda, was the Belus or Bel of the Inscriptions—that "the lofty capital of Vala" in the Rig Veda, was "the lofty citadel of Bel" in the Inscriptions, that the Asuras, Panis, (Sanskrit Panayas) of the Veda, were identical with the Phinides of classical history or mythology—that the river crossed by Saramá, or whatever detective was indicated by that term, was the Euphrates. As far then as the subject of this chapter is concerned, we find that the Arians who emigrated to India were once familiar with the lofty citadel of Bel, and must have then lived not very far from the Euphrates.

Our idea of searching westward for the primitive home of the Arians is thus singularly corroborated by the Vedic story of the captured and recovered cows. But we must now add a few observations on the importance of the canine lady herself in this detective process. The very conception of such an animal in the Brahminical mind is a fact which requires accounting for. How did the Vedas get at such an idea as a "divine dog?" The canine species has never been in much favour on Indian soil. It has always been reckoned an unclean animal fit only

---

[55] *Ibid*, pp. 269, 36.

to be treated with stones of the roughest kind.[56] How came an animal, whose very touch is pollution, to be dignified with the title of "divine?" The gods have indeed certain favourite animals for their *chargers.* Indra has his elephant, Siva his bull, Vishnu his Garuḍa, Durga her lion, Kártikeya his peacock. Even the cat and the rat and the snake have their respective riders of celestial origin. The fish, the tortoise, the boar, have also been honoured as divine vehicles. But the dog has never enjoyed such a dignity in the pantheon of India. How then came the authors of the Rig Veda to entertain the idea of a "divine dog?"

There is nothing in human nature to induce such an exaltation of the canine species—certainly not in Asia. The merchant in the Bagh-o-Bahar, who had manifested a peculiar interest for a dog, to which he had owed many obligations, and even his life, had a narrow escape with his head, when arraigned as a *sag-parast* (dog-worshipper). Asiatics have never been such fox-hunters as to patronize hounds,[57] nor had they the Spartan spirit which produced the "Laconian bitch," and made it the subject of learned dissertations and eulogies. But the Spartans themselves were innocent of the idea of a "divine dog." The

---

[56] Sankaracharia in his well known commentary on the Vedant takes occasion to speak of three classes of stones—*highly precious, of middling water,* and low rough clods *fit only for casting at dogs and crows:* पृथिवीत्वसामान्यात्मतानामप्यश्मनां केचिन्महार्हा मणयो वज्रवैडूर्यादयोऽन्ये मध्यवीर्याः सूर्यकान्तादयोऽन्ये प्रहीणाः श्ववायसप्रक्षेपणार्हाः । II. 1, 23.

[57] The Assyrian Inscriptions do not speak very flatteringly of

Grecian Cerberus was a creature or denizen of *hell*, not heaven. The Egyptians, indeed, had their Anubis, but how came Indian Brahmins to be infected with notions peculiar to the land of Ham? How came the authors of the Rig Veda to devote a whole hymn to the glorification of Saramá—a hymn in which she is alternately a "deity" and a holy "Rishi." Even Anubis had never been worshipped as a *sage*-diplomatist, such as the following Dialogue indicates.

The Panis. "With what object has Saramá come hither? The way back is far, and shut out from her. 'What do you require from us? How have you travelled here? How have you crossed the waters of the aerial river?' "

Saramá. "I come as an emissary, deputed by Indra. I am seeking, O Panis, your great wealth. The river itself saved me from the fear of passing over. Thus I crossed the waters of the aerial river."

The Panis. " 'O Saramá, what sort of a person is Indra? What army has he whose emissary, thou hast come hither from such distance?" (*Turning to themselves*) "Let *Saramá* come. Let us receive her as a friend. And let her be mistress of our Cows."

Saramá. "I do not consider him (Indra) to be destroyable by you. He destroys (all enemies), whose emissary, I, have come from such a distance. Deep

the canine species—the following are specimens of their complimentary language: "gilbu, gilbilu"—a *dog*, a *vile wretch.* Norris's Assyrian Dictionary, p. 177.

"Kalbi [ur-ku] tarbit hekal-ya" *dogs the growth of my palace* (meaning treacherons and seditious officers). Ibid, p. 511.

streams cannot overwhelm him. You shall, O Panis, yourselves lie slain by Indra."

The Panis. "O Blessed Saramá, these cows which thou seekest, coming round from the extremity of the sky, are thine. Who shall without a fight escape hence? Moreover our arms are sharp."

Sarama. "O Panis, your words are unworthy of soldiers. Your bodies are not fit for arrows, because they are vile. Let your ways be passable or impassable, but Brihaspati will not, in either case, impart pleasure to you with those two attributes."

The Panis. "This treasure, O Saramá, is secured by rocks, obtained by means of cattle, horses and wealth. The Panis, who are excellent protectors, guard the sites of the cows, which, by their lowing thou suspectest. In vain hast thou come."

Sarama. "Here are some Rishis, sharpened by the Soma liquor, Ayásia and the Angiras, who had been engaged for nine months in the sacrifice. They will divide among themselves that multitude of cows. Therefore, O Panis, renounce this language you have uttered that I have come in vain."

The Panis. "O blessed Saramá, thou hast come hither prevented from going back by divine power. We shall therefore make thee our sister. Do not go back. We shall share thy cows between ourselves.

Sarama. "I know neither brotherhood nor sisterhood. Indra and the fierce Angiras know it. They have now surrounded my desired cows for which I have come. Therefore, O Panis, surrender the great multitude of cattle and depart hence. *Saramá continues.* Do ye, O Panis, go to some large distant country. Let the cows come out breaking through the gates by the force of them. Brihaspati, Soma, the stones and the Rishis shall take them."[58]

Such virtues in a dog had never entered into Brahminical conceptions. How is this psychological marvel to be accounted for? Here "the missing link" comes to our relief. The Zend Avasta solves our problem. The Vendidad comes with a whole chapter, the Fargard XIII., devoted to the glorifica-

---

[58] किमिच्छंती सरमा प्रेदमानड् दूरे ह्यध्वा जगुरिः पराचैः ।
कास्मेहितिः का परितक्म्यासीत् कथं रसाया अतरः पयांसि ॥
इंद्रस्य दूतीरिषिता चरामि मह इच्छंती पणयो निधीन्वः ।
अतिष्कदो भियसा तन्न आवत्तथा रसाया अतरं पयांसि ॥
कीदृङ्ङिंद्रः सरमे का दृशीका यस्येदं दूतीरसरः पराकात् ।
आ च गच्छान्मित्रमेना दधामाथा गवां गोपतिर्नो भवाति ॥
नाहं तं वेद दभ्यं दभत्स यस्येदं दूतीरसरं पराकात् ।
न तं गूहंति स्रवतो गभीरा हता इंद्रेण पणयः शयध्वे ॥
इमा गावः सरमे या ऐच्छः परि दिवो अंतान्सुभगे पतंती ।
कस्त एना अव सृजादयुध्व्युतास्माकमायुधा संति तिग्मा ॥
असेन्या वः पणयो वचांस्यनिषव्यास्तन्वः संतु पापीः ।
अधृष्टो व एतवा अस्तु पंथा बृहस्पतिर्व उभया न मृळात् ॥
अयं निधिः सरमे अद्रिबुध्नो गोभिरश्वेभिर्वसुभिर्न्यृष्टः ।
रक्षंति तं पणयो ये सुगोपा रेकु पदमलकमा जगंथ ॥
एह गमन्नृषयः सोमशिता अयास्यो अंगिरसो नवग्वाः ।
त एतमूर्वं वि भजंत गोनामथैतद्वचः पणयो वमन्नित् ॥
एवा च त्वं सरम आजगंथ प्रबाधिता सहसा दैव्येन ।
स्वसारं त्वा कृणवै मा पुनर्गा अप ते गवां सुभगे भजाम ॥
नाहं वेद भ्रातृत्वं नो स्वसृत्वमिंद्रो विदुरंगिरसश्च घोराः ।
गोकामा मे अच्छदयन्यदायमपात इत पणयो वरीयः ॥
दूरमित पणयो वरीय उद्गावो यंतु मिनतीर्ऋतेन ।
बृहस्पतिर्या अविंदन्निगूळ्हाः सोमो ग्रावाण ऋषयश्च विप्राः ॥

tion of the canine race, commencing with its ancestor Vaṇhápára. "Which is the creature created by Spenta-Mainyus among the creatures which Spenta-Mainyus has created which every morning at the rising of the sun comes forth as a thousand slayers of Aṇgra-Mainyus? Then answered Ahura Mazda: The dog with the prickly back and woolly muzzle, Vaṇhápára, upon whom evil-speaking men impose the name of Dujaka."[59] Then follows a catechetical dissertation on the virtues of Vaṇhápára and his whole species, including both their physique and morale, occupying some 160 or 170 verses, to the very end of the chapter. We do not wish to class ourselves with the "evil-speaking men" who give a bad name to Vaṇhápára, nor either to join the great scholar[60] who had ridiculed the Vendidad for it. We shall only take note of this extravagant description of the dog as a peculiar feature in the Zend-Avesta, and the Veda, by supplying a fitting illustration of the same in its character of the "divine bitch," Saramá, exhibits an unmistakable resemblance to the same features, and thus indicates the quondam connection of Indian Arians with sites where the Zend Avesta passed for a sacred Record. The story of the stolen cows in the citadel of Vala is consequently corroborated, for our purpose in this chapter, by the fact of such a conception as "Saramá, the divine bitch," in

---

[59] Bleeck, vol. i. p. 103.

[60] Sir William Jones, quoted in the Rev. Dr. Wilson's *Religion of the Parsees*, pp. 325-327.

Hymns of the Rig Veda. And thus in our search for the original Arian home, we already find unmistakable vestiges in Central and Western Asia which cannot fail to place us on the right track.

Having done with the dog, we shall now revert to the story of Vritra, the *restrainer of waters*. The opening of rivers by Indra is referred to in numerous hymns, which explain the sense, in which, the benefits, conferred by his successful conflict with Vritra, were appreciated by the undivided Arians. It was not, as Sáyana imagined, a local allegory of thunder and lightning, turning the collected clouds into a refreshing shower. It was, as appears from various passages, Indra's opening rivers, the Parushni, (Euphrates ?) being especially named, the natural course of which had been, by some secret manœuvre, perhaps during night, obstructed by a besieging enemy, that drew down upon him the thanks and acknowledgments of the grateful Arians, and inspired their doxologies, songs, and odes at his wonderful success.

One doxology of this kind is contained in R. V. x. 133, which is attributed to Sudás, son of Pijavana. The first mantra addresses Indra as "Vritrahá," or destroyer of Vritra, and calls upon all ceremonial panegyrists to laud him—concluding with a sentence (which continues as a refrain throughout the hymn, the last mantra only excepted) "let the vile bowstrings of all others (our enemies) be broken." The second mantra recounts Indra's killing the Serpent (Vritra) and opening the streams, and concludes with the same refrain.[61] Now the author of this hymn was a king as well as a Rishi. He was probably ruler of the place which the enemy had intended to storm by a night march through a ford, caused by a manœuvre in the dark. The author of the hymn x. 133 had therefore himself mainly benefited by "the opening of streams." The benefits he had derived are given in detail in vii. 18 (attributed to Vasistha) the first four mantras of which indicate the intention of the doxologist to recount Indra's benefactions to a past generation.

1. "That, O Indra, even our fathers, extolling (or supplicating) thee, obtained all their desires, [it was quite befitting] because thou hast good-milking cows, thou hast horses. Treasure itself desires thee for its lord, thou being most bountiful to the sacrificers.[62]

2. "As a king with his wives, thou dwellest with lights, being thyself a wise performer of ceremonies. Protect us, O Maghavan, with cows, horses and treasure. Train us, thy own devotees, for the acquisition of riches.

---

[61] R. V. x. 133, 1, 2. प्रो ष्वस्मै पुरोरथमिंद्राय शूषमर्चत ।
अभीके चिदु लोककृत्संगे समत्सु वृत्रहास्माकं बोधि चोदिता
नभंतामन्यकेषां ज्याका अधि धन्वसु ॥
त्वं सिंधूँ रवासृजोऽधराचो अहन्नहिं ।
अशत्रुरिंद्र जज्ञिषे विश्वं पुष्यसि वार्यं तं त्वा परिष्वजामहे नभंतां &c.

[62] R. V. vii. 18, 1-4. त्वे ह यत्पितरश्चिन्न इंद्र विश्वा वामा जरितारो असन्वन् । त्वे गावः सुदुघास्त्वे ह्यश्वास्त्वं वसु देवयते वनिष्ठः ॥ राजेव हि जनिभिः क्षेष्येवाव द्युभिरभि विदुष्कविः सन् । पिशा गिरो मघवन् गोभिरश्वैस्त्वायतः शिशीहि राय अस्मान् ॥ इमा उ त्वा पस्पृधानासो अत्र मंद्रा गिरो देवयंतीरुपस्थुः । अर्वाची ते पथ्या राय एतु स्याम ते सुमताविंद्र शर्मन् ॥
धेनुं न त्वा सूयवसे दुदुक्षन्नुप ब्रह्माणि ससृजे वसिष्ठः । त्वामिन्मे गोपतिं विश्व आहा न इंद्रः सुमतिं गंत्वच्छ ।

3. "May these cheering encomiums, boldly coveting thee for their divine object, reach thee here. May thy way unto wealth come before us. May we remain at ease in thy good will.

4. "Vasistha has offered these mantras desiring to milk thee, like a cow in a good green pasture. All my people call thee the owner of cows. May Indra come unto our well-intentioned devotions."

The hymnist then goes on giving in detail the acts of Indra in the interest of Sudas.[63]

"Even waters, dispersed by the enemy, Indra made easily passable by Sudas.

"Turvasa came forward (against Sudas) for wresting his treasure. The Bhrigus and the Druhyas were the respective auxiliaries of Sudas and Turvasa. Indra by a flank movement delivered his friend.

---

[63] अर्णांसि चित्पप्रथाना सुदास इंद्रो गाधान्यकृणोत्सुपारा ।

पुरोळा इत्तुर्वशो यक्षुरासीद्राये मत्स्यासो निशिता अपीव । श्रुष्टिं चक्रुर्भृगवो द्रुह्यवश्च सखा सखायमतरद्विषूचोः ।

दुराध्यो अदितिं स्रेवयन्तोऽचेतसो वि जगृभ्रे परुष्णीं । मह्ना विव्यक् पृथिवीं पत्यमानः पशुष्कविरशयच्चायमानः ।

ईयुरर्थं न न्यर्थं परुष्णीमाशुश्चनेदभिपित्वं जगाम ।

अध श्रुतं कवषं वृद्धमप्स्वनु द्रुह्युं नि वृणग्वज्रबाहुः ।

वि सद्यो विश्वा दृंहितान्येषामिंद्रः पुरः सहसा सप्त दर्दः ।

व्यानवस्य तृत्सवे गयं भाग्जेष्म पूरुं विदथे मृध्रवाचं ॥

निगव्यवोऽनवो द्रुह्यवश्च षष्टि शता सुषुपुः षट् सहस्रा ।

आवदिंद्रं यमुना तृत्सवश्च प्रात्र भेदं सर्वताता मुषायत् ।

अजासश्च शिग्रवो यक्षवश्च बलिं शीर्षाणि जभ्रुरश्व्यानि ॥

न त इंद्र सुमतयो न रायः संचक्षे पूर्वा उषसो न नूत्नाः ।

देवकं चिन्मान्यमानं जघंथाव त्मना बृहतः शंबरं भेत् ॥

प्र ये गृहादममदुस्त्वाया पराशरः शतयातुर्वसिष्ठः ।

न ते भोजस्य सख्यं मृषंताधा सूरिभ्यः सुदिना व्युच्छान् ॥

"The wicked and evil-minded (enemy of Sudas) broke down the embankments of Parushni. Sudas, through the grace of Indra, reclaimed the lands. And Kavi, the son of Chayamána, fell like a sacrificial victim.

"The waters of Parushni went to their natural place, and no longer flowed where they were not intended to flow. The horses of Sudas too moved in their natural place.

"Then the thunderbolt holder, Indra, inflicted death on Sruta, Kavasha, and Druhya, by drowning them in the waters.

"Then Indra at once destroyed all their cities and strongholds, and gave away to Tritsu the habitation of the followers of Anu.

"The followers of Anu and Druhya to the number of six thousand lay in the sleep of death being killed by Sudas.

"Then Yamuna and the sons of Tritsu gratified Indra who had in this battle killed Bheda. The people of Aza, the Sigrus, and the Yakshus, presented him the heads of horses, slain in war, as offerings.

"Neither thy good will nor thy wealth, whether of yore or now-a-days, can be sufficiently described. Even Devaka, the son of Manyamána, thou didst kill, and Sambara thou didst hurl down from an eminence.

"O Indra, Parásara himself, capable of subduing hundreds of Yatus, together with Vasistha and other Rishis, having by thy favour got a home, and sought to propitiate thee, are by no means forgetful of thy kindness as their patron."

This hymn was evidently written, after the hymnists had "got a home" in India, recounting the deeds of Indra in the course of their migration. It shows that Vritra's meditated night attack was after the manner of what Cyrus afterwards did so successfully against Babylon itself. The appearance of the sun and morning light, which some hymns mention, only meant that the enemy's plot was frustrated during the night, and morning dawned immediately after,—the sun rose with his gratifying brilliance, when Indra saw no enemy, for his foes were all submerged by the returning waters.[64] From the number of persons punished and humbled by Indra after Vritra's death, it would seem that many neighbouring princes and people had leagued with the enemy, and the situation of those princes and people must give material help

---

[64] यदिंद्राहन् प्रथमजामहीनामान्मायिनाममिनाः प्रोत मायाः।
आत्सूर्यं जनयन्द्यामुषासं तादीत्ना शत्रुं न किला विवित्से॥
नदं न भिन्नममुया शयानं मनो रुहाणा अति यन्त्यापः।
याश्चिद्वृत्रो महिना पर्यतिष्ठत्तासामहिः पत्सुतःशीर्बभूव॥
नीचावया अभवद्वृत्रपुत्रेन्द्रो अस्या अव वधर्जभार।
उत्तरा सूरधरः पुत्र आसीद्दानुः शये सहवत्सा न धेनुः॥

"When, O Indra, thou struckest the first-born of serpents (Vritra), then thou didst completely baffle the tricks of the deceivers. Then producing the sun, the sky, and the morning, thou indeed couldst observe no enemy. The heart-cheering waters had passed over Vritra, lying on the ground, like a river with embankments broken. Vritra lay under the feet of the very waters which by the force of his arts he had restrained.

The mother of Vritra fell prostrate on her son, struck by Indra. There lay the mother Dánu over, and the son below, like a cow with her calf." Rig Veda I. 32. 4, 8, 9.

in ascertaining the quarter where the Arians resided at the time and their line of march towards India.

Many names of places, peoples, and individuals are mentioned in the above hymn (vii. 18) of which Indian tradition knows next to nothing. The Assyrian inscriptions, however, throw much light. Turvasa may be easily recognized as Tubusu of the Inscriptions, king of Nirdun.[65] The A'navas, or followers of Anu, and the Ajása, liege subjects of Aja, readily find their respective objects of homage and allegiance in Anu[66] and Aza.[67] The former, as a deified prince, the first member of the Assyrian triad, is constantly mentioned in the Inscriptions, and the latter appears as a son of Sanzu, king of Manna. Kavasha may have been a chief connected with Kabsu, a city on the mountains above Nipar.[68] Devaka, son of Manyamána, may be claimed by Dabigu[69] (a frontier town of Syria) as its chief, and Sambara, so well known throughout the Rig Veda, and (in iv. 30, 14) called a *son or descendant of Kulitara*, will perhaps be hailed as a relative by Kíliteru,[70] prince of Commukha. The Yatus usually

---

[65] Norris's Assyrian Dictionary, p. 650.

[66] "Anu king of the great divine chiefs and Anunnaki." *Ibid*, p. 471. Rawlinson's Herod. vol. i, p. 485.

[67] Talbot's contributions, &c. Journal Royal Asiatic Society, 1867, p. 57.

[68] *Ibid*, p. 527.

[69] *Ibid*, p. 692.

[70] "Kiliteru son of Kaliteru son of Serupin-sihusuri their king in the midst of the fight my hand took." *Ibid*, p. 564. This was in the reign of Tiglathpileser I., or the 12th century B. C. which is a curious confirmation of the age of the Vedas as calculated by the

called Yátu-dhánas or holders of Yatu, and reproached as eaters of human and equine flesh, without a local habitation assigned to them, will perhaps gladly accept a home and a safe asylum in the country called "Yatu"[71] in the Inscriptions, and escape at once the railleries, both of the Veda and Zend Avesta, content with their "horse flesh," which, in the vicinity of the Scythians, will be coveted as a dainty, rather than execrated as an abomination.

Yamuna cannot be intended for the river of that name in India, as the word is joined with the sons of Tritsu and the people of Aza and others. It may more reasonably stand for a Hittite (possibly an ancestor of the) usurper Yamani,[72] mentioned in the Assyrian Inscriptions.

The A'navas whom Sáyana takes, in two places at least, as sons of Anu, or *men*, (Anu being held as the progenitor of mankind in the same sense as Manu), may suggest other reflections for which this chapter, however, is not the proper place.

We thus find that most of the characters concerned in the encounter of Indra with Vritra belonged to Assyrian regions, in the West of Asia.

We shall now direct the reader's attention to another passage in the Rig Veda, not only most important for our object in this chapter, but, curiously enough,

---

late Archdeacon Pratt, from an astronomical conjunction mentioned by Bentley. Mr. Pratt placed it in the 12th century before Christ. (*Scripture and Science not at variance*, p. 153.)

[71] *Ibid*, p. 491. [72] *Ibid*, p. 484.

throwing light on a point, in Assyrian history, on which further light was held as a desideratum in the outer learned world. The question is thus stated by Professor Rawlinson: "It only remains to notice the name of Σάνδης which is applied by Agathias to the Assyrian Hercules, [the god *Nin* or *Bar*] on the authority of Berosus. This name has been much canvassed by classical and Oriental scholars, but without any definite results. It may be interesting, then, to add that *Bar* is explained in one of the Babylonian vocabularies by *Zindu*, as if the one name meant "the binder with chains," and the other, "the binder to the yoke," and both being sufficiently applicable to the god in question, either as Hercules or as the Man-Bull."[73]

Sanda-Marka have from time immemorial been popularly held in India as the twin names of the *Asura-guru*, but the Rig Veda sanctions only the *first*, thus:

"Do thou, O Saraswati, save us. Joined with the Maruts, boldly overthrow the enemy. Indra has killed that daring powerful [Asura] hero, the very chief of the disciples of Sanda."[74]

This verse not only confirms the name applied by

---

[73] Rawlinson's Herodotus, vol. i. p. 514.

[74] सरस्वति त्वमस्माँ अविड्ढि मरुत्वती धृषती जेषि शत्रून्।
त्यं चिच्छर्धन्तं तविषीयमाणमिन्द्रो हन्ति वृषभं शण्डिकानां ॥ R. V. ii. 30. 8.

Sáyana interprets "Sandikánám" शण्ड वंश्यानां *of the race of Sanda*, but "Sandika" would more properly stand for a follower or disciple of Sanda, just as Platonic would mean a follower, rather than a descendant, of Plato.

Berosus and Agathias to the "Assyrian Hercules," but also sustains the idea of the "man-bull,"—for "Sanda" means a *bull.* And as far as our object in this chapter is concerned, its success becomes undoubted from the above passage. The Asuras are clearly identified, and the Arians are *proved to have had conflicts* with the *Assyrians* whose *guru* or *god* was *Sanda* alias *Hercules*, *Nin*, or *Bar.*

Numerous other names may be found in the Vedas with outlandish traces, but we shall content ourselves here with one more example only. Ambarisha, a well-known royal Rishi, is mentioned in the Rig Veda as making obeisance to Indra in company with several others. He may also be claimed by the Cuneiform Inscriptions as a hero of Assyrian regions, perhaps the founder of a dynasty which had the courage to slight the fortunate star of a great Assyrian monarch.[73] Ambarisha, again, had a son who like himself was one of the Rishis or authors of the Rig Veda, bearing the name of "A'mbarisha Sindhudwipa." This very name would tend to confirm what the Inscriptions say of Ambarisha. Sindhudwipa may stand for an island in the ocean, or a country on the other side the sea or the River Indus. In any case it would be an *un*-Indian

---

[73] "Whose king Ambarissi the power [fortunate star] of Sargina disregarded." *Norris*, p. 243. The Ambarissi of the Inscription appears to have been a contemporary of Sargon, whose age would be posterior, at least by two or three centuries, to the age of the Vedas. But as the descendants of the Vedic Ambarisha were also called A'mbarisha, the initial vowel of the original name being only lengthened, Sargon's opponent might have been a descendant of the original Ambarisha.

locality. The prince who bore that name or surname must have had *foreign associations.*

We shall here conclude this chapter. We think sufficient traces of Arian connection have been discovered in the West of Asia to encourage us to persevere in the inquiry after the original settlement of our ancestors in that direction, and this will be our business in the next chapter.

CHAPTER III.

Arians' original settlement. Foreign evidence. Evidence of language. Objections answered. Zend Avesta and Persian tradition considered.

In dealing with the foreign evidence, bearing on the question of the primitive settlement of the Arians, one great difficulty consists in our own misfortune. We are unable to concur in the opinion, maintained by many eminent scholars, that the original Arian home was on the slopes of the Hindu Kush. We shall therefore first state the exact question at issue. We seem to be all agreed that the ancestors of the Brahmins came to India from beyond the Indus, that when they came they were themselves strangers to India, and India was a strange soil to them, that whether they came as conquerors, adventurers, or fugitives, the aboriginal inhabitants showed them no hospitality, nor allowed them to settle in the country without a struggle. Thus far we seem to be agreed. And as far as our own domestic interests are concerned, one main point is concurred in with the unanimous consent of scholars, and without any perceptible dissentient voice from the representatives of Brahminism. The position thus gained by the friends of Progress is itself of vast importance. The great bulwark of Brahminism is yielded without a struggle. For after this concession, those who have raised an enormous structure of *Caste*, on the system, introduced by the Arian immigrants, can no longer hold *Ariavarta* to be the original settlement of the A'ria (आर्य्य) race, nor the ancestors of Brahmins, either, to have been "autochthones" of Indian soil. They must, for consistency's sake, abandon their superstructure. For, the maintenance of the Brahminical system would compel them to hold that *Ariavarta* was the primitive home of the Arians. Without such a historical finding, Brahminism cannot stand, except as a spectacle of contempt and derision, a huge fabric founded on an admittedly exploded myth. If the ancestors of the Brahmans were themselves emigrants from an outlandish soil, "the earthly gods"[1] of India must be proved to be descendants of a Mlecha race. And then the boast of a Brahminical pedigree, co-eval with the creation of gods and the heavenly bodies, mountains and rivers, must vanish.[2] Such pretensions cannot be consistent with the fact of the Arian emigration from the other side of the Indus.

But so strong is the evidence of Comparative philology, and so numerous are the admissions and allusions in the Vedas themselves, that no one, laying any claims to the position of an educated man, can dare

---

[1] So the Brahmins call themselves—भूसुर, भूदेव, महीसुर &c.

[2] यावत् मेरुस्थिता देवा यावद् गङ्गा महीतले ।
चन्द्रार्कौ गगने यावत्तावद्विप्रकुले वयं ॥

to deny the fact of the Arian immigration. Even vernacular manuals, composed by authors who are strict observers of the caste system, inculcate that fact as a lesson of undoubted history.

Our difficulties commence from this point. After tracking the migratory path of the Arians to the other side of the Indus, many are inclined to look toward the slopes of the Hindu Kush as the quarter whence they had come. But as that mountain range continues to the Caspian gates, it is difficult to say what, in their opinion, are the limits of the Hindu Kush. We cannot derive from their theory any definite idea of the actual locality of the Arians' primitive home.

But, however appalling a position of antagonism to scholars of high reputation must confessedly be, we cannot at once abandon the chain of argument followed in the last chapter, and based, if we may venture to say so, on indisputable facts. The testimony of the Rig Veda, confirmed by the Zend Avesta and the Cuneiform Inscriptions, has brought us within Assyrian territory in our course. We have found Indra and Brihaspati fighting against "the lofty citadel of Bel," across the "great river" Euphrates. We have found Twastri fabricating weapons for Indra in his conflict with Vritra on the river Parusni (probably Purrati, or the same Euphrates, *Græce*). We have seen that the followers or votaries of the Assyrian god, or deified hero, Anu, engaged in that conflict, with many other individuals and peoples, traceable to places, within the limits of the Assyrian influence, in Mesopotamia, and to the furthest meandering of the Euphrates.

These pre-emigration events naturally point to the westward of Asia in our inquiry after the primitive home of the Arians.

This, again, is confirmed by a legend, which Dr. Muir has cited from the *Satapatha Brahmana*, evidently indicating the migratory path of the Devas and Asuras, or the undivided Arians, to have been from "the West to the East."[1]

"The gods and Asuras, who were both sprung from Prajápati, strove together. Then the gods were, as it were, worsted, and the Asuras thought, 'this world is now certainly ours.' 2. Then they spake, 'Come let us

---

[1] देवाश्च वा असुराश्च । उभये प्राजापत्याः पस्पृधिरे ततो देवा अनुव्यमिवासुरथ
हासुरा मेनिरेऽस्माकमेवेदं खलु भुवनमिति ॥ १ ॥ ते होचुः । हन्तेमां पृथिवीं
विभजामहै तां विभज्योपजीवामेति तामौक्ष्णैश्चर्मभिः पश्चात् प्राञ्चो विभजमाना
अभीयुः ॥ २ ॥ तद्वै देवाः शुश्रुवुः । विभजन्ते ह वा इमामसुराः पृथिवीं प्रेत
तदेष्यामो यत्रेमामसुरा विभजन्ते के ततः स्याम यदस्यै न भजेमहीति ते यज्ञमेव
विष्णुं पुरस्कृत्येयुः ॥ ३ ॥ ते होचुः । अनु नोऽस्यां पृथिव्यामाभजतास्त्वेव नोऽप्यस्यां
भाग इति ते हासुरा असूयन्त इवोचुर्यावदेवैष विष्णुरभिशेते तावद्वो दद्म
इति ॥ ४ ॥ वामनो ह विष्णुरास । तद्देवा न जिहीडिरे महद्वै नोऽदुर्ये नो
यज्ञसंमितमदुरिति ॥ ५ ॥ ते प्राञ्चं विष्णुं निपाद्य छन्दोभिरभितः पर्यगृह्णन् गाय-
त्रेण त्वा छन्दसा परिगृह्णामीति दक्षिणतस्त्रैष्टुभेन त्वा छन्दसा परिगृह्णामीति
पश्चाज्जागतेन त्वा छन्दसा परिगृह्णामीत्युत्तरतः ॥ ६ ॥ तं छन्दोभिरभितः परि-
गृह्य । अग्निं पुरस्तात्समाधाय तेनार्चन्तः श्राम्यन्तश्चेरुस्तेनेमां सर्वां सपत्नां सर्वं
पृथिवीं समविन्दन्त तद्यदेनेमां सर्वां समविन्दन्त तस्माद्वेदिर्नाम तस्मादाहुर्यावती
वेदिस्तावती पृथिवीत्येतया हीमां सर्वां समविन्दन्तैवं ह वा इमां सर्वां सपत्नानां
संवृङ्क्ते निर्भजत्यस्यै सपत्नान्य एवमेतद्वेद ॥ ७ ॥ सोऽयं विष्णुर्ग्लानः । छन्दोभिरभितः
परिगृहीतोऽग्निः पुरस्तान्नापक्रमणमास स तत एवौषधीनां मूलान्युपमुम्लोच ॥ ८ ॥
ते ह देवा ऊचुः । क्व नु विष्णुरभूत् क्व नु यज्ञोऽभूदिति ते होचुश्छन्दोभिरभितः
परिगृहीतोऽग्निः पुरस्तान्नापक्रमणमस्त्यत्रैवान्विच्छतेति तं खनन्त इवान्वीषुस्तं त्र्यङ्गुले-
ऽन्वविन्दंस्तस्मात्त्र्यङ्गुला वेदिः स्यात्तदु हापि पाञ्चिस्त्र्यङ्गुलामेव सौम्यस्याध्वरस्य वेदिं
चक्रे । *Sanscrit Texts*, vol. iv, 107.

divide this earth, and having divided it, let us subsist thereon.' They accordingly went on dividing it with ox-hides from west to east. 3. The gods heard of it, [and] said, 'The Asuras are dividing this earth; come, we shall go to the spot where they are dividing it. Who shall we become (i. e. what shall become of us), if we do not share in it?' Placing at their head Vishnu, the sacrifice, they proceeded [thither], 4. and said 'put us in possession of this earth; let us also have a share in it.' The Asuras, grudging as it were, answered, 'We give you as much as this Vishnu can lie upon.' 5. Now, Vishnu was a dwarf. The gods did not reject that offer; [but said among themselves], 'They have given us much, [these Asuras], who have given us what is co-extensive with sacrifice.' Then having placed Vishnu to the east, they surrounded him with metres; [saying], on the south side, 'I surround thee with the Gáyatrí metre;' on the west, 'I surround thee with the Trishṭubh metre;' on the north, 'I surround thee with the Jagatí metre.' 7. Having thus surrounded him with metres, they placed Agni (fire) on the east, and thus they went on worshipping and toiling. By this they acquired the whole of this earth; and since by this they acquired (*samavindanta*) it all, therefore [the place of sacrifice] is called *vedi* (from the root *vid*, 'to acquire).' Hence men say, 'as great as is the altar, so great is the earth;' for by it (the altar) they acquired the whole of this [earth]. Thus he who so understands this, conquers all this [earth] from rivals, expels from it rivals. 8. Then this Vishnu, being wearied, surrounded by metres, with

Agni to the east, did not advance; but then hid himself among the roots of plants. 9. The gods then exclaimed, 'What has become of the sacrifice?' They said, 'Surrounded by metres, with Agni to the east, he does not advance; search for him here.' So digging, as it were, they searched for, and found him at a depth of three fingers; therefore let the altar [have a trench] three fingers deep; therefore, also, *Páñchi* made an altar of this description for the soma sacrifice. 10. But let no one do so," etc.—(*Sanskrit Texts, Vol. IV,* p. 108.)

If now we advert to the well known testimony of Herodotus on the subject, we only introduce evidence which remarkably harmonizes with the vestiges of Arian migration in Western Asia, contained in the Vedas themselves. Herodotus tells us that the Medes, were, from time immemorial, called Arians until the age of Medea of Colchis, who changed their name on her arrival in their country. Herodotus declares that they were of yore called Arians πρὸς παντων *by all parties,* or *universally.*[4] It is remarkable that he gives us no insight into the *reason* of their being originally so called, and that he only assigns a mythical cause for the cessation of that name. But he has nevertheless noted a living memorial—a standing witness of the *fact* of Arians having once had their home in that quarter. Among the six tribes of the Medes he has named, one was called the Arizanti,[5] or descendants of

[4] Herod. vii. 62.
[5] Herod. i. 101.

Arians. Another vestige of Arian connexion with the Medes, noticed by him, was in the equipment of the Arians in the army of Xerxes. They were all inhabitants of the Central Asian Province of Aria, where they had doubtless settled on their migration or expulsion from Media. They were *furnished with Median bows*, but were, in other respects, like the Bactrians.[6]

We know that much reliance cannot be placed on unsupported statements of Herodotus. But we know also that his testimony *supported by other evidence* becomes most satisfactory. He has here recorded a tradition that in times of yore Media was peopled by "Arians," and, again, that they had already moved out before the age of mythology had given place to that of history. The tradition is not only corroborated by the evidence of the Vedas and the Assyrian Inscriptions, but by many other considerations which we shall state presently. Indeed the record of Herodotus supplies an explanation of what the Rig Veda says, without which the Vedic descriptions, to which we adverted in the last chapter, would have presented the appearance of a *mirage* in the desert, or the wild reveries of an insane mind.

Bochart proves by a learned dissertation that Media was called Ara or Aria from *Hara*, a place where the Assyrian Kings Pul and Tiglathpilnesar had banished the Reubenites, the Gadites, and half the tribe of Manasseh. "Hara," he says, "stands in 1 Chron. v.

---

[6] Ibid, vii. 65.

26 for Media in Ezra. Omitting the aspirate, Jerome reads it Ara. Indeed by the Greeks also, Media is called Aria, and the Medes, Arians." He then cites the passage in Herodotus to which we have already referred. He next cites Pausanias in Corinthiacis de Medéa, where he says that *Medéa went to the region then called Aria, and gave to the people thereof the name of Medes.* Apollodorus is then quoted, who says, that *Ariania was a country near Cadusia.* Xenophon is referred to after this, whose testimony is as remarkable as it is curiously satisfactory. He says, "The Thamnerians of Media are near Cadusia." Now Thamneria is derived from תֵּימָן "theman" *South*, and Aria, meaning *the southern Arians.* And so Bochart concludes : "Porro Aria est Hara."[7]

Here we have a chain of evidence leading us to Media as the original home of the Arians. We may safely say that in this investigation we have conjectured, or assumed nothing, we have put forth no pet theory of our own, we have followed our evidence, link after link, each link being independent in itself, without any inter-dependence of one on another. And if in the chain any link adds strength to its .neighbour, it is after the fashion of a Company of troops wherein each combatant supports his comrade, and, only so far as, in every chain of sound reasoning, logically established, the several arguments necessarily corroborate each other. The whole chain may be thus stated in a few words. (1) We find the Arian, a stranger, pro-

---

[7] Bocharti Geographia Sacra, Phaleg, p. 220.

bably a fugitive in India. He speaks of his "old home," but cannot definitely give its geography. He only says he came from *West to East*. He is a learned man, but is more fond of poetry than prose. He is certainly not a Xenophon. Unlike the author of the *Anabasis*, he kept no notes of his journeys and travels before he reached this country. He cannot give a coherent account of his marches, or halting stages in his journey. But he speaks of his gods and priests. He calls them Asuras, and yet he sometimes curses the Asuras, (some of whom he describes as the disciples of one "Sanda,") not in the language of a profane reprobate, but as a serious moralist, who knew how to distinguish good from evil. He is indeed so impatient of evil, that he imprecates his chief Asura, (whom he calls *eminently wise*,[8] and to whom he ascribes the creation of the Heavens and earth), to banish to a distant land, the baneful author of evil, named "Nir-riti," or unrighteousness incarnate.

2. Then, again, he speaks of a "lofty citadel," of an Asura named "Vala," which could only be reached by crossing a "great river." He speaks also of certain officers of Vala, who were brothers or cousins with the common surname of "Panis." The Panis, he says, had captured some cattle belonging to the spiritual preceptor of his chief, Indra, who recovered the animals after fighting and conquering the captors.

3. He speaks also of a conflict between his Indra, and an Asura called Vritra. The latter had attempted

---

[8] R. V. i. 24, 8, 9, 14, viii. 42, 1.

to cause a ford, in a certain river by restraining its waters, with a view to storm, by a night march, some town of which one of Indra's friend's (Sudas) was the ruler. Indra baffled the enemy's plots and stratagems, and saved his friend's territories. He then punished, by death or deprivation, many individuals and peoples who had leagued with the enemy, and gave away their territories and substance to others, who were friends and allies.

4. He names some of these peoples and individuals concerned in the above conflict. Some of these are Turvasa, Kavasha, Yamuna, Devaka, Sambara, together with the followers of Anu, the people of Aja, the Sigrus, the Yatus, &c.

Such being the statements of the Arian stranger, we make inquiries about the individuals and peoples named by him, and we find them verified in Central Aria and the Assyrian empire, by the testimony of the Cuneiform Inscriptions and other equally undoubted evidence, almost exactly as he has described them. And now Herodotus and some other Greek historians recognize him as an old resident of Media, missing for a long time, supposed to have been roving like a truant, or perhaps expelled from his original home by the incursion of some ruffian bands.

We ask whether this is not a chain of evidence which would satisfy even a judicial tribunal?

We fail to see anything like evidence in the conjectures of great men who have assigned the slopes of the Hindu Cush as the original home of the ancestors of Hindus, Persians, Greeks, and Teutons,—as, indeed, at the same time, the great nursery and rendezvous of the whole Arian family, that is to say, of the progenitors of all the most civilized races in the world.

Let us hear the most eminent scholar of the day as a supporter of the same side of the question :—

"At the first dawn of traditional history we see these Aryan tribes migrating across the snow of the Himalaya southward toward the "Seven Rivers" (the Indus, the five rivers of the Panjab and the Sarasvati), and ever since India has been called their home. That before that time they had been living in more northern regions, within the same precincts with the ancestors of the Greeks, the Italians, Slavonians, Germans, and Celts, is a fact as firmly established as that the Normans of William the Conqueror were the Northmen of Scandinavia. The evidence of language is irrefragable, and it is the only evidence worth listening to with regard to ante-historical periods. *Max. Müller's Hist. of Anct. Sanscrit Literature*, p. 12.

* * * *

But while most of the members of the Aryan family followed this glorious path, the southern tribes were slowly migrating towards the mountains which gird the north of India. After crossing the narrow passes of the Hindukush or the Himalaya, they conquered or drove before them, as it seems without much effort, the aboriginal inhabitants of the Trans-Himalayan countries. They took for their guides the principal rivers of Northern India, and were led by them to new homes in their beautiful and fertile valleys. It seems as if the great mountains in the north had afterwards closed for centuries their Cyclopian gates against new immigrations, while, at the same time, the waves of the Indian Ocean kept watch over the southern borders of the peninsula. None of the great conquerors of antiquity—Sesostris, Semiramis, Nebuchadnezzar, or Cyrus, who waged a kind of half-nomadic warfare over Asia, Africa, and Europe, and whose names, traced in characters of blood, are still legible on the threshold of history, disturbed the peaceful seats of these Aryan settlers. Left to themselves in a world of their own, without a past, and without a future before them, they had nothing but themselves to ponder on. *Ibid*, p. 15.

We yield to no one in our admiration of the great feat achieved by the learned editor of the Rig Veda Sanhita. It is therefore with extreme diffidence that we are obliged to give expression to our wonder that with the proofs of his Rig Veda in hand, the editor himself could have said that the Arian settlers, when they arrived in India, were "without a past, and without a future before them." What were "the ancient exploits" of Indra, if they were "without a past?" What meant the fights of Brihaspati and Angiras before the "lofty citadel" of Vala on the Euphrates, whether historical or mythical, if they were "without a past," in fact and in fancy? What meant their dealings with the names we have already mentioned, and perhaps scores more that we can yet mention, if the Arians were "without a past" on the plains of India? How could they have known the names of the great Assyrian gods, Anu and Sanda, if they were never in Assyria, nor had any dealings with that people, and—if they were really "without a past?"

We dare not say more. We can only regret that we are unable to accede to such confident assurances from one to whom multitudes justly look up for instruction and intellectual enlightenment. Sacred interests compel us, or we could not have presumed to give expression to our dissent from an authority so high—from a scholar so ripe, and from a philosopher at whose feet we would willingly receive lessons.

But the language of the Rig Veda Sanhita is plain. The voice of the Rishis, whose compositions he has

12

himself brought within our reach, gives no uncertain sound. There is nothing in it to manifest a journey to or over the Himálayá or the Hindu Kush. The Rishis point to many traces of a journey through Assyria and Central Asia, but none through the passes of the Hindu Kush and the Himálayá.

We believe that the story of the slopes of the Hindu Kush, having been the original settlement of the Arian family, was a conjecture entertained before the evidence of the Rig Veda was examined or noticed—certainly before it was compared with the notes of the Cuneiform Inscriptions. Critical scholars had generally a distrust of Herodotus, and they did not think that his assertion about a *Median* Aria was at all better than many other stories which he had recorded, only to be repudiated, in the republic of letters, as glaring untruths. They did not therefore think it worth their while to notice or examine evidence about it. Their motto seems to have been—*farthest from Herodotus, nearest to the truth.*

We do not however know what fate has overtaken that unfortunate historian's statement about the *Germans* having at one time been a Persian tribe—whether *that* has been assented to or not. If this has been credited, it will itself lead to a moral presumption that the Arian family in its integrity lived in Central and Western Asia, rather than the neighbourhood of the Hindu Kush. The Germans of whom Herodotus makes mention (i. 125) were probably the Carmanians, and, as such, Asiatic remnants of the great nation which now occupies such proud eminence on the continent of Europe—before whose arms France has been prostrated, and whose intellectual energy and vigour the whole world acknowledges with admiration.

It may be said we have proved too much. We have carried Arian relations even beyond Mesopotamia—into Syria, and almost on the borders of Palestine. All this, Apelles the Jew may credit—not men of understanding and intellect.

But we have not carried Arian relations an inch beyond where the stream of accredited evidence has impelled us. After traces of relationship have been discovered between "the swarthy natives of India and their conquerors, whether Alexander or Clive," nothing can in itself be incredible with reference to human movements on the face of our common globe. And all we have proved is that there were conflicts in Mesopotamia between the Arians and certain Assyrian chiefs who were joined by people from all parts of the Assyrian empire—from the south of the Caspian, to the land of the Hittites on the other side of the Euphrates.

But the Assyrian Inscriptions prove a great deal more than we have yet had occasion to show. They speak of towns on the Euphrates, and in Mesopotamia, which were evidently relics of Arian relations in those parts—indeed, of Indo-Arian relations, that is to say, those of the future ancestors of the Hindus : such as Hardispi (Haridaswa, the *yellow-horsed*, *Indra*, or perhaps the *sun* under an Indian title) Hindanu, Hindan, Hindaru, &c.[9] What is still more surprising, the Inscriptions note the existence of a tribe called "Haya-páda," in the neighbourhood of Samaria.[10] This is a pure unmixed Sanscrit word, meaning *horse-footed*, *i. e.* swift of foot, and the tribe so named must have remained at least till the reign of Sargon, (in whose tablet the record is found) as a living monument of Arian adventures in that quarter. It was as great a proof of Arian connection in Western Asia, as would a tribe called "Podas-ókus" have been of Grecian relations in India, if such a tribe had really been found near the Punjab.

The derivation of the word "Arian," as the Cuneiform Inscriptions indicate it, is also a proof of our primitive ancestors' sojourn in Western Asia. The meaning of the term appears in the Inscriptions from its use with the negative particle "la," *i. e.* "la-Ari" which means *barren*. Thus, "edis ipparsu asar *la-ari*; "*away they fled* (*to*) BARREN *places*." Again, "Tudat *la-ari* ... rabis etettiqa," *morasses* BARREN *greatly I passed over*. "Arian" accordingly meant *productive* or *cultivated*, and is given there as derived from "Heb. אָרָה *to gather fruit*," and it is compared with the Ethiopian "arara" *to reap*.[11] It may also be compared with the Greek ἀρόω and the Latin "aro" *to plough*, for without sowing, there could not be reaping—and surely "Arian" did not mean a *plunderer who reaped what another sowed.*

---

[9] Norris's Assyrian Dictionary, pp. 345, 417, 434, 443.

[10] Ibid, 417.

[11] Ibid, 662.

The above derivation of Arian accords with the Zend idea. Referring to the creation of Airyana Vaejo, Mr. Bunsen says, "The meaning of the verse is this: In the earliest time Airyana Vaejo was the only cultivated country; all the rest was a desert."[12] And the meaning attached to the word in Sanscrit was probably based on the same idea. A tiller of the ground is, in the Rig Vedas, (i. e. *Krishti* or *Charshani*), held synonymous with *man*,[13] and the Arian was considered *excellent* or *noble*, because he was exemplary as a *tiller of the ground*.

The Greek idea of Arian ἄρειος is doubtless derived from ἄρης *Ares* Mars, and Ares again comes probably from the Heb. אֲרִי Ari a *lion*. This word, if aspirated, turns into the Sanscrit *hari*, which, among various other meanings, stands also for "lion."

The name "Arian" appears thus to be of Semitic origin, but adopted and naturalized in Sanscrit. We have seen that the Arians left behind them, in the very heart of Semitic regions, a living monument of their wanderings in Western Asia. The tribe Hayapáda, if the testimony of language be allowed any authority as evidence of their Arian origin, bore, in their persons,

---

[12] Among the extracts in Bleeck's Avesta, p. 9.

[13] धर्तारा चर्षणीनां "ye two that are upholders of men" (*cultivators*) R. V. i. 17. 2. वृषा यूथेव वंसगः कृष्टीरियर्त्योजसा । ...... य एकश्चर्षणीनां वसूनामिरज्यति इंद्रः पंच क्षितीनां । The "Showerer (Indra) rules over men (*cultivators*) by his strength like a bull over his herd. Indra alone rules over the men (*cultivators*) and their wealth of the five regions. R. V. i. 7. 9. राजा कृष्टीनामसि मानुषीणां "Thou ar the king of human creatures (*cultivators*) R. V. i. 59, 5.

an unmistakeable sign of *Japhet dwelling in the tents of Shem.* And Arian records themselves exhibit, linguistically, manifest traces of familiar intercourse on the part of their authors with the children of Shem. This they could not have done if their original home had been so far away from Semitic regions as the slopes of the Hindu Kusḫ.

The Rig Veda Sanhita contains a good number of words which belonged clearly to the Semitic stock, but which have failed to take root in Sanscrit. This fact would show that while the Arians at one time had sufficient intercourse with the Semitics to accept or interchange certain vocables of their respective languages, that intercourse did not continue long enough to allow all the grafts, so accepted, to take root, and become incorporated in their respective languages. Two remarkable instances of this kind we shall mention here, as regards Sanscrit. These are the two forms of the ineffable Hebrew name for the Supreme Being, that is to say, यहु *Jahu* (if we may dispense with the prevailing but very questionable fashion of representing the semivowel of *i* by *y*, and use the natural *j* after the example of the "Worterbuch,") and यह्वः *Jahvah.* The former occurs seven times in combination with the word सहसः *sahasah*, and has (according to Sáyana बलस्य पुत्र) the sense of the "son of power." And once it is used in the sense of "great" or "supreme" (so Sayana renders it) and applied to Indra. As "son of power," it is applied six times to Agni, and once to Angiras. It is an unusual word in Sanscrit either in the sense of "great" or of a "son." And its use seems to have subsided after the eight passages just referred to.[14]

As a word for a "son" it has some resemblance to the Greek υἱός, but it is evidently a form of the sacred Hebrew name already mentioned. The word did not take root in Sanscrit and has gone out of that language entirely The exact import of the word appears in the following paragraph from Mr. Talbot's "Contributions," where he has dealt with it as an Assyrian word derived from the Hebrew.

"IAHU-KHAZI. Ahaz, king of Judah. The name Iahu-khazi signifies "Iahu is my possession (or my treasure)," from Hebrew אחוזה "a possession." The final vowel *i* should not be overlooked, since it is the pronoun "*my.*" Iahu = Ιαω of the Greeks,[15] which is the same as Jah or Jehovah. In 2R67, 61, this Iahu-khazi (who is there called the King of Judah), is named as one of those who paid tribute to Tiglath Pileser II. But we know from 2 Chronicles xxviii.

---

[14] The eight passages in which Jahu occurs are the following:
R. V, i. 26, 10 ... ... चनो धाः सहसो यहो ।
i. 74, 5 तमित्सुहव्यमंगिरः सुदेवं सहसो यहो । जना आहुः सुबर्हिषं ॥
i. 79, 4 अग्न वाजस्य गोमत ईशानः सहसो यहो ।
vii. 15, 11 स नो राधांस्या भरेशानः सहसो यहो । भगश्च दातु वार्य ।
viii. 4, 5 विश्वे त इंद्र इसमानयो यहो-नि इषा इव येमिरे ।
viii. 19, 12 विप्रस्य वा स्तुवतः सहसो यहो मक्षूतमस्य रातिषु ।
viii. 84, 5 द्यामेम कस्य मनसा यज्ञस्य सहसो यहो । कदु वोच इदं नमः ॥
viii. 60. 13 शिशानो वृषभो यथाग्निः ... ...
... ... सहसो यहः ।

[15] See Diodorus, Clemens Alexandrinus, and Hesychius. The name Ιαω is very common on the Gnostic gems and amulets.

20, that Ahaz was the king who paid tribute to Tiglath Pileser: therefore Iahu-khazi was Ahaz. No doubt the name Jeho-ahaz (who was a different king) corresponds more nearly to the Assyrian name. Indeed it agrees with it exactly. But I am disposed to conjecture that Ahaz was originally named Jeho-ahaz, and that the Assyrians knew him by that name only; but that when Ahaz lapsed into idolatry, and no longer worshipped Jehovah, he dropped that holy name, being reluctant to bear it, "while making molten images for Baalim, burning incense in the valley of Hinnom, and while he sacrificed and burnt incense on the high places, and on the hills, and under every green tree."

We can hardly conceive the possibility of the Arians finding such a word at all, if they had been, from the beginning, isolated on the slopes of the Hindu Kush. And we think that it fell into desuetude very much for the same reason as its abandonment by Ahaz.

The other form of the sacred word, as used in the Rig Veda, was in the garb of an adjective, यह्वः "Jahvah." This was a nearer approach to the word Jehovah—wanting only the vowel *o* between *h* and *v*. In this form it has been used pretty largely in the Rig Veda. It was even forced into the Unadi sutras to accept an etymology concocted for it. It was held to have been derived from या (*ja*) *to go*.[16] The affix, which the etymologist assigned to it, in common with some

[16] प्रेषयकञ्जिकाभीवाघामीया । यान्स्यनेम यकः । ह्रस्वो ऊगामसच । Unadi 1—152.

other words, would not, however, account for the vocable under consideration, and therefore a second arbitrary affix, unusual, if not unprecedented, in itself, was impressed on it. But even that affix could not answer for the meaning attached to it by Sáyana, namely *great*, or *supreme*. Professor Wilson takes it, in his Dictionary, in the sense of *sacrifice*. The word could not, however, for that etymology, take any deeper root in Sanscrit than the twin vocable यह्न, *Jahu*, and both have alike disappeared from post-Vedic Sanscrit.

In the Rig Veda the word "Jahvah" is found in various senses. As an adjective, it is used 14 times to express the dignity of Agni, 11 times that of the "seven Rivers," and other streams, and waters, as offspring of the sky, 7 times that of heaven and earth, as "mothers of sacrifice," twice that of Indra, and once, that of each of the following nouns, *viz.* luminous herbs, soma, hymns, horses, and wealth. Twice it stands as a substantive for *offspring* or *strength*, and twice, again, for the importance of *day and night*.

The following are examples of its use in the Rig Veda. It is found in every *Mandala*, and continues in Vedic literature as a memorial of Arian residence in Western Asia.

i. 36, 1 प्र वेा यह्वं पुरूणां विशां देवयतीनां ।
अग्निं सूक्तेभि र्वचोभि रीमहे यं सीमिदन्य ईळते ॥

"We supplicate the *Great* (jahvam) Agni with hymns for the benefit of you," &c.

i. 59, 4 बृहती इव सूनवे रोदसी गिरो होता मनुष्यो न दक्षः ।
स्वर्वते सत्यशुष्माय पूर्वी र्वैश्वानराय नृतमाय यह्वीः ॥

"This expert invocator has addressed many various *great* (jahvih) hymns to the excellent moving Fire," &c.

i. 142, 7 आ मंद्माने उषाके नक्तोषासा सुपेशसा।
यह्वी ऋतस्य मातरा सीदतां बर्हि आ सुमत्।

"O ye excellent Day and Night, *great* (jahví) mothers of Sacrifice, &c."

ii. 35, 9 ......हिरण्यवर्णाः परि यंति यह्वीः।

"The golden-coloured *great* (jahvíh) rivers circulate its greatness."

ii. 35, 14 आपो नप्त्रे घृतमन्नं वहंतीः स्वयमत्कैः परि दीयंति यह्वीः।

"The *great* (jahvíh) waters pass by its own streams."

iii. 1, 9 गुहा चरंतं सखिभिः शिवेभि र्दिवो यह्वीभिर्न गुहा बभूव।

Here *jahvah* is used in the sense of "offspring" like *jahu*—qualifying the *waters, offspring of the sky.*

iii. 3, 8 विश्पतिं यह्वमतिथिं नरः....

"The leaders exalt the *supreme* (jahvam) Fire, the cherisher of the creation, &c."

iii. 2, 9 तिस्रो यह्वस्य समिधः परिज्मनोऽग्नेः

"The gods sanctified the three forms of the circumambient *great* (jahvasya) Agni," &c.

iii. 28, 4 अग्ने यह्वस्य तव भागधेयं न प्र मिनंति विदथेषु धीराः।

"O *great* (jahvasya) Agni, the sage priests do not grudge thee thy allotted butter in the Sacrifices."

vii. 70, 3 यानि स्थानान्यश्विना दधाथे दिवो यह्वीष्वोषधीषु विक्षु।

"O Aswins, the places you make from heaven among the *great* (jahvíshu) herbs and sacrificers, &c.

viii. 13, 20 तदिद्रुद्रस्य चेतति यह्वं प्रत्नेषु धामसु।

That *offspring* (jahvam) of Rudra is manifested in the old habitations, &c.

viii. 23, 14 तमीमहे पुरुष्टुतं यह्वं प्रत्नाभिरूतिभिः।

"Him, *great* (jahvam) Indra, lauded by many, we supplicate with the old gratifying hymns."

iv. 13, 3 तं सूर्यं हरितः सप्त यह्वीः स्पशं विश्वस्य जगतो वहंति।

"The seven *great* (jahvih) horses carry that sun, &c."

v. 41, 7 उप व एषे वंद्येभिः शूषैः प्र यह्वी दिवश्चितयद्भिरर्कैः।
उषासानक्ता.......

"O ye *great* (jahvíh) day and night, &c."

vi. 17, 7 पप्राथ क्षां महि दंसो व्युर्वीमुप द्यामृष्वो बृहदिंद्र स्तभायः।
अधारयो रोदसी देवपुत्रे प्रत्ने मातरा यह्वी ऋतस्य॥

"O Indra, thou upholdest Heaven and Earth, parents of the gods, and the *great* (jahvíh) mothers of sacrifices."

x. 59, 8 सं रोदसी सुबंधवे यह्वी ऋतस्य मातरा ॥
भरतामप यद्रपो द्यौ पृथिवि क्षमा रपो मो षु ते किं चनाममत् ॥

"May the heavens and earth, the *great* ((jahví) mothers of Sacrifice confer happiness, &c."

ix. 75, 1 अभि प्रियाणि पवते चनोहितो नामानि यह्वो अधि येषु वर्धते ।
आ सूर्यस्य बृहतो बृहन्नधि रथं विष्वंचमरुहद्विचक्षणः ॥

"The delightful waters in which the nourishing *great* (jahvah) Soma thrives, &c."

ix. 92, 4 तव त्य सोम पवमान निण्ये विश्वे देवास्त्रय एकादशासः ।
दश स्वधाभिरधि सानो अव्ये मृजंति त्वा नद्यः सप्त यह्वीः ॥

"O Soma, the seven *great* (jahví) rivers purify thee."

But we must now take notice of possible objections to our theory, or rather of the only ground to which the propounders of "the Hindu Kush" theory have referred, as evidence *on their side*. Leaving, out of the question, the compliments which one theorist has passed on another, by citing him as authority, that ground may be considered under two heads: (1) the antecedent presumption against distant migrations, and against the idea of introducing remote nations as progenitors of others, thousands of miles away, and (2) the Persian tradition, as recorded in the Zend Avesta.

The first point is of course entitled to every consideration. The antecedent presumption, just mentioned, must be rebutted by adequate evidence before our theory can be admitted. We have all along been ourselves under the same impression. It is from the conviction that the burden of proof is on us that we have been expatiating so long on the question. And now we contend we have rebutted the antecedent presumption, quite sufficiently for our purpose, by the mass of evidence given against it. We may further remark that the objection is nullified by its inherent inconsistency. The fact that the original home of the Indo-Arians was also the nursery of the ancestors of the Greeks, Romans, Germans, &c. is fatal to it. If the objection be of any worth, as against our theory, in regard to the Indo-Arians, it must, by a parity of reasoning, be suicidal, *exactly to the same extent*, in regard to the Greeks, Romans and Germans. That which is *nearer* to India, in this respect, must be so much the *farther* from Greece, Italy, and Germany.

We must now deal with the second ground of the objection, namely, the Persian tradition as recorded in the Zend Avesta. We fail to find the *point* of the objection. Persian tradition and the Zend Avesta have been vaguely mentioned as favouring the *Hindu Kush theory*. This does not certainly follow from the statement with which the Vendidad commences, that the first creation of Ahura Mazda was the delightful *Airyana Vaejo*. For, its locality is not mentioned, its geography is not given. "Airyana Vaejo" means the *Àrian residence*. There is nothing in it conflicting with our theory. We also say, what indeed may be called a truism, that there was an Arian residence, since there was undoubtedly an Arian family of the human race. The question is about its geography. On this point, not only does the Vendidad throw no light, but those that adduce it as evidence against our theory, themselves admit that *Airyana Vaejo became* a "fabulous region."[17] We cannot understand how a geographical site can be developed into a "fabulous region," nor again how an *un*geographical "fabulous region" can be placed in opposition to a defined geographical site. The Parsees themselves look upon it as "an abode, typical of faith or belief."[18] The ingenuity of European scholarship may have fixed a place as the local habitation of the Zend ideal. But that is not Persian tradition.

According to the Vendidad, as interpreted by its own doctors, "Airyana Vaejo" or "Iran vaeja" was the

---

[17] This country must be placed in the farthest east of the Iranian highlands, at the sources of the Oxus and Jaxartes (*cf.* Lassen Ind. Alterthk. I., p. 527). In later times Airyana-vaêja becomes a purely fabulous region. Thus the Minokhired says (p. 332 ff.): "The Dev of winter is most vehement in Erân-vej. It is stated in the law that in the Erân-vej the winter lasts ten months and summer two months, and these two summer months are cold as to water, cold as to the earth, cold as to the trees; and they have, as opposition, the winter and many snakes. They have few other oppositions. And it is manifest that Ahura-Mazda created Erân-vej good beyond other places and localities; and the good is this that men live 3000 years and cows and cattle 150 years, and that they have little pain or sickness, and that they do not lie, and have no falling off of nails or hair, and the Dev of lust has less power over them, and ten men eat of one loaf and become full therewith, and every forty years a child is born of one man and one woman, and their law is the law of the Paŏiryo Ṭkaêsha, and when they die they are sanctified. Their chief (raṭ) is Gopatishâh (*cf.* my Pârsî Grammar, pp. 142, 172), their king and ruler is Çĕrosh." *Bleeck.* 6. See also Note, p. 14, *supra.*

[18] See Wilson on the Religion of the Parsees, p. 155.

Elysium of the Zendavesta, and, practically, it can lead to no other inference than that, in the conception of the authors of that work, primeval man enjoyed a state of sanctified happiness which the Greeks have described under the figure of the "golden age," and the Brahmins of the "Satya-Yuga." "Airyana-Vaejo" was the *ideal residence of the Arians.* It is impossible to turn it into a veritable geographical locality—and the attempt to define it on the authority of the Vendidad, would be like an attempt to fix the locality of Elysium, either *on* or *under* the surface of the earth, on the authority of classical poets.

But it may be said that although "Airyana Vaejo" is a fabulous region, yet historical places are mentioned in the Vendidad as the next successive creations of Ahura Mazda, such as Gau Sugdha, Mouru, Balkdhi, Nisa, Haroyu, &c. It is therefore supposed to be only reasonable that the original residence of the Arians should be in the vicinity of these places. This is not an unfair argument in itself; and it certainly admits of discussion. But the places created after Airyana Vaejo are not declared to be successive residences of Arians. On the contrary, it would seem that they were made to prevent the sanctity of Airyana Vaejo from being violated and profaned by a press of crowds. "I created," said Ahura Mazda, "O holy Zarathustra, a Creation of delight (but) nowhere was created a possibility (of approach). For had I not, O holy Zarathustra, created a place, a creation of delight, where nowhere was created a possibility, the whole corporeal would have gone after Airyana Vaejo." It would not follow from this that the next creations were intended as Arian seats, and therefore there was no necessity for their being in the immediate vicinity of the first creation. The probability would indeed be on the opposite side, considering the jealousy with which the first creation was made inaccessible and unapproachable. It was obviously intended for an isolated residence of a select few, to the exclusion of the non-Arian nations, against whose approach it was carefully guarded. And it would ill harmonize with this intention to allow the select few themselves to sally out into regions designed for the non-Arians.

At any rate we have no right to assume that the Vendidad itself, not only meant the creations after Airyana-Vaëjo to be all of them Arian settlements, but, also, that they represented Arian movements in the same order of succession as their creation. And even on the supposition of such an intention on the part of the writers of the Vendidad, we have no right to force historical evidence into servility to its dicta. As far as mere tradition is concerned, why must Western Asian tradition, as recorded by Herodotus and the other historians, cited by Bochart,[19] so curiously concurrent and explicit, be necessarily subservient to the Persian tradition, the basis of which is admitted by the Parsee *dasturs* themselves to have been idealistic, parabolical, and mythical. "What is written in the Vendidad," says Dosabhai, "about Hormuzd and Ahriman, and light and darkness, is a *parable* of

[19] See p. 85, *supra*.

our prophet Zartusht...The explanation of the matter is this. The description is of the [good] qualities and evil qualities which are in a man, and which in Arabic are called *fazilat* and *razilat*, and in English *virtue* and *vice*. Hormazd and Light are good works; and Ahriman and Darkness are evil works; as what is good is Hormazd, and what is bad is Ahriman. Liberty is light, and Stinginess darkness; the restraining of Anger is Hormazd, and indulging it is Ahriman; Humility is Hormazd, and Pride is Ahriman. So, in like manner, may the other good and evil qualities be spoken of. The explanation of what is written in the Vandidád about Ahriman running forth with the other Devas is, that to each side of a good quality there is an evil quality attached. For example, to Humility there are two evil qualities attached; for if it exceeds its proper bounds, it becomes Lowness and Meanness; and if it fall short of its bounds, it is not Liberality but Extravagance and Immorality, as it is called in English; and if Liberality falls short of its bounds, it becomes Pride. In like manner, if Liberality is, in excess it is Stinginess. In this way, every good quality which is in man has its opposing bad quality. Connected with this the Vandidád has given a parable; and learned Pársis and Musalmáns have consequently written in their books that the prophet Zartusht is a speaker of parables."[20]

It, again, notwithstanding the protests of Parsee Dasturs, the successive creations after Airyana-Vaejo

---

[20] Wilson on the Religion of the Parsees, p. 150.

were held veritably to represent the successive movements of the Arians, *in the same order*, it would lead to palpable absurdities. The creations referred to were, 1. Airyana Vaejo, 2. "Gaû the dwelling-place Sugdha," 3. "Mouru, the high, the holy," 4. Bakdhi, 5. Nissa, 6. Harôyu, 7. Vaekereta, 8. Urva, 9. Khnenta, 10. Haraquiti, 11. Haetumat, 12. Ragha, 13. Chakra, 14. Varena, 15. Hapta Hendu, 16. to the east of Ranha.

The meaning forced on the Vendídád by the advocates of the Hindu Kush theory, without any authority from the Vendidád itself, and despite the protests of the Parsee dasturs, its authorized interpreters, would imply that the Arians having, from a "fabulous region," called Airyana Vaejo, arrived in the dwelling-place of Sugdha, proceeded by a circuitous route to Ragha[21] (well known to be a principal town in Media), and then again, by some route which we cannot satisfactorily verify, they came to "Hapta Hendu," or India. But even here they get no rest. They are still in a state of motion, and that motion is like that of the sun after a *solstice*. They are carried back "to the east of Raṇha." The verse which gives the 16th creation "to the east of Raṇha" is thus rendered by Bunsen. "As the sixteenth best of regions and countries, I, Ahura Mazda,

---

[21] Bleeck refers to a Behistan Inscription which mentions Ragha. He also cites Isidore of Charax who calls Raghu "the greatest of all Median cities, near Mount Caspius from which the Caspian gates have their name." Strabo says: *ἐισι δε ἀπὸ Κασπίων πυλῶν ἐις μεν* Ραγὰς *στάδια πεντακόσιοι ὥς φησιν* Απολλόδωρος.

created those who dwell without ramparts on the sea-coasts." The learned archæologist adds a foot-note to this: "As the Caspian was the sea nearest to the old Iranians, we must here understand the shores of that sea. The Indian Ocean is out of the question, in consequence of the mention of cold."[22]

Here then we have the movements of the Arians, like the apparent motion of the sun, India and Ragha (south of the Caspian) being the two solstitial points. And we are seriously asked to gulp all this on the credit of the Persian tradition, against the dictum of history, the dictum of the Vedas, and the dictum of Assyrian Inscriptions, and despite the protests of the Parsees themselves! It might have been more intelligible to us, and less disrespectful to the Zend Avesta, if the Arian movements, thus described, were given out as allegorical of the solar revolution.[23] But to do justice to the Zend Avesta, we must say that, by the creation of Airyana Vaejo, it means nothing more than the quondam existence of some blissful and innocent state of primeval man, (agreeably to the relics of some significant tradition which seems to have reached almost all nations) whom, as an exemplary *tiller of the ground*, it called "Arian." Zoroaster had admitted-

---

[22] *Bleeck's Avesta*, p. 12.

[23] It is a curious coincidence that the Zend Avesta *did* regard the Median Aria, because of its Western position, as the closing point of the sun's diurnal motion. "The Taera, says the Yaçna xli, of the Hara-berezaiti, praise we." "Taera" says Mr. Bleeck "is the mountain opposite Alborj, on which the sun finishes his course." Bleeck's Avesta ii, 100.

ly been in Assyrian regions, and was aware of the derivation of "Aria," which we have already quoted from Mr. Norris's Assyrian Dictionary. The Vendidád then mentioned certain places, famous for traditions or events grateful to Arian or Iranian recollection, but it never intended that the successive creations of Ahura Mazda were to be taken for successive stages of Arian movement, exactly in the order of the creations. To one broad fact, however, it bore testimony. Media and India were the two extreme points of Arian migrations, longitudinally and, in a great measure, latitudinally too. So that the so-called Persian tradition, instead of being in conflict with our theory, or an objection to it, is rather confirmatory of it.

Ranha, which is fixed by Bunsen on the coast of the Caspian sea, is in the Huzverash translation identified with Rúm ארום This would carry the western limits of Ariana into Mesopotamia, for there is contained "Arumu,"[24] which, without the Semitic redundant initial, is Ruma or Rum. The Rig Veda confirms this extension of Arian range, by mentioning the names of two sovereigns, Ruma and Rusama,[25] as worshippers of Indra, who were doubtless either themselves called after the names of their territories,

---

[24] Norris, p. 52. The redundant initial *A* appears in many Assyrian words, *e. g.* Azaba (Zab), p. 22.

[25] R. V. viii. 4, 2. यद्वा रुमे रुशमे श्यावके कृप इंद्र मादयसे सचा ।
कण्वासस्त्वा ब्रह्मभिः स्तोमवाहस इंद्रा यच्छंत्या गहि ॥

"Although, O Indra, thou delightest in Ruma, Rusama, Siavaka, Kripa, yet the sons of Kanwa, carrying thy praises, offer to thee hymns. Do thou, O Indra, come."

or their territories called after their names. Rum may also be connected with Armenia, the capital of which, "Erz-rum," is *the land of Rum.* The Rig Veda joins Ruma and Rusama with two others, Siabaka, and Kripa. Siabak reminds one of the Ethiopian Sabacon in Herodotus, but we cannot say that his time and site will allow him to be identified with the Siabak of the Veda.

In all this we see nothing conflicting with our theory of the Arians' original home. On the contrary, we find a great deal in the Zend Avesta that confirms our theory. The sixth best creation in the Vendidad is called Haroya, the Hareva and Areva of the Inscriptions, both Behistan and Assyrian proper. It is the Aria of Central Asia, the site of the modern Herat. "Har" for a mountain is not a Zend, but Hebrew or Semitic, expression. How could the Zend Avesta light on such a word, if it was not already familiar with the name as the original home of the Arians?

But we are not left merely to the testimony of Inference. We have more direct evidence. The original Hara, or Hara-berezaiti, is identified with the Alborj of later writers, or "Elburz," placed south of the Caspian, in Murray's Encyclopædia of Geography, at the foot of which is the modern city of Teheran. It is the Median Hara, distinct from Hareva. It is thus described in the Khordah-Avesta: "Mithra... who as the first heavenly Yazata, rises over Hara before the sun, the immortal, with swift steeds, who first, with golden form, seizes the fair summits, then surrounds the whole Arian place, the most profitable, where rulers, excellent, order round about the lands, where mountains, great with much fodder, abounding in water, afford wells for the cattle, where are canals deep full of water, where flowing waters, broad with water, hurry to Iskata, and Pourata, to Mouru and Haraeva, to Gau, Sugdha, and Quarizao."[26]

Here we have the Median Hara described as distinct from Hareva, and spoken of as the chief or first Arian dwelling, superior and senior to the second and other successive creations of Ahura Mazada.

We have it described again in terms which would correspond only to the picture which Parsee expositors have given of the Airyana Vaejo of the Vendidad. "Mithra...for whom Ahura Mazda has created a dwelling on Hara-Berezaiti, the far reaching, lofty, where is neither night nor darkness, neither cold wind nor hot, nor sickness with much death, nor dirt created by the Devas, no mist ascends the high mountain,—which (dwelling) the Amesha-spentas have made, which all have the same will with the Sun, towards the believing mind out of memory (?), who, on the high mountain, comprehends [in his survey] the whole corporeal world."[27]

The same description occurs again. "Since thou, O pure Rashnu, art at the great Hara, the very aspiring, lofty, where [are] neither night nor darkness, neither cold wind nor hot, neither dissolution which

---

[26] Bleeck, p. iii. 58.

[27] Ibid, p. iii. 62.

draws to itself many deaths, nor filth created by the Devas, nor do clouds ascend the high mountain—we invoke and praise &c."[28]

Accordingly in the deliberate judgment of the authors of the Zend Avesta, Hara or Hara-Berezaiti, *alias* Alborj, or Elburz of Murray's Encyclopædia, was the first and most delightful settlement of the Arian family—the Airyana Vaejo of the Vendidad, as far as it may have indicated anything like an actual earthly place. It is needless to repeat how it directly confirms the tradition recorded by Herodotus, and explains the numerous allusions in the Rig Veda to Western Asian characters and events. Persian tradition, far from being opposed to our theory, is thus strongly corroborative of it.

How and why the Arians left their Median home we cannot confidently say. A Turanian invasion of Media, as was suggested by Professor Oppert at the International Congress of Orientalists in London, was probably the cause of the introduction of the name Media, and the consequent expulsion of the Arians from their primitive Ariana. The adoption of the word "tur" in Assyrian and Sanscrit very much, in the same concurrent sense of youth, quickness, and vigour, establishes a presumption in favour of that idea. In the Assyrian, it is often used instead of "pal" for a youthful son, and the Sanscrit "tura" stands for quickness and vigour. The Assyrian "pal" or "bal" corresponds also to the Sanscrit "bála" for *young*.

---

[28] Bleeck, p. iii. 79.

We accordingly conclude that the original home of the Arian family was in Media, the chief city having been Hara. On their expulsion by a Turanian invasion they dispersed on all sides. Some went westward to Europe, others eastward. It is difficult to define their routes, but that as they came eastward, they had, probably on their way, the conflicts adverted to in the Vedas and the Zend Avesta. The Indo-Arian tradition of their coming with Vishnu (personified as Sacrifice) surrounded by *metres* on the West, North, and South, with Agni, in their front,[29] probably meant that their marches were like religious processions, regularly performing their devotional ceremonies, the rear and flank guards chanting hymns in the Vedic *seven* metres,[30] and the vanguard carrying the sacred Fire in front. The temporary disappearance of Vishnu betokened the reverses they experienced in the way. There may have been many defections, portions of them may have remained behind, such as the Arizanti, and some may have left the main body, and stopped to settle in the east of the Caspian, and other sites by the side of their route. The main body did not probably settle down before they reached Haroyu (Herat) in the province which, thenceforward, was called Aria after them. They may have either sent

---

[29] See p. 82 *supra*. Agni was placed *in front*, or *the East*. The original words are अग्निं पुरस्तात् समाधाय. "Purastat" means *in front* as well as *in the East*. Here both senses are equally applicable. The march having been *eastward*, whatever was *in front* was necessarily *in the east*.

[30] R. V. i. 22, 16.

colonies to Sugdha and Balkdhi, or some may have branched off in those directions. Or, possibly, the main body itself may have first stopped in those places, and then moved down to the province of Aria. The Indo-Arians may have afterwards found their way to the banks of the Indus, and crossed over to India. Such a view of primitive movements accords at the same time with the allusions in the Vedas and Zend Avesta, with Herodotus and other Greek writers, and with the cuneiform Inscriptions themselves.

CHAPTER IV.

On the Creation.

"In the beginning God created the Heavens and the Earth." Such was the short but pithy declaration of Moses at the very commencement of the Bible. The simplicity of the declaration is only equalled by its sublimity, and yet neither the one nor the other can transcend its *authoritative truthfulness*. No faltering here, no question or disputation, no faint-hearted hesitation to betray any scruple or conscious weakness—no ambiguity for the cover of a lurking uneasy suspicion in the mind, no apologetic appeal to logic or metaphysics. It is, on the contrary, a clear declaration, in full confidence of its truth, and of its immediate acceptance by all classes of mankind. Indeed its simplicity is such that an untutored child can understand it, and yet its sublimity transcends the heights of science, and the dialectics of logic. The philosopher and ripe scholar can only admire it, but, (as far as facts can justify an induction) he could not from his own resources teach it as an indisputable truth. This does not, however, detract from the truth implied in the declaration, for its truthfulness must commend itself to all minds that are not traitors to human nature. And it is to human nature that the declaration is addressed. The fact only confirms the Apostolic dogma, that "through faith we understand that the worlds were framed by the word of God, so that things which are seen were not made of things that do appear."[1]

It may be asked who ever denied such a truth—who ever doubted that "in the beginning God created the heavens and the earth?" It may be all very well to ask such a question, now that the world has for ages been educated to it—but look to the disputations of philosophers in ancient times. What a circuitous path was trodden by those who found or accepted that truth, if they ever found and accepted it. And how many never found it at all! How many could never comprehend the very idea of a *Creation*, the production of things which are seen, out of nothing.

A declaration like the above no other writer has been able to excogitate from his own resources. None, untaught of Moses, has been able to describe the act of creation, discriminating, as above, between the Creator, Himself eternal and uncreate, and the creature made by Him—and, at the same time, recording the fact as an independent act of God,—an actual production of all things out of nothing, a real universe called into existence from a state of nonentity. This view of Creation involves three ideas: (1) A God, perfect in Himself, eternal and uncreate, *as the only Agent of the creation*; (2) A real universe, including all existent substances, *as the object created*;

---

[1] Hebrews xi. 3.

(3) A act of creation *out of nothing*—with no preexistent materials.

The Arian family could not come up to this conception. Some of them had no idea of one Eternal and all-perfect Supreme Intelligence and Power. They fancied that there were two independent principles, one being the representative of Good, the other of Evil. To neither, therefore, could they attribute the creation of the *whole* Universe. Moreover, such as those two principles were, they were themselves reputed as created beings, born as brothers of one "Zervam akaran," or *causeless Time.*

Others, again, believing in a plurality of gods, held that they were themselves creatures, born of Heaven and Earth. And there were also those who conceived that the gods were originally but men and mortals, though they afterwards attained to Heaven, immortality, and godhead, by virtue of their works. None of these ideas could consist with the notion involved in the work of Creation such as Moses represented.

The duality of Principles was maintained by the followers of the Zend Avesta, and was also acknowledged by the Rig Veda. The theory of the production of gods from Heaven and Earth was especially inculcated in the writings of Greek poets, and also generally sanctioned by the Rig Veda. That the gods were originally but men and mortals is repeatedly taught in the Vedas.

The *dualism* of the Zend Avesta is so well known that it does not require much comment. "Ormuzd" and "Ahriman" are familiar terms in the literary world. The former is properly "Ahura Mazda." "The meaning of *Ahur* (Sanscrit Asur) is Lord (*Khuda*) and the meaning of Mazd is wise (*dáná*)."[2] "Ariman" is "Anghro-Mainyus" or the Evil Spirit. We have had occasion to refer to both. The Parsees endeavour to allegorize this dualism—but they cannot by such a device cast away the second and save the first. If the statement be an allegory, both must share the same fate, and then in the result a blank alone will be left.

But without entering into discussion on debated questions, we shall confine ourselves to acknowledged facts. The Vendidad itself expressly attributes to Ahura Mazda but a moiety of the Creation by admitting many things as *self-created.* Thus:

> "Praise thou, O Zarathustra, the self-created firmament, the infinite time, the air, which works on high.
>
> I praise the heaven, the self-created firmament, the never-ending time, the air which works above."[3]

The Zend notion of creative agency is also different from the Mosaic idea. It was limited to the act of *arranging*, *establishing*, and *directing* what was already pre-existing in some form. Thus the word for "O Creator," is *datar*, equivalent to the Sanscrit धातः *dhatar.* "Self-created," again, is *Kha-dhatahe*, or self-established. And the phrase, "created by Mazda," is *Mazd-dhato.* The idea is not that of a creation of something out of nothing.

---

[2] Edal Dárú, in Wilson on the Religion of the Parsees, p. 110.

[3] Fargard xix 44, 45 Bleeck, p. 139.

In justice to the Zenda Avesta, we must, however, acknowledge here, that, despite the worship of Fire, it has boldly and uncompromisingly resisted idolatry, and disavowed polytheism. It falls short of Moses, but contrasts favourably with other Arian systems on this cardinal point. Ahura Mazda represents a divine unity which the Rig Veda cannot produce. Indra and Varuna alternately act in that capacity, but it is not natural to either, and both have since been degraded to inferior positions by the descendants of the authors of the Vedas.

The Rig Veda, as we have said, sanctions the dualism of the Avesta, and, we may add, its limited idea of creative agency too. We may refer to a passage already cited (i. 24. 9,14) where Varuna as "Asura pracheta" (Zendice, *Ahura Mazda*) is represented as opposed to "Nir-riti," or *the principle unrighteousness*, interpreted by Sáyana *Pápa-devatá*,[4] or the sin-deity. He also appears in viii. 42, 1 as "Asura viswaveda"[5] (Zendice, Ahura Mazda, the all-knowing Ahura) and, in both hymns, his creative agency is limited to the fixing of the Sun in the bottomless sky, the directing

---

[4] See p. 32 *supra*. Nir-riti is also referred to in x. 76, 8 (where Sáyana again calls him *Pápadevatá*), in i. 38, 6 (where Sáyana styles him as *Rakshas deva*), in vi. 74, 2 (where the commentator regards him as *Alakshmi*, Ill-luck) and x. 10, 11 ; x. 16, 10 ; x. 36, 2, 4 (where Sáyana call him *Mrityu-devatá*, the death-god,) In x. 59, again, the first four mantras conclude with the refrain परातरं सु निर्ऋति र्जिहीतां । the hymnist desiring to be rid of Nirriti, called by Sáyana, *Pápa-devatá*.

[5] See p. 44, *supra*.

of his path, the establishment of the heavens, and setting of limits to the Earth—the objects themselves being supposed to have been pre-existent.

But while seconding in this manner the teaching of the Zend Avesta on the questions before us, the Vedas say, with reference to their own gods, that they were originally but *men* and *mortals*, but had attained, by virtue of the sacrificial ceremony, diligently performed, to immortality and divinity in heavenly regions. "The gods were formerly mortals. As soon as they accomplished the Sanvatsara (by certain ceremonial rites) they became immortals." "By means of Sacrifice the gods got to heaven." And they are constantly addressed as *men* and *heroes*.[6]

The Vedas were therefore incompetent for such a declaration of Creation as Moses made.

The Greek ideal was similar to the Vedic. It commenced with Chaos, which appears like the self-created firmament of the Avesta, to have been self-produced. Out of it proceeded the *spacious and broad Earth*, and "the earth first produced the starry Heaven equal to herself." And, by the combination of the two, was generated (after many other beings) "the wily Saturn, the fiercest among the offspring" of heaven and earth. And he was the parent of *the*

---

[6] मर्त्या ह वा अग्रे देवा आसुः। स यदैव ते संवत्सरमापुरथामृता आसुः।
Satapatha Brahmana, p. 828.

यज्ञेन हि देवा दिवं गताः। *Tait. Bráhmana*, p. 821.

Indra is called नृतम *most excellent among men in* R. V. iv. 22. 2, Aswins are called नरा in i. 3, 2.

father of gods and men.[7] Here again we see plainly that there could be no room for such a view of the Creation as that of Moses.

It is curious that the Rig Veda also contains this Greek ideal of the generation of gods from heaven and earth. There is no consolidated narrative, nor any complete statement on the subject, such as Hesiod has given, but the fact is assumed, and the Heavens and Earth (or *Rodasi*) are frequently described as "parents of the gods," (*Devaputre*) and in some passages as "parents of the gods and ancient mothers of Sacrifice."[8] Sáyana was evidently much bewildered by such an idea, and, although generally interpreting the phrase (Devaputre) as a Bahuvrihi compound, meaning, as Rosen has in one place rendered it, "quorum filii dii sunt," *whose sons the gods are*, yet the Brahmin interpreter often endeavoured to reduce the gods into men—as ministers or officers of the Sacrifice.

Ovid, whose notion of the Creation was in one important point borrowed from Hesiod, had, however, given utterance to something like a theistic idea on the establishment of order and harmony following the discord involved in "chaos," But this we shall consider further afterwards. On the question of the original creation of matter and material, he is as silent as Hesiod, looking upon Chaos as a self-produced or self-existing discordant mass.

---

[7] Hesiod, *Theogony* 116, 117, 126, 127, 137, 447.

[8] R. V. vi. 17, 7 अधारयो रोदसी देवपुत्रे प्रत्ने मातरा यह्वी ऋतस्य । The same idea pervades many other passages such as i. 106, 3 ; i. 159, 1 ; i. 185, 4 ; iv. 56, 2 ; vii. 53, 1 ; x. 11, 9 ; x, 62, 4.

On the question of the creation of the substance or material of Heaven and Earth, the Arian records can give no other testimony in confirmation of the Mosaic idea than by their evident failure to reach it. Like a defendant's confession of judgment, they practically acknowledge their shortcomings, and sustain the Psalmist's observation—"In Jewry is God known, His Name is great in Israel."

The Mosaic idea of God, as the original Creator of the Universe, without the assistance of any pre-existing materials, appears to have been unknown, or if it was suggested anywhere by report or tradition, to have been misunderstood, in communities which had constructed systems of faith, laid on other foundation than the Word of God. This may appear strange and singular, but it was nevertheless only too true, especially in the ancient world.

After declaring that the Universe had a beginning, and that God *created* the heavens and the earth out of nothing, Moses goes on to state how, and in what order of succession, arose the present arrangement of the world, the scene of man's probation, in which we are especially interested. With the ages that were past to human nature, it was no object of the sacred record to interfere. Their story was left to be told by their own subterranean remains, for the special study of persons competent to unravel the hieroglyphics of Nature. It was not the inspired historian's vocation to record them. He proceeds to tell us only those things which we might not otherwise have been able to discover from natural sources.

"And the earth was without form, and void: and darkness *was* upon the face of the deep. And the Spirit of God moved upon the face of the waters." *Gen.* i. 2.

In these two or three concise sentences is described the state of our globe, (previous to the arrangement of the present order of things) on some catastrophe which had overtaken it immediately preceding. And this concise description receives remarkable corroboration from the speculations of all civilized nations, Arian and un-Arian, of Europe and of Asia, who have left any records on the subject. Whatever their sources of information may have been, and whatever mutual discordances and contradictions there may have existed *inter se*, they have all borne testimony to the record of Moses, which indeed appears to represent the only points in which they are almost all at one. Our professed object is to exhibit the Arian testimony of Asia. We shall keep within the scope of our self-chosen subject, with perhaps an occasional glance at peculiarly striking passages out of that scope.

In the verse above cited five things are noticed as among the ruins of a preceding world: (1) the state of the earth, "without form and void;" the original Hebrew words being "tohu va bohu"; (2), the existence of darkness; (3), the existence of a "deep" (Tehom); (4), the existence of waters; (5), some divine operation indicated by the word "moving" in the authorized English Version, which, however, does not represent the original term "merahephet" so correctly as the word in Milton's Epic, "*brooding* on the vast abyss."

This state of things, antecedent to the present creation, which Hesiod designated by the word "chaos," is strongly corroborated by the Brahminical Scriptures. How, and on what data, the Indo-Arians formed their conception of that state of things, it is difficult to say with any confidence. We have, however, seen that from the very position of their original settlement, and their rambles still more to the West, as appears from a colony they left under the designation of Hayapâda, they had good opportunities of knowing and hearing what was popularly known or talked about in Palestine. But whatever might have been their sources of information, Vedic writers have described the condition of our globe, before the existing arrangement was formed, very much in the same way as Moses. The five pre-existing things noticed by the Hebrew prophet are also noticed by them. They are wanting in the simplicity, confidence, and authoritativeness which could only be expected from an inspired writer, making statements under divine instruction. But they have nevertheless borne remarkable testimony to the facts contained in the second verse we have cited from Genesis. They had pondered them in their minds, and recorded their mature reflections, though in the midst of a great deal that is falteringly speculative. In truth, what they have written with any confidence may be regarded as a paraphrase or commentary on the above text—with many puerile superadditions, and conjectures, indeed, but as far as the fundamental facts are concerned, they are precisely the same as those which Moses had so neatly summarized.

In the 10th Maṇḍala of the Rig Veda, Hymn 129, reference is made to the state of the world previous to the creation, and the Mantras have been thus translated by Dr. Muir: "There was then neither nonentity nor entity; there was no atmosphere, nor sky beyond it. What covered (all?) where was the receptacle of each thing? was it water, the deep abyss? Death was not then, nor immortality; there was no distinction of day and night. That One breathed calmly with *svadhá* (nature); there was nothing different from It (that One) or beyond it. Darkness there was; originally enveloped in darkness, this universe was undistinguishable water; the empty [mass] which was concealed by a husk [or by nothingness] was produced, single, by the power of austerity (or heat). Desire first arose in It, which was the first germ of mind. This the wise, seeking in their heart, have discovered by the intellect to be the bond between non-entity and entity. The ray which shot across these things—was it above, or was it below? There were productive energies, and mighty powers; Nature (*swadhá*) beneath, and Energy (*prayati*) above. Who knows, who here can declare, whence has sprung this creation? The gods are subsequent to its formation; who then knows whether any one created it or not. He who in the highest heaven is its ruler, He knows or He does not know."[7] (*Dr. Muir's Translation—Sanscrit Texts*, Vol. iv, p. 4.)

There is here a great deal of speculation, a great want of confidence, even as regards the existence of an Omnipotent and All-knowing Author and Framer of the Universe. *The wise, who sought in their hearts*, could not, *by their intellect*, determine whether any one created, or framed, this universe or not. It is strange that in this respect, the Rig Veda betrays greater uncertainty in the independent mental musings

---

[7] R. V. x. 129 नासदासीन्नो सदासीत्तदानीं नासीद्रजो न व्योमा परो यत्।
किमावरीवः कुह कस्य शर्मन्नंभः किमासीद्गहनं गभीरं ॥
न मृत्युरासीदमृतं न तर्हि न रात्र्या अह्न आसीत्प्रकेतः।
आनीदवातं स्वधया तदेकं तस्माद्धान्यन्न परः किंचनास ॥
तम आसीत्तमसा गूळ्हमग्रेऽप्रकेतं सलिलं सर्वमा इदं।
तुच्छ्येनाभ्वपिहितं यदासीत्तपसस्तन्महिनाजायतैकं ॥
कामस्तदग्रे समवर्तताधि मनसो रेतः प्रथमं यदासीत्।
सतो बंधुमसति निरविंदन्हृदि प्रतीष्या कवयो मनीषा ॥
तिरश्चीनो विततो रश्मिरेषामधः स्विदासीदुपरि स्विदासीत्।
रेतोधा आसन्महिमान आसन्स्वधा अवस्तात्प्रयतिः परस्तात् ॥
को अद्धा वेद क इह प्र वोचत्कुत आजाता कुत इयं विसृष्टिः।
अर्वाग्देवा अस्य विसर्जनेनाथा को वेद यत आबभूव
इयं विसृष्टिर्यत आबभूव यदि वा दधे यदि वा न।
यो अस्याध्यक्षः परमे व्योमन्सो अंग वेद यदि वा न वेद ॥

The translation of this hymn we have given above from Dr. Muir's book is excellent. It is as faithful as it is accurate and dispassionate. The only amendment we might be disposed to submit is in the last line. The word *Adhyaksha* literally means a *supervisor*, and although supervision is generally associated with directing and *ruling*, yet, for ought we know to the contrary, the hymnist may have intended it in the sense in which Kapila and his followers, in a later age, used it as synonymous with a simple *sákshí* or witness.

of its Rishis, than when, after the fashion of the Zend Avesta, it described the creation, or rather arrangement of the universe, by Varuna under the title of the *wise* or *all-knowing Asura* (Zendice, Ahura Mazda). The independent speculations of the Rishis were so far inferior to the Zend Avesta in respect of theistic knowledge. Although an existing principle as" adhyaksha," or superintendent, is acknowledged, it is no more than the atheistic Sankhyas themselves allowed, but as to his creative agency, *whether He or any one* created the visible world or not, the Rishis could not tell. They could not even say that the " supervisor" himself was in possession of the secret. " He knows, or He does not know !"

The assertion of the existence of " Desire" or rather Love (káma) in that unformed state of things is curiously similar to Hesiod's declaration of Ἔρος as existent with " Chaos." Assuming, after Professor Max-Müller, that the above hymn was not a later speculation of philosophy, but unable to join in his enthusiastic laudation of it, we are compelled to recognize germs, which afterwards, assisted by Buddhism, grew up into the Sankhya system of Kapila, in which a Purusha was acknowledged as " adhyaksha," but he was denied any hand in the creation or arrangement of the universe.

It is satisfactory, however, to notice that the description of the unformed *state* itself is a strong corroboration of Moses. The hymn gives us *tuchhen-ábhu-apihitam* for the *tohu va bohu* of Genesis. " Tuchhen-ábhu," if read rapidly will sound very much like " tohu-va-bohu"—having regard to the peculiar and varying sound of *chh.* The last two syllables of the Sanscrit will certainly echo the Hebrew *bohu.* And the meaning is almost alike. The Hebrew is rendered "unformed and void." The Sanscrit is "an empty (mass) covered with a husk," or a quasi nothing. The hymnist's description of that mass is exquisite—"neither non-entity nor entity." Not "non-entity," because there were the material elements present—nor "entity," because nothing was yet formed. And the things which Moses recognized in that state are all mentioned in the above Hymn. "*Darkness* there was." "This universe was undistinguishable *water.*" "The abyss," or *deep*, identified with the *water*, was also allowed. The *productive* "energy above" and "Nature beneath," in the Veda, were an apt representation of the *Spirit moving upon the face of the waters.* Here then we find the elementary existences mentioned by Moses all confirmed in the Hymn. And it is in this confirmation that the best part of the hymn consists. As to the rest, we can only admire it as a candid recognition of the short-comings of human nature, and a confession of the apostolical adage, *the world by wisdom knew not God.* We cannot, however, absolutely admire this ignorance or scepticism on the very foundation of all religion. There cannot be any religion in man unless it had for its basis the relation of the creature to the Creator. But when a philosopher doubts whether there was any creation at all, or whether any supreme Intelligence himself created it, and again, whether He knew any thing on the subject, we cannot recognize in it anything to laud or admire. We can only exclaim with the apostle : "Where is the wise ? where is the scribe ? where is the disputer of this world ? Hath not God made foolish the wisdom of this world ?"[8]

We do not mean to say that the Rig Veda is tinged throughout with sceptical notions like the above on the very foundation of all religion. We gladly acknowledge purer sentiments on the opposite side : "He who is our father (or cherisher) and generator, who as disposer knows all sites and worlds, who is the one assigner of names to the gods, to him have all other worlds recourse as the solution and end of all questions (and doubts)."[9]

We have seen that the Rig Veda X. 129 confirms the Mosaic statement of darkness, water, and productive power on the face of the waters, in the unformed state of the earth. The same is frequently referred to, not only in other places of that Veda itself, but in other Vedas and post-Vedic Scriptures. We shall cite a few passages from Dr. Muir's book. R. V. X. 121. 7. "When the great waters pervaded the universe, containing an embryo, and generating fire, thence arose the one spirit (*asu*) of the gods," p. 15.

The commentator on the above, citing a verse from the Satapatha Brahman, says: "'This (universe) was

---

[8] 1 Cor. i. 20.

[9] X. 82. 3 यो नः पिता जनिता यो विधाता धामानि वेद भुवनानि विश्वा ।
यो देवानां नामधा एक एव तं संप्रश्नं भुवना यन्त्यन्या ॥

in the beginning waters, only water,' and also containing an embryo distinguished as the golden embryo (*Hiranyagarbha*)," p. 15.

The *Atharva Veda*, 2. 6 "In the beginning, the waters, immortal and versed in the sacred ceremonies, protected (covered ?) the universe, containing an embryo; over these divine waters was the god,[10] &c." p. 16.

This is a close approximation to "the Spirit of God moving over the face of the waters."

Manu says: "This universe was enveloped in darkness, unperceived, undistinguishable, undiscoverable, unknowable, as it were entirely sunk in sleep,......He ...first with a thought created the waters, and deposited in them a seed." *Muir's Sanscrit* "*Texts*, vol. iv. p. 26.

The *Mahábhárata* says:[11] "This (Universe) having been without light, without luminaries, covered on all sides with darkness, there became a great egg, the indestructible seed of the creation." I. 29.

The Arian records in all this bear indisputable testimony to their own short-comings in missing the cardinal point in Cosmogony—the creation of all things out of nothing, and thereby virtually confess the superiority of the Mosaic conception. And at the same time they confirm the Biblical description of the *unformed state* of our globe previous to the

[10] आपो अग्रे विश्वमावन् गर्भं दधाना अमृता ऋतज्ञा। यासु देवीष्वधि देव आसीत ॥

[11] निष्प्रभेऽस्मिन्निरालोके सर्वतस्तमसावृते। बृहदण्डमभूदेकं प्रजानां बीजमव्ययं ॥

existing arrangement of the earth. Darkness, waters, and the deep, with the Spirit moving or brooding over the face of the waters, are all acknowledged.

It is not our intention to say much on other Arian records than those of Asia, but on this subject we are induced to say a few words on Ovid's description of it. The Romans had doubtless derived the word and idea of "Chaos" from Hesiod, but while the Greek poet said that "first of all Chaos became, or came into existence, (*egeneto*)," before the production of Earth or Heaven, Ovid maintained, that, "In the beginning, Ocean, Earth, and, what covered everything, Heaven, were but one face of Nature, in the whole world, which they called Chaos."[12] This approached nearer, than the Greek account, to the Mosaic description of the wreck of the world before the present formation. In Hesiod, again, the development of Chaos to a state of order was apparently without any divine agency, and before the production of the gods, while Ovid distinctly recognized a divine Framer of the Universe, co-operating with Nature, though He was to him an *unknown* God, he himself not being able to say which god it was.[13] The Mosaic idea of an independent and all-Perfect God creating, by the fiat of His own

---

[12] Ante, mare et tellus, et, quod tegit omnia, coelum,
Unus erat toto Naturae vultus in orbe,
Quem dixere Chaos ;

[13] Hanc Deus et melior litem Natura diremit.
... ...
Sic ubi depositum, quisquis fuit ille Deorum,
Congeriem secuit,

word, the whole universe out of nothing, and without any external help, is not reached by any writer whether Greek or Roman, Iranian or Indo-Arian. But Ovid is so far better than Hesiod that he distinctly confessed a divine Framer, as "mundi melioris origo," which the former did not. Later Greeks did, however, make the same acknowledgment, and the Roman poet was doubtless aware of it, and improved himself by it.

Ovid's cosmogony was an improvement on Hesiod's, in the same sense in which the later followers of Kapila and Kanáda had improved on their original masters by introducing a God, as co-operator with the pre-existing matter, in whatever form, conceived by the founders of their respective schools. The founders themselves held the sufficiency of *Prakrita* or *Atoms* for the purposes of the Creation. Their followers in a later age ascribed the arrangement of the existing matter to a divine agency, and so far these were not essentially unlike Ovid.

Ovid's account is on one important point peculiarly corroborative of Moses. While the Rig Veda confirms the Mosaic order of creation by describing "light as the first production,"[14] Ovid speaks of man as the last creation, and, referring to the irrational creatures, previous to the appearance of man, he says: "But an animated being, holier than these, and more capable of high culture, and one who could exercise dominion

---

[14] X. 55. 2 महन्नाम गुह्यं पुरुस्पृग्येन भूतं जनयो येन भव्यं ।
प्रत्नं जातं ज्योति र्यदस्य प्रियं प्रियाः समविशंत पंच ॥

over the rest, was still wanting. Accordingly man was produced."[15] Such a description beautifully harmonizes with Moses, and must have been based on the tradition or report which had reached the poet of the account in Genesis: "And God said, Let us make man in our image, after our likeness: and let them have dominion over the fish of the sea, and over the fowl of the air, and over the cattle, and over all the earth, and over every creeping thing that creepeth upon the earth."[16]

Ovid, however, falls short of Moses in his description of the *agency* to which the human race owed its original. He gives utterance to an uncertain sound, and casts doubts on the subject. He does not know whether it was the very "Deus," he had before mentioned, "the Framer of all things, and the Author of the reformed world, that made man from a divine energy,"[17] or whether (Prometheus) the son of Japetus, formed him into an image of the gods, who ruled over all things, out of some celestial material which the earth, but lately reclaimed from a

---

[15] Sanctius his animal, mentisque capacius altae
Deerat adhuc, et quod dominari in cetera posset.
Natus homo est:

[16] Gen. i. 26.

[17] Sive hunc divino semine fecit
Ille opifex rerum, mundi melioris origo:
Sive recens tellus, seductaque nuper ab alto
Æthere, cognati retinebat semina coeli,
Quam satis Japeto, mixtam fluvialibus undis,
Fixit in effigiem moderantum cuncta Deorum.

state of Chaos, and separated from the lofty ether, still retained in itself.

Notwithstanding this uncertainty, the statement substantially confirms the Mosaic narrative: "So God created man in his own image, in the image of God created he him; male and female created he them."[18] It is a curious corroboration of sacred history, inasmuch as it is neither a translation nor a paraphrase, but a record of primitive tradition, in which are found only such necessary distortions as are always incident in such cases, and which, for all that, place the substantial facts upon a firmer basis.

Perhaps Ovid's account was a figurative narrative. That which was doubtfully declared may have been intended for a description of the origin and progress of human society, the former from the direct hand of God, the latter by the cultivation of the arts, of which Prometheus and the *stolen fire* were held as types.

Thus we see that Arian writings substantially confirm the sacred history of the creation. They are all conspicuous by their failure to reach the Mosaic conception of a Perfect God, creating the worlds, in the beginning, out of nothing: and some of them differ, both from Moses and from the rest of themselves, by denying or doubting the agency of God in reclaiming the world from Chaos. But in other respects they all confirm the Mosaic account, more or less, on the pre-existent elements which constituted the unformed state of the world.

---

[18] Gen. i. 27.

There are two more points on which the Vedas propound ideas curiously corresponding to the Biblical history. Referring to the formation of the world from its unformed and void state, the Psalms declare that "By the word of the Lord were the heavens made: and all the host of them by the breath of his mouth." "He spake the word, and they were made; he commanded and they were created.[19] The Vedas represent a way of calling things into existence from their chaotic state which is strikingly similar to the above. "While they were performing austerity, a golden egg came into existence. Being produced, it then became a year....From it in a year a man (*purusha*) came into existence, who was Prajápati....In a year he desired to speak. He uttered "bhuh," which became this earth; *bhuvah*, which became this firmament; and *svah*, which became that sky.[20] *Muir's Sanscrit Texts &c.*, Vol. iv, p. 22.

Sankarácharia, the great commentator of the Sariraka Sutras of the Uttara mimánsa, or the Vedant, cites various passages to prove the fact of a creation *by utterance of words*. Thus: "They show that the Creation was preceded by utterance of words. For the Veda says: By the word "ete," Prajápati created the gods. By the word "asrigram" he created men. By the word "indava" he created the

---

[19] Ps. xxxiii. 6; cxlviii. 5.

[20] तासु तपस्तप्यमानासु हिरण्मयमण्डं संबभूव आजातो ह तर्हि संवत्सर आस। ... ततः संवत्सरे पुरुषः समभवत् स प्रजापतिः। ... स संवत्सरे व्याजिहीर्षत। स भूरिति व्याहरत् सा इयं पृथिव्यभवत्। भुव इति तदिदमन्तरिक्षमभवत् स्वरिति सा असौ द्यौरभवत्।

pitris. By the words "tirah pavitram" he made the planets. By the word "ásava" he created the hymns. By the word "visváni" he made eulogies. By the word, "abhi saubhagá" he made the other creatures."[21] In all this we see an unmistakeable reflection of the Biblical truth, however faint and somewhat distorted. The Vedic words, above cited, are found in a group forming the first mantra of Hymn ix. 62 of the Rig Veda. Their meanings, however, have no obvious or apparent connection with the objects, alleged to have been created by their utterance.[22]

The other point has reference to the passage "And the Lord God formed man of the dust of the ground and breathed into his nostrils the breath of life; and man became a living soul."

Ths *Satapatha Brahmana* furnishes a similar idea, though somewhat tinged with pantheism. Indra is identified with the vital breath that is in the midst of man, and he is said to have "kindled these breaths."[23]

Before concluding this Chapter on the Creation, we cannot help adverting to an Assyrian Calendar, noticed by Mr. George Smith, which, though not an Arian record, is far too important to be omitted here. Mr. Smith says: "In the year 1869, I discovered

---

[21] ते हि शब्दपूर्विकां सृष्टिं दर्शयतः। एत इति वै प्रजापति र्देवानसृजत असृग्रं इति मनुष्यान् इन्दव इति पितॄं स्तिरः पवित्रमिति ग्रहान् आशव इति स्तोत्रं विश्वानीति शस्त्रमभिसौभगेति अन्याः प्रजा इति श्रुतिः।

[22] एत असृग्रमिन्दवस्तिरः पवित्रमाशवः। विश्वान्यभिसौभगा।

[23] स योयं मध्ये प्राण एष एवेन्द्रः। तानेष प्राणाम मध्यत इंद्रेणैन्ध।

among other things a curious religious calendar of the Assyrians, in which every month is divided into four weeks, and the seventh days, or 'Sabbaths,' are marked out as days on which no work should be undertaken." (*Assyrian Discoveries*, p. 12.) The division of time into weeks of seven days has prevailed elsewhere, but, that the seventh was to be observed as a day of rest, is a testimony to the truth of the Mosaic record, as strong as it is curious.

CHAPTER V.

On the Fall.

The existence of sin and evil is a fact so indisputable that it needs no evidence to prove it. Every man has experience of it in the world external, and is conscious of it in the mind internal. Societies and communities make laws and rules to protect themselves from evils accruing from the depravity of their own common nature. The principal duties which press on governments are to ensure security of human life and property against external attacks and internal disorder, caused by men themselves. The great struggle of life is for every one to hold his own against aggressive injustice and wrong on the part of his neighbours. And the state of things we observe in our own days, we learn to have existed in the days of our ancestors and predecessors. The earliest history of man is principally a record of man's devices against man, whether aggressive or defensive.

And yet there must have been a commencement of sin and evil. Everything had a beginning. The beginning of the world, the creation of the heavens and the earth we attribute—we cannot help attributing—we are compelled by every sentiment that is good in our nature to attribute—to the SUPREME BEING—to a POWER, an INTELLIGENCE, a GOODNESS, and a WISDOM, transcending all our thoughts, baffling all our calculations, and therefore INFINITE and BOUNDLESS. Few will refuse their response to the Psalmist's assurance: "Be ye sure that the Lord he is God: it is he that hath made us, and not we ourselves; we are his people, and the sheep of his pasture." Few will hesitate to acknowledge: "The heavens are thine, the earth also is thine: thou hast laid the foundation of the round world, and all that therein is." Or, "The Lord is gracious, his mercy is everlasting: and his truth endureth from generation to generation." Or either that, "righteousness and judgment are the habitation of his throne."[1]

But what about the introduction of Sin and evil? Is the creation of Sin to be attributed to the Supreme Being? To such an idea we can only respond—none but an irreverent and ungodly mind can help responding, "God forbid!" If any person can seriously entertain such a question, we can only turn aside with the exclamation, "monstrous blasphemy!" Even loyalty to an earthly sovereign will recoil from the idea of attributing injustice or wrong to the person of Royalty. And loyalty is *next* to Piety.

We cannot, at the same time, attribute the introduction of sin to a second but opposite co-ordinate and co-eternal Being. We cannot admit another independent Principle,—whether it be a Pápa-devatá, or

[1] *Psalms* c. 2; lxxxix. 12; c. 4; xcvii. 2.

an Angro-mainyus, as opposed to a Spenta-mainyus—without detracting from the Infinite power, which as we have said before, we are bound to attribute, to the Supreme Author of the Universe. Here then lies our difficulty. How to account for the origin of evil without any derogation from the Power, Goodness and Wisdom which constitute the glory of God. This is indeed a formidable difficulty—in fact the real difficulty in theology of any kind. It is not peculiar to Revealed Religion. It affects Natural theology itself.

The fact of evil cannot be denied, and yet the glory of God must be maintained. Here we have constant need to bear in mind that the finite cannot comprehend the Infinite. We criticised in the last chapter the faltering voice of the Rig Veda X. 129 on the subject of the Creation—not because the Hymnist confessed his ignorance or the short-comings of human nature, but because, admitting some One *as supervisor in the highest heaven*, he doubted the sufficiency of His creative agency, and His knowledge of the mystery of the Creation. That writer did not, like his colleague of Hymn 82 in the same Mandal, refer to *the Author of all things as the solution of all questions and doubts.* The writer of Hymn 129 aspired after a transcendental position from which to suggest uncertainties on the Creator and the creation, and to undermine the fundamental Source of all knowledge and belief.

Human discussions must have some ascertained principle as their basis, or they would be like a ship without anchor or rudder at sea. In religious discourses, we must have faith and hope in a God, perfect and independent, of boundless power, knowledge, and goodness, *as the anchor of the soul* and mind. There must not be a derogation from any of these acknowledged attributes of the Deity. Whatever we may say must be in consistence with those attributes. And this maxim must be recognized as a principle, a postulated axiom, in every branch of religious controversy.

Such being the case, the perfect solution of the problem involved in the origin of evil transcends human ingenuity. And we must be satisfied with what is given to us to know and understand.

Moses has told us that at the Creation *all things were good*, and that man *was made after the image of God.* But he has not said that man was indefectible, infallible, or impeccable. The state of the present world was a state of probation, but there could be no probation where there was not a possibility of deflection, and a liability to fall. And a fall there was, of which we have a concise account given us, not as a question decided dialectically, but as the narrative of an actual event.

"Now the serpent was more subtle than any beast of the field which the LORD God had made. And he said unto the woman, Yea, hath God said, Ye shall not eat of every tree of the garden? And the woman said unto the serpent, We may eat of the fruit of the trees of the garden: but of the fruit of the tree which is in the midst of the garden, God hath said, Ye shall not eat of it, neither shall ye touch it, lest ye die.

And the serpent said unto the woman, Ye shall not surely die: for God doth know, that in the day ye eat thereof, then your eyes shall be opened: and ye shall be as gods, knowing good and evil. And when the woman saw that the tree was good for food, and that it was pleasant to the eyes, and a tree to be desired to make one wise, she took of the fruit thereof, and did eat, and gave also unto her husband with her, and he did eat.... And the Lord God said unto the serpent, Because thou hast done this, thou art cursed above all cattle, and above every beast of the field: upon thy belly shalt thou go, and dust shalt thou eat all the days of thy life. And I will put enmity between thee and the woman, and between thy seed and her seed; it shall bruise thy head, and thou shalt bruise his heel."[2]

The duty we have undertaken in this chapter is to see what portions of this narrative are confirmed by any statements in old Iranian or Indo-Arian records. Traditions of ante-diluvian facts or narratives may have been transmitted through Noah to the post-diluvian world. The Assyrians have a legend, that on warning having been given of a coming flood, their King Xisuthrus wrote a "a history of the beginning, procedure, and conclusion of all things," and buried it "in the City of the Sun at Sippara,"[3] and that, after the Flood, they had searched the same out. Whether this account was true or false, it showed the

---

[2] *Gen.* iii. 1—6, 14, 15.

[3] Mr. George Smith's *Assyrian Discoveries*, pp. 209, 211.

possibility of the transmission of ante-diluvian accounts. Our business now is to see what, if any, traditions or ideals of the event under consideration are recorded in Arian Scriptures. In the narrative of the Fall we have (1), the Serpent; (2), his instigation to disobedience of a divine injunction; (3), his sentence and the sentence against his victims.

The serpent was identified with the Devil. "And the great dragon was cast out, that old serpent, called the Devil and Satan, which deceiveth the whole world: he was cast out into the earth, and his angels were cast out with him."[4]

There could be no direct testimony to the above narrative in its integrity from human records. But both Iranian and Indo-Arian Scriptures testify to traditional recollections of substantial portions of that account. "The evil spirit," says Dr. Smith, "in the form of a serpent appears in the Ahriman, or Lord of Evil, who, according to Zoroaster, first taught men to sin under the guise of this reptile."[5] Whether Ahriman was identical with "the enemy Serpent" of the Zend Avesta is not quite clear, but it is certain that the latter was his chief representative, if not his own self. The reason of our doubting the actual identity of these two personalities of evil is that, in one place, a distinction seems to be implied in the Vendidad. "Zarathustra asked Ahura-Mazda: "Ahura Mazda! Heavenly, Holiest, Creator of the corporeal world,

---

[4] Rev. xii. 9.

[5] *Dictionary of the Bible*, p. 1213.

Pure one! How shall I combat the Druksh (enemy) which flies from the dead upon the living: how shall I subdue the Naçus which defiles the living from the dead?" "Mazda: Speak the words which are called in the Gáthás Bishámrúta."..."After the Bishámrúta speak these victorious wholesome words. 'I combat Añra-Mainyus away from this dwelling, away from this clan, from this tribe, this land, away from my own body, away from unclean (or dead) man, the unclean woman, from the lord of the house, the clan, the tribe, the region, away from all pure creatures. I combat the Naçus. I combat direct uncleanness. I combat indirect uncleanness away from the dwelling, the village, the town, the region, away from my own body, away from the unclean man, the unclean woman, the lord of the house, the village, the town, the region, away from all pure creatures."[6]

Here are two exorcisms—first of the Añro-Mainyus, and then of the "Naçus." It may be that the second was intended for adding intensity to the first. The first or Ahriman was certainly called "Satan" in the Khordah-Avesta, although the passage in which it occurs was "in Pársi," not Zend, and therefore of a later date. The passage is "Broken, broken, be Satan Ahriman, whose deeds and works are accursed."[7] But "Satan" שָׂטָן which, in Hebrew means *an enemy*, corresponds to the Sanscrit शातन (*sátana*) which signifies *oppression*, or an *oppressor*, and may stand for an

[6] Bleeck. p. i. 92.

[7] Bleeck. iii. 3.

"enemy." Indeed, the Sanscrit शत्रु is from the same root शत.

The most remarkable confirmation of the sacred narrative here, is, in truth, the linguistic view, the word Naçus, by which the Zend Avesta designates the "Druksh" or enemy. It is the same as the Hebrew word "Nachas" (in Genesis iii) and also means a serpent. It also closely corresponds to the Sanscrit "Nagas" and Nahush"—both words having some bearing, as we shall presently see, on the question before us.

As far then as the principal instrument of man's fall into sin is concerned, the narrative of the Bible is curiously confirmed by the Zend Avesta. The worker of evil appears the same, both in name, form and ideal. Considering that the languages are widely different, it is a remarkable coincidence, that the Zend Avesta should designate, by the word "Naçus," the same character for which in Genesis the word "nachas" is used. It would be difficult to account for such a concurrence except on the supposition of both having received and approved the prevailing tradition of the same primeval event. The Mosaic account is thus strongly supported by the legend of the Zend.

With reference to the sentence pronounced against the serpent, that *it should be cursed above all cattle, and above every beast of the field, and go upon its belly, and eat dust all the days of its life*, some eminent interpreters have maintained that before the event mentioned in Genesis iii, the serpent was not a reptile, but an erect animal, others, equally learned, have held, on scientific grounds, that the serpent was always a reptile, and that the sentence did not intend a change in its structure. It is not our purpose here to interfere between learned critics and interpreters on such a question. We have only to say that, even on the assumption of the theory of an organic change in the serpent, consequent on the above curse, the account of Moses would still have the support of Arian records. The Zend Avesta speaks of "Serpents with two feet, the very deadly two-footed, the wolves with four feet."[8] The Indo-Arians, also, had certain mythical legends, occasioned, probably, by traditional interpretations of the above account of the Fall, which, incidentally, and therefore the more curiously, show that they were cognizant, as approvingly as the old Iranians themselves, of the Mosaic narrative of the origin of evil. They had (1) a legend about the "Nágas," corresponding to the Zend "Naçus" and the Hebrew "nachas," that the serpent tribe, so called, had Cadru, the wife of Kasiapa, for their mother. They were looked upon as "demi-gods, in the human shape, with a serpent's tail, and dilated neck, like the Coluber Naga."[9] They play an important part in Hindu mythology. They are classed with other demigods or demoniacal beings, such as Gandharvas, Rákshasas, Yakshas, and Kinnaras, and appear with them at festivals and ceremonies of Rájás and Rishis, sometimes as acceptable guests, welcomed as friends, and

---

[8] Bleeck. ii. 52.

[9] Colebrooke's Amara Kosha.

not seldom, as hostile intruders to be expelled or guarded against by mantras or amulets. They are represented as capable of sexually attracting, and being attracted by, human beings. Mainâka, brother of Parvatí, was married to a "nâga-vadhu," or a wife who was a Naga's daughter.

In the story of king Nahusha we have again a curious Indo-Arian ideal of the curse pronounced against the serpent. Nahusha was originally a *righteous king, of a very ancient family, who by sacrifices, austerity, sacred study, self-restraint, and valour, had acquired the sovereignty of the three worlds. Being then intoxicated with the conceit of his lordly power, he was corrupted by pride.* The result is thus related by himself according to the Mahâbhârat in "the Serpent-section." "Yudhisthira said: "O thou best of the wise! That you have such excellent intelligence! Why do you ask me what is or ought to be known to you? How has delusion entered thee, who knowest all things and wast a dweller of heaven and a worker of such wonders? This perplexes me." The serpent replied: "Prosperity deludes even the hero of intelligence. I believe that all persons living at ease fall into delusion. And so myself, O Judhisthira, was filled with pride by the delusion of lordly power. But now I am addressing you, being awaken to better thoughts by my fall. You have, O great king, done me a great service. By speaking with you, a holy person, my curse has become attenuated. Formerly I moved through the sky on a celestial car. Intoxicated with self-conceit, I regarded no one but myself. All the inhabitants of the three worlds, Brahmanical Rishis, gods, gandharvas, yakshas, rakshasas, pannagas, paid me tribute. Such was the power of my gaze, that on what creature I fixed my eyes, I straightway robbed him of his energy. A thousand of the great sages bore my vehicle. That misconduct it was, O king, which hurled me from my high estate. For then I touched with my foot the muni Agastya who was carrying me. Agastya in his wrath cried out to me, "Fall, thou serpent." Hurled therefore from that magnificent car and fallen from my prosperity, as I descended headlong, I felt that I had become a serpent."[10]

---

[10] नहुषो नाम राजाहमासं पूर्व्वस्तवानघ ।
प्रथितः पञ्चमः सोमादायोः पुत्रो नराधिपः ॥ ११ ॥
क्रतुभिस्तपसा चैव स्वाध्यायेन दमेन च ।
त्रैलोक्यैश्वर्य्यमव्ययं प्राप्तोऽहं विक्रमेण च ॥ १२ ॥
तदैश्वर्य्यं समासाद्य दर्पो मामगमत्तदा ।
* * * * *
युधिष्ठिर उवाच ।
अहो बुद्धिमतां श्रेष्ठ शुभा बुद्धिरियं तव ।
विदितं वेदितव्यं ते कस्मान्मामनुपृच्छसि ॥ २८ ॥
सर्व्वज्ञं त्वां कथं मोह आविशत् स्वर्गवासिनम् ।
एवमद्भुतकर्म्माणमिति मे संशयो महान् ॥ २९ ॥
सर्प उवाच ।
सुप्रज्ञमपि चेच्छूरमृद्धिर्म्मोहयते नरम् ।
वर्त्तमानः सुखे सर्व्वो मुह्यतीति मतिर्म्मम ॥ ३० ॥
सोऽहमैश्वर्य्यमोहेन मदाविष्टो युधिष्ठिर ।
पतितः प्रतिसंबुद्धस्त्वान्तु सम्बोधयाम्यहम् ॥ ३१ ॥
कृतं कार्य्यं महाराज त्वया मम परन्तप ।
क्षीणः शापः सुकृच्छ्रो मे त्वया संभाष्य साधुना ॥ ३२ ॥
अहं हि दिवि दिव्येन विमानेन चरन् पुरा ।
अभिमानेन मत्तः सन् कञ्चिन्नान्यमचिन्तयम् ॥ ३३ ॥

The name of the person thus reduced to the condition of a reptile serpent was "Nahusha," or, according to popular parlance, *Nahus*. This, it will be observed, was almost identical with *nachas*, the word for the serpent in Genesis, the Hebrew ח sometimes standing for a deep aspirate, like the Arabic ح with which it is frequently commutable. Now whatever the actual meaning of the divine sentence against the offending "nachas" might have been, there is no doubt that many interpreters, and especially Oriental expositors, held that a structural change was thereby caused in the serpent. Such a conception had existed in the East, and the Indo-Arian legend of Nahus, as it represents that ideal, gives at the same time a strong confirmation of the sacred record on which the ideal was founded.

Adverting, now, to another clause in the sentence pronounced against the serpent, we find both Iranian and Indo-Arian legends, again, to be curiously corro-

---

ब्रह्मर्षिदेवगन्धर्वयक्षराक्षसपन्नगाः ।
करान्मम प्रयच्छन्ति सर्वे त्रैलोक्यवासिनः ॥ २४ ॥
चक्षुषा यं प्रपश्यामि प्राणिनं पृथिवीश्वर ।
तस्य तेजो हराम्याशु तद्धि दृष्टेर्बलं मम ॥ २५ ॥
ब्रह्मर्षीणां सहस्रं हि उवाह शिबिकां मम ।
स मामपनयो राजन् भ्रंशयामास वै श्रियः ॥ २६ ॥
तत्र ह्यगस्त्यः पादेन वहन् स्पृष्टो मया मुनिः ।
अगस्त्येन ततोऽस्म्युक्तो ध्वंस सर्पेति वै रुषा ॥ २७ ॥
ततस्तस्माद्विमानाग्रात् प्रच्युतश्च्युतभूषणः ।
प्रपतन् बुबुधेऽऽत्मानं व्यालीभूतमधोमुखं ॥ २८ ॥

A considerable portion of the translation given above is taken from Dr. Muir's *Sanscrit Texts*.

borative of it. "And I will put enmity between thee and the woman, and between thy seed and her seed, it shall bruise thy head, and thou shalt bruise his heel." In the Ardibehesht, "the killing of the serpent seed' (*azhi-chitra*) *i. e.* of all noxious animals, such as, wolves, frogs, mice, ants, snakes, &c., which are believed to be the mere covers of evil spirits, is enjoined as meritorious, and contributing largely towards the growth of nature, and preservation of light, which both are represented by the archangel Ardibehesht."[11]

In Yasna XLVII it is said:

> "When the coming Asha (Holy one) shall smite the Druksh
> When there comes what was announced as delusive:
> Immortality for men and Daevas,
> Then shall Thy profitable land increase, O Ahura."[12]

Druksh Naçus was the *enemy serpent* of the Zend Avesta, and Asha, the holy one. Whatever the peculiar signification of the above lines may be, it is evident that it involved the general ideal of the sentence against the serpent as recorded in Genesis. But there is an Indo-Arian legend still more remarkable. We allude to the story of Rama.

Whether the conception of Rama, the antagonist of Rávana, be an allegory or a myth, or whether it be a historical Romance, is a question we need not discuss here. There are German scholars who have pro-

---

[11] Haug's Essays, &c., p. 177.

[12] Bleeck, ii. p. iii.

nounced it to be a myth borrowed from the ideal of Homer's Iliad, and there are others, again, who hold exactly the opposite opinion. Our business, now, is not to judge between the two conflicting theories. But whether allegorical or historical, we have in the very notion of his Incarnation, a most curious confirmation of the last words in the sentence against the Serpent, the Devil. We need not stop to explain what *the seed of the woman* means, and how Gospel Truth is intimately linked with it. It is said in the Rámáyana that gods and men were both anxious to encompass the overthrow of the arch-demon Rávana, under whose iron rod and oppressive rule the whole world was piteously groaning. But the monster was as powerful as he was cruel, and Indra, the king of the gods, was reduced to the condition of his vassal. They had recourse to Brahmá, the creator of the Universe, who told them that the salvation of the world from the tyranny of the prince of demons could only be achieved by the descent of Vishnu on the earth, born of human parents, and incarnate in human form. No other species of animated beings in the creation could prevail against Rávana. It must be a man, armed with divine omnipotence, who alone could save the world by destroying that demon.[13]

Thus advised, the gods resorted to Vishnu, the

---

[13] सन्तुष्टः प्रददौ तस्मै राक्षसाय वरं प्रभुः ।
नानाविधेभ्यः भूतेभ्यो भयं नान्यत्र मानुषात् ॥
तस्मात् तस्य वधो दृष्टो मानुषेभ्यः परन्तपः ।

second person of the Indian triad, beseeching him to assume human form and destroy the demon.[14]

Now this is the very ideal of the verse just cited from Genesis. *The seed of the woman was to bruise the serpent's head.* "Verily he took not on him the nature of angels, but he took on him the seed of Abraham." "Wherefore in all things it behoved him to be made like unto his brethren." That the Saviour of mankind must partake of human nature—and that "forasmuch as the children were partakers of flesh and blood, he must himself likewise take part of the same," were, according to Christian records, among the mysteries of the Divine Counsel with regard to human salvation. The mystery was first revealed after the fall, and the passage quoted from the Rámáyan may be considered a strong corroborative evidence of the fact.

We thus see that the Scriptural narrative of the Fall is supported by Arian records in such parts of it as concern human interests, human duty, and human regeneration. We know who, in the highest sense of the term, was *the seed of the woman.* And it is as remarkable as it is assuring to Christian faith, that the same ideal appears to have prevailed in the Indo-Arian mind of old. We know also what was meant by *the Serpent and his seed.* And we see what the Arian conception was. Rávana, as the chief of Rákshasas, represented the Evil One, whom the Ira-

---

[14] एवमुक्ताः सुराः सर्व्वे प्रत्यूचु र्विष्णुमव्ययं ।
मानुषं रूपमास्थाय रावणं जहि संयुगे ॥

nians called *the Serpent enemy*, and the Indo-Arians, "Pápa-devatá" (Sin-deity), and "Rakshas-deva," (chief or god of Rakshasas). Brahmá, the first member of the Brahminical triad, was solicited for the destruction of that archdemon. He confessed his inability to give relief against the Evil One, who had a charmed life against all opponents, man alone excepted. The only person capable of affording relief, was Vishnu, the second member of the triad. But it would be necessary for him to come into the world in the likeness of man. He must be born as man—become *the seed of the woman*, assume human nature, be in all respects as man, and then he would be sufficient for the deliverance of the world from the oppression of Rávana. The legend of Ráma is thus founded on the old prevailing tradition of *the seed of the woman*, as alone capable of bruising the Serpent's head. We accordingly see the large extent to which the divine sentence against the Serpent had influenced human ideas even so early as the age of Ráma.

To the same ideas must be attributed the peculiar conception of Ráma's incarnation. It was not the advent of a god for a momentary purpose in the disguise of a man or animal. It was different from the occasional descents of Apollo, or Jupiter, as Greek mythology has recorded. Nor was it to be confounded with the appearance of the *divine fish*, or the *divine boar*, or even *Nri-Singha*, the man-lion. None of those characters is represented as born in those forms, nor partaker of those animated natures. The incarnation of Ráma was so far unique. There were two or three other incarnations in Indian records of which we may afterwards have to speak. But we have now to declare in concluding this chapter that to the Mosaic narrative of the Fall must be attributed the great idea with which the incarnation of Ráma was fraught, that it was necessary for a divine person *to be made flesh*, and assume human nature, in order to encompass the destruction of *the Devil and his works*.

CHAPTER VI.

On the Deluge and certain after events.

Man's wickedness after the Fall multiplied to a fearful extent. "The earth also was corrupt before God; and the earth was filled with violence. And God looked upon the earth, and behold, it was corrupt: for all flesh had corrupted his way upon the earth."

One honourable exception is, however, noticed. Noah *was found righteous*, and grace was in store for him. "And God said unto Noah, The end of all flesh is come before me; for the earth is filled with violence through them; and behold, I will destroy them with the earth. Make thee an ark of Gopher-wood: rooms shalt thou make in the ark, and shalt pitch it within and without with pitch."

The dimensions of the ark were next prescribed, and Noah was warned of "a flood of waters" coming upon the earth "to destroy all flesh." He was advised to enter into the Ark with all his house, and take pairs of all animals to keep them alive, and ample provisions for the use of all in the ark.

The flood is then described in its waters increasing, assuaging, abating and ultimately drying up. In the seventh month the ark rested upon the mountains of Ararat. In the tenth month were the tops of the mountains seen. Forty days after that, Noah opened the window of the ark, and, to try the state of things below, he sent forth a raven, which went forth to and fro, until the waters were dried up from off the earth. Then he sent forth a dove, but the dove found no rest for the sole of her foot, and she returned into the ark. After seven days he again sent forth the dove, and the dove returned in the evening with an olive leaf in her mouth. Noah perceived now that the waters had abated, and after another seven days sent the dove a third time when she no more returned.

Then Noah removed the covering of the ark and saw that the surface of the earth was dry, and on receiving another divine mandate, he came out of the ark with his family, and got out all that were with him.

"And Noah builded an altar unto the Lord; and took of every clean beast, and of every clean fowl and offered burnt-offerings on the altar."[1]

The above may be considered a brief summary of the Mosaic account of the deluge. The principal points that are noticeable are (1), the increase of human wickedness which occasioned it; (2), the timely warning given to Noah, singled out as a *righteous* man in that generation; (3), the instruction for the building of an ark of given dimensions; (4), the number of persons that entered the ark with pairs of living crea-

---

[1] Gen. viii. 20.

tures, and adequate provisions; (5), the resting of the ark on "the mountains of Ararat"; (6), Noah's sending out birds to try if the waters had dried up; (7), Noah's building an altar, and offering burnt-offerings.

We shall now see to what extent this narrative is confirmed by Arian legends. The Iranian scriptures appear to be silent on the subject. The Indo-Arians have several legends of which the first is the following from the *Satapatha Bráhmana.* We give it as it has been rendered by Dr. Muir, the most accurate and faithful translator of the passage.

"In the beginning they brought to Manu water for washing, as men are in the habit of bringing it to wash with the hands. As he was thus washing, a fish came into his hands, (which spake to him) 'Preserve me; I shall save thee.' (Manu enquired) 'From what wilt thou save me?' (The fish replied) 'A flood shall sweep away all these creatures; from it will I rescue thee.' (Manu asked). 'How (shall) thy preservation '(be effected)?' The fish said: 'So long as we are 'small, we are in great peril, for fish devours fish; 'thou shalt preserve me first in a jar. When I grow 'too large for the jar, then thou shalt dig a trench, 'and preserve me in that. When I grow too large 'for the trench, then thou shalt carry me away to 'the Ocean, I shall then be beyond the reach of 'danger.' Straightway he became a large fish; for he waxes to the utmost. (He said). 'Now in such and such a year, then the flood will come; thou shalt therefore, construct a ship, and resort to me; thou shalt embark in the ship when the flood rises, and I shall deliver thee from it.' Having thus preserved the fish, Manu carried him away to the sea. Then in the same year which the fish had enjoined, he constructed a ship, and resorted to him. When the flood rose, Manu embarked in the ship. The fish swam towards him. He fastened the cable of the ship to the fish's horn. By this means he passed over this northern mountain. The fish said, 'I have delivered thee; fasten the ship to a tree. But lest the water should cut thee off whilst thou art on the mountain, as much as the water subsides, so much shalt thou descend after it.' He accordingly descended after it as much (as it subsided). Wherefore also this, *viz.*, 'Manu's descent' is (the name) of the northern mountain. Now the flood had swept away all these creatures; so Manu alone was left here. Desirous of offspring, he lived worshipping, and toiling in arduous religious rites. Among these he also sacrificed with the *páka* offering. He cast clarified butter, thickened milk, whey and curds, as an oblation into the waters. Thence in a year a woman was produced."[2]

---

[2] Muir's Texts, vol. i. p. 183. The following is the original Sanscrit passage:

मनवे ह वै प्रातरवनेग्यमुदकमाजह्रुर्यथेदं पाणिभ्यामवनेजनायाहरन्त्येवं तस्यावनेनिजानस्य मत्स्यः पाणी आपेदे । स हास्मै वाचमुवाद । बिभृहि मा पारयिष्यामि त्वेति कस्मान्मा पारयिष्यसीत्यौघ इमाः सर्वाः प्रजा निर्वोढा ततस्त्वा पारयिष्यामीति कथं ते भृतिरिति । स होवाच । यावद्वै क्षुल्लका भवामो बह्वी वै नस्तावन्नाष्ट्रा भवत्युत मत्स्य एव मत्स्यं गिलति कुम्भ्यां माग्रे बिभरासि स यदा तामतिवर्धा अथ कर्षूं खात्वा तस्यां मा बिभरासि स यदा तामतिवर्धा अथ मा समुद्रमभ्यवहरासि तर्हि वा अतिनाष्ट्रो भवितास्मीति । शश्वद्ध झष आस । स हि

The name of the woman thus produced was Iḍa. "From Manu and Iḍa, we are expressly told, the race, known as that of Manu, *i. e.* the race of men, was produced."[3] Manu, according to the above legend, was the progenitor of all post-diluvian men.

But the Rig Veda leads us to predicate the same attribute of another character also. And that character was Anu, whom, as we shall presently see, the Matsia Purána considers the progenitor of Mlecchas. The words "anava" and "ánava" from Anu, are in the Rig Veda used, according to Sayanacharia, in the same sense or senses as "manava" and "mánava" from Manu. Thus; "anavah" stands in v. 31, 4 for "manushiah," *men*, just as "manavah" does for the very same in iv. 18, 22; x. 11, 3; 43, 4, 8; 66, 12; 91, 9. "A'nave" loc. sing. stands in viii. 4. 1 for *a son of Anu*, and "manavam" acc. sing. stands in x. 62. 1 for *a son of Manu.* Thus Anu and Manu are both described as kings and first parents of mankind.

We may therefore fairly conclude that in the con-

ज्येष्ठं वर्धत अथेतिथीं समां तदौघ आगन्ता तन्मा नावमुपकल्प्योपासासै स औघ उत्थिते नावमापद्यासै ततस्त्वा पारयितास्मीति । तमेवं भृत्वा समुद्रमभ्यवजहार स यतिथीं तत्समां परिदिदेश ततिथीं समां नावमुपकल्प्योपासांचक्रे स औघ उत्थिते नावमापेदे तं स मत्स्य उपन्यापुप्लुवे तस्य शृङ्गे नावः पाशं प्रतिमुमोच तेनैतमुत्तरं गिरिमतिदुद्राव । स होवाच अपीपरं वै त्वा वृक्षे नावं प्रतिबध्नीष्व तं तु त्वा मा गिरौ सन्तमुदकमन्तश्छैत्सीद्यावदुदकं समवायात्तावत्तावदन्ववसर्पासीति स ह तावत्तावदेवान्ववससर्प तदप्येतदुत्तरस्य गिरेर्मनोरवसर्पणमित्यौघो ह ताः सर्वाः प्रजा निरुवाहाथेह मनुरेवैकः परिशिशिषे । सोऽर्चञ्छ्राम्यंश्चचार प्रजाकामः । तत्रापि पाकयज्ञेनेजे स घृतं दधि मस्त्वामिक्षामित्यप्सु जुहवांचकार ततः संवत्सरे योषित्सम्बभूव ।

[3] Ibid, p. 185.

ception of the Rig Veda, Anu and Manu are different names of the same representative character. But Anu was the very name which occurs frequently in the Cuneiform Inscriptions for the principal god of the Assyrians. He is constantly associated with Bel, Assur and other tutelar gods of Assyria.[4] And if we read the Cuneiform Inscriptions with the allusions in the Rig Veda, Anu stood among the Assyrians in the same light as Manu among the Indo-Arians, *viz.* as the progenitor of mankind. Considering, then, that the Assyrians frequently used a redundant *a* as the initial letter of a proper name,[5] Anu probably was a modification of Nu or Nuh (the common Oriental transliteration of Noah) deified as the grandfather of Ashur, the founder of their nation and the original source of their national name Assur. And if Anu could thus stand for Nu or Noah among the Assyrians, "Manu" must have been the Indo-Arian ideal of Noah. And it is a remarkably significant fact that, while the Rig Veda assimilates Anu with Manu, as the progenitor of mankind, a later Indian legend declares that Anu was the first parent of the "Mlecchas," or aliens from the Brahminical faith. The Puránas generally associate Anu with Yadu, Turvasu, Druhu, and Púru as sons of

---

[4] "The gods Anu, Assur, Bel, Vul, and Istar, to his (the first Vulnirari's) feet have subjected (diverse foreign rulers)." "Anu, Bel, Hea, and Ziru, the great gods," &c. *Smith's Assyrian Discoveries*, pp. 243, 245. See also Norris's Assyrian Dictionary, p. 471. Rawlinson's Herodotus, vol. i, p. 485.

[5] See p. 107 *supra*.

king Yayáti, and the *Matsia* Purána adds: "From Yadu were produced the Yadus. The sons of Turvasu were Yavanas. The sons of Druhu were the Bhojas, but the sons of Anu were the Mleccha or alien races."[6] Turvasu and Anu are thus described in the Indian records themselves to have been connected with outlanders, which the Assyrian inscriptions also show. This is another conclusive proof of the coincidence between Indian and the Cuneiform records of Western Asia.

The above assimilation of Manu with Noah is further confirmed by another consideration. In the Vedic account we have given of the Deluge, the ship is said to have passed over the "Northern mountain." The commentator of the Veda, writing perhaps some fifteen hundred years after the Vedic period, identifies the *northern mountain* with the "Himaván" or Himálaya. Doubtless that was the Brahminical notion in the age of the commentary. But the earliest recollections of the Indo-Arians of such a primitive event must have been cherished while they were yet in their original home, which we have already shown to have been in Media. The "Northern mountain" must therefore have referred to the same range as "the mountains of Ararat", which the Vulgate renders, *super montes Armeniæ.* The Hebrew "Ararat" is elsewhere translated in the authorized English

---

यदोस्तु जाता यदवस्तुर्वसोर्यवनाः सुताः।
द्रुह्योस्तु तनया भोजा अनोस्तु म्लेच्छजातयः।
पुरोस्तु पौरववंशो यत्र जातोऽसि पार्थिव।

Version itself *the land of Armenia*,[7] which accords also with the Septuagint. Ararat is also mentioned in the Assyrian Inscriptions in the same sense, and referring to the same period.[8] Viewing from the point of their original settlement, the Indo-Arian recorders of the Diluvian tradition must have meant that very locality by the "Northern mountain."

This will appear still more clear from the consideration of another fact noticed in the above legend from the Veda. "He accordingly descended after it *as much* (*as it subsided*). Wherefore also this, viz. 'Manu's descent' is (the name) of the northern mountain." Now there is no peak or point in the Himálaya called "Manu's descent." Nor does any other Indian tradition of the deluge, subsequently recorded, in the Mahábhárat, the Matsia Purána, or the Sribhágavata, make any mention of a mountain or peak called "Manu's descent." But there is an account elsewhere given of *Noah's first stage* or *descent*. "That the scene of an event," says Dr. Smith "so deeply interesting had even at that early age been transferred, as was natural, to the loftiest and most imposing mountain in the district, appears from the statement of Josephus, that the spot,

---

[7] 2 Kings xix. 37.

[8] "Sarduri of Ararat with me revolted," &c. "Sarduri of Ararat in the city of Turupsa his city I besieged him." "For 70 Kaspu the land of Ararat entirely from top to bottom I destroyed." *Smith's Assyrian Discoveries*, pp. 271, 272. And in the Inscriptions of Sennacherib we have: "Concerning the news of Ararat (Armenia) the *daili* I send." Mr. Smith remarks, "It (Turupsa) was the capital of Ararat or Armenia." *Assyrian Discoveries*, p. 309.

where Noah left the ark, had received a name descriptive of that event, which he renders 'Ἀποβατήριον, and which seems identical with *Nachdjevan*, on the banks of the Araxes. To this neighbourhood all the associations connected with Noah are now assigned by the native Armenians, and their opinion has been so far endorsed by Europeans, that they have given the name Ararat exclusively to the mountain which is called *Massis* by the Armenians, *Agri-Dagh*, *i. e.*, *Steep mountain*, by the Turks, and *Kuh-i-Nuh*, *i. e.* *Noah's mountain* by the Persians."[9] The Vedic legend, therefore, itself not naming any mountain, and yet recognizing the idea of a peak, *nominally* expressive of the surviving man's "descent" from the ship or ark, may be considered as an additional corroboration of the Biblical account of the descent "on the mountains of Ararat."

This conclusion will follow still more clearly from a stricter examination of the above facts. The Vedic legend gives the name of "Manu's descent" to the spot where, under the advice of the Fish, he had got out of the ship, *as much as the waters had subsided*, *i. e.*, where he had *first* got out and *stopped*, before the waters had wholly subsided. Now this very idea is involved in the literal meaning of the Armenian word *Nachdjevan*, or rather, phonetically, "Nah-chevan," equivalent in meaning to the Persian *manzale áwel*, or the first stage.[10]

---

[9] Dictionary of the Bible, p. 99.

[10] The author's authority for the above phonetic representation

The legend of the deluge contained in the Mahábhárata introduced the fish as coming to Manu, who was engaged in devotion on the banks of the Chírní, and asking his protection, and then afterwards evincing his gratitude by warning his benefactor of the coming deluge. "The time for the purification of the world has now arrived. I therefore inform thee what is for thy greatest good .....Make for thyself a strong ship, with a cable attached; embark in it with the seven Rishis, and stow in it, carefully preserved and assorted, all the seeds which have been described of old by Brahmins." Manu did as he was advised. The flood came, and, "for many years, the fish, unwearied, drew the ship over the waters; and brought it at length to the highest peak of Himavat. He then, smiling gently, said to the Rishis, 'Bind the ship without delay to this peak.' They did so accordingly. And that highest peak of Himavat is still known by the name of Naubandhana ('the binding of the ship')."[11]

This legend states that eight persons were saved from the waters, that seeds were preserved, and gives the duration of the flood as "for many years." It also points to the highest peak of "Himavat" as the

---

and literal signification of Nachdjevan is the Most Reverend the Armenian Archbishop of Ispahan, now on a visit to Calcutta, who spoke of that place as the seat of the "Catholicus" of Armenia, showed Photographs of the church in that locality, and gave the litera meaning of the word, in Persian, "Manzale Awel."

[11] Muir's Texts, vol. I, p. 200.

place where the ship was tied, and for which it was called *Naubandhana.*

The word "Himavat," in the above extract from the Mahábhárat, would, according to modern usage, doubtless stand for the *Himálaya.* In the Rig Veda, however, the word had a different signification. It simply meant *a mountain*, as opposed to the ocean, rivers and other earthly regions. Its literal meaning being *snowy*, it might be an epithet for any lofty mountain. The Rig Veda does not mention the *Himálaya* at all in its pages. *Himavat* occurs only once in the plural ("himavantah") to signify *mountains.* "Whose greatness these mountains, whose (greatness) the ocean and the river declare, whose (greatness) these regions (the cardinal points) which are his arms, (declare), to him, Prajapati, do we offer oblations."[12] It may be reasonably supposed that the Mahábhárat, in recounting such a primeval event as the Deluge, uses the word "Himavat" in the same sense as the Rig Veda, and then the interpretation of the passage would be: "and brought it (the ship) at length to the highest peak of a mountain." There is nothing in the context of the Mahábhárat to require a different meaning of "Himavat," from what it has in the Rig Veda.

The Matsia Purana gives a part of Malaya or Malabar as the scene of Manu's encounter with the Fish. A small *saphari* comes into his hands while

---

[12] यस्येमे हिमवंतो महित्वा यस्य समुद्रं रसया सहाहुः ।
यस्येमाः प्रदिशो यस्य बाहू कस्मै देवाय हविषा विधेम ॥ R. V. x. 121-4.

making offerings of water to the manes. He takes pity on it and places it in his pitcher. The fish in a single night outgrew the pitcher, when the devout Rishi removed it to a larger vessel. That proving in one day too small for the rapidly growing animal, he took it successively to a well, a lake, the river Ganga, (!) and the ocean, where it grew 200,000 yojanas (one or two millions of miles) in size ! The fish, who was no other than Vishnu himself, said to Manu, "In a short time the earth with its mountains, groves, and forests, shall be submerged in the waters. This ship has been constructed by the company of all the gods for the preservation of the vast host of living creatures. Embarking in it all living creatures,...preserve them from calamity. When driven by the blasts at the end of the Yuga, the ship is swept along, thou shalt bind it to this horn of mine."[13] On the occurrence of the event, Manu did as he was instructed.

The legend in the Sribhágavata resembles the above in the Matsia Purana, with some variations. The scene is laid in the south of India, and Manu is represented in the character of Satiavrata, king of Draviḍa. A demon named Hayagriva also appears as a sacrilegious robber, having seized and carried off the Vedas as they issued from Brahma's mouth. His destruction and the recovery of the Vedas were among the results of the universal dissolution. Satiavrata and his company were saved by "a large ship,"

---

[13] Muir's Texts, vol. I, p. 206.

sent him at the time, for that purpose. The ship was fastened to the horn of the Vishnu-fish.

The supposed peak "Naubandhana" is ignored by both the *Matsia* and *Bhágavata* Purânas. "Manu's Descent," as represented in the *Satapatha Bráhmana*, probably meant the very same place in the *Northern mountain* which was popularly called *Nachdjevan*, rendered by Josephus Ἀποβατήριον meaning *descent*. The Vedic writer must have got the traditional idea of the original word, and substituted or added Manu's name to it. Had the original word been itself Sanscrit, it would have been, agreeably to the Sanscrit idiom, one compound word, instead of a phrase comprising two *padas* "Manoh avasarpanam." On the whole we find the Biblical account of the Deluge to be strongly confirmed by the Indo-Arian traditions, the later ones becoming, as was natural, by lapse of time more faint in truthful parts, and more extravagant in fictitious additions.

The above traditions all represent the timely warning given of the deluge, though the Sanscrit idea of a fish giving the warning may appear strange. In the first two of the above legends, the Fish advises Manu to build a ship against the approaching flood, but in the third he presents him a ready-made vessel, of divine manufacture, expressly made for that purpose, and in the fourth he promises to send a large ship.

The Indo-Arian idea of a Fish giving the warning of the Deluge may have been borrowed from the Assyrian pantheon. Berosus mentions a tradition about a strange animal appearing in Assyria, at a remote period, out of the Erythraean, or Persian Gulph, endowed with reason, and instructing the Chaldeans in letters, and in all arts and sciences. It was called Oannes, having a body like that of a fish, but under the head of the fish that of a man, with woman's feet added to its tail. The animal performed the office of a public teacher during the day, but plunged into the sea at night. The above conception seems to have been worked out by the Assyrians into the form of a Fish-god. "To the body of a man as far as the waist was joined the tail of a fish."[13]

Now this is the very form of the *Matsia avatar*, or the Fish-manifestation, of Vishnu, as annually exhibited to this day in the pictorial pantheon over the group of images at the Durga puja. The warning of the Deluge was, according to Assyrian legends, given, as we shall presently see, by Hea, their god of the ocean, and the Indo-Arians appear to have represented the same tradition by an aquatic animal, afterwards deified under the same form as the Assyrian Fish-god.

Our reason for holding the Assyrians as the *lender*, and the Arians as the *borrower*, of this *ichthyolatry* is (1) that the Arians had hardly settled in India at such a remote period. (2) Although there was a maritime tribe in Gedrosia called Ichthyophagi, as there was another in Ethiopia, there is no record of a similar ancient tribe in India itself. (3) The oldest Indo-Arian pantheon, as represented in the Rig Veda,

---

[13] *Layard's Nineveh and its Ruins*, vol. ii. p. 466.

had no *niche for a Fish-god.* (4) The *Satapatha Brahmana,* while introducing the Fish in the Diluvian legend, does not invest it with a divine or (formally) even a super-natural character. (5) Piscicultus in India, as far as the *Matsia avatar* betokened it, belonged to a later date.

With reference to the number of persons in the ark, the *Satapatha* names only one, all the others add the seven Rishis: while the *Matsia* and the *Sri Bhágavata,* give indefinite numbers of animals and plants. The resting of the ship was on the "Northern mountain" according to the first legend, and a Himaván, or mountain, according to the second: the remaining two, name no locality whatever. Noah's trial of the state of things by sending out birds is not mentioned in any of these legends, but the *Satapatha* notices Manu's offering of sacrifice on descending from the ship.

Such are the Indo-Arian legends of the Deluge. Leaving the reader to consider for himself how curiously the Mosaic account is confirmed by them, we shall now turn to the Assyrian inscriptional legends which are too remarkable to be overlooked here. Although they are not strictly Arian records, yet we may well consider them *quasi*-Arian, and so far, not entirely beyond the range of our scope. We have already shown that the Assyrian legends and traditions account in some measure for the otherwise unaccountable phenomenon of an aquatic animal warning a royal Rishi of the coming flood, and thus saving the human race from entire extinction. And the very "flood series of legends," as Mr. Smith calls them, opens with a story, in which a goddess (Ishtar, *i. e.*, Venus), not a great sampler of feminine virtue, appears with her maidens, whose names are genuine Arian words, *viz.*, Samhati and Harimati (or in Sanscrit letters संहति and हरिमति), and Izdubar, the hero of the legends, whose slight of Ishtar's personal attractions appears to have given occasion for the discovery of the Diluvian facts, himself bore a *quasi*-Arian name, which might be transliterated ईशुवर or ईश्वर signifying *ruler* or *lord*, the *zd* being equivalent to the Hebrew צ and therefore to our palatal sibilant श.

Mr. George Smith says: "It appears that at that remote age the Babylonians had a tradition of a flood which was a Divine punishment for the wickedness of the world; and of a holy man who built an ark and escaped destruction; who was afterwards translated and dwelt with the gods."[14] The tradition, as is usual in such cases, is mixed up with many fabulous legends. The Inscriptions refer to a king, Izdubar by name, whose chief city was Erech. "For the favour of Izdubar the princess Ishtar (the Assyrian Venus) lifted her eyes, (and said) "I will take thee Izdubar as husband, thy oath to me shall be thy bond, thou shalt be husband and I will be thy wife." Izdubar did not accept her hand. Enraged by his slight, "Ishtar went to the presence of Anu her father, and to the presence of Anunit her mother she went, and said; "Father, Izdubar hates me, and Izdubar despises my

---

[14] Smith's Assyrian Discoveries, p. 205.

beauty, and my charms." The divine father and mother sympathize with their daughter, and at her request a winged bull was formed for the destruction of the obnoxious Izdubar, who, however, succeeds in killing the bull and baffling the efforts of the gods. But the wrath of the gods was not to be evaded. Izdubar had a sage friend, a seer, named Heabani. The rage of the gods struck him down and killed him.

Izdubar mourns disconsolately over his friend and seer, and seeks Hasisadri, *alias* Xisithrus, the holy man who had escaped the flood. Hasisadri, moved by his importunity, relates the story of the Deluge, of which the following is a brief summary. The gaps indicated by three dots ... represent mutilated parts of tablets.

" Hea opened his mouth and spake to me his servant ... thou shalt say unto them ... he has turned from me and ... fixed over me ... like caves ... above and below ... closed the ship ... the flood which I will send to you, into it enter and the door of the ship turn. Into the midst of it thy grain, thy furniture, and thy goods, thy wealth, thy woman servants, thy female slaves, and the young men, the beasts of the field, the animals of the field all, I will gather and I will send to thee, and they shall be enclosed in thy door."

* * *

" Its (the ship's) interior I examined on the eighth time. With planks the waters from within it I stopped. I saw rents and the wanting parts I added. 3 measures of bitumen I poured over the outside. 3 measures of bitumen I poured over the inside."

* * *

"All I possessed the strength of it, all I possessed the strength of it silver, all I possessed the strength of it gold, all I possessed the strength of it the seed of life, the whole I caused to go up into the ship; all my male servants and my female servants, the beast of the field, the animals of the field, the sons of the people all of them, I caused to go up. A flood Shamas made and he spake saying in the night: "I will cause it to rain heavily, enter to the midst of the ship and shut thy door." That flood happened (of which) he spake saying in the night: "I will cause it to rain (*or* it will rain) from heaven heavily."

* * *

"The surface of the earth like ... it swept, it destroyed all life from the face of the earth ... the strong deluge over the people, reached to heaven. Brother saw not his brother, it did not spare the people."

* * *

"To the country of Nizir went the ship; the mountain of Nizir stopped the ship, and to pass over it, it was not able. The first day, the second day, the mountain of Nizir the same. The third day, and the fourth day, the mountain of Nizir the same. The fifth, and sixth, the mountain of Nizir the same. On the seventh day in the course of it I sent forth a dove and it left. The dove went and turned, and a resting-place it could not enter, and it returned. I sent forth a swallow and it left. The swallow went and turned, and a resting-place it could not enter, and it returned. I sent forth a raven and it left. The raven went, and the drying up of the water it saw, and it did eat, it swam, and wandered away, and did not return. I sent the animals forth to the four winds, I poured out a libation. I built an altar on the peak of the mountain, by seven herbs I cut, at the bottom of them I placed reeds, pines, and spices. The gods collected at its burning, the gods collected at its good burning; the gods like flies over the sacrifice gathered. From of old the great god in his course the great brightness of Anu had created."

* * *

"Adrahasis a dream they sent, and the judgment of the gods he heard. When his judgment of the gods he heard. When his judgment was accomplished, Elu went up to the midst of the ship. He took my hand and raised me up, he caused to raise and to bring my wife to my side; he made a bond, he established in a covenant and gave his blessing, in the presence of Hasisadra and the people."[15]

We shall next cast a glance at the account of Berosus which has now recovered its deserved credit by the late Assyrian discoveries. It states that king Xisuthrus and his relatives and friends were the survivors that had escaped from the catastrophe of the Deluge. That king on being warned by a vision had written an account of antediluvian events and buried it in the city of the Sun at Sippara, and had built a ship in which his friends and relatives with birds and beasts, and ample

---

[15] Smith's Assyrian Discoveries, between pp. 172-193.

provisions for all, were received. After the waters had abated he sent out forth birds which, not finding any rest for their feet, returned to the ship. He made a second trial after some days when they returned with mud on their feet. On a third trial the birds returned no more, and Xisuthrus concluded that the waters had dried off from the surface of the earth. He then made an opening in the vessel, and discovered that it was stranded upon the side of some mountain. He then came out of the vessel with his family, and having made an altar offered sacrifices to the gods. He found afterwards that the place where the vessel had rested was the land of Armenia. He had been translated to the etherial regions, whence he informed his friends, whom he had left behind, that the land where the ship had struck, was Armenia. He exhorted them to search for the records, buried in the city of the Sun at Sippara, and pay due regard to the rules of religion. As an earnest of their obedience to his admonitions, they offered sacrifices to the gods and proceeded to Babylonia.

The legends of the Cuneiform Inscriptions and the account of Berosus may be considered together as the consolidated Chaldean tradition of the Deluge. Though self-inconsistent in minor points of detail, it confirms the Mosaic records in all points of importance. The previous warning to the excepted person of the forthcoming disaster; its cause, the wickedness of mankind; the instruction to build a ship, pitching it within and without, and to embark *with all his house*, taking on board birds, beasts and other animals; the trial of the state of things by sending out birds for three times successively; the resting of the vessel on the mountains in Armenia (which country is constantly called Ararat in the Inscriptions) all these are curiously confirmed. The Inscriptions give the name of "Nizir" to the mountain where the vessel rested. Mr. Smith says: "The indications as to the place of Nizir fix it between the 35th and 36th parallels of latitude, east of the river Tigris."[16] Considering that "the Babylonians, although learned in some things, had no knowledge at this time of geography,"[17] their indications of the place where the ark rested remarkably approximated to the "land of Armenia" in Berosus, the difference being only one or two degrees in latitude. We do not know in what sense the word "Nizir" is used in the Inscriptions, unless it be in the sense of a *Protection from the waters*, and the term be referred to the Heb. "natsar" as it occurs in Deut. xxxii. 10; Ps. xii. 7; xxxii. 24, &c.

All the Chaldean legends confirm the Biblical account of the surviving man building an altar and offering sacrifices, while the Cuneiform Inscriptions appear to refer also (albeit somewhat obscurely) to the covenant which God made *with Noah and his seed after him* (Gen. ix. 9).

The diluvian legends from Indo-Arian records also confirm the Biblical representation of the Unity of the human race, all nations having sprung from the same

---

[16] Assyrian Discoveries, p. 216.

[17] Ibid, p. 207.

human parents. It was Manu and Iḍa that, according to the *Satapatha*, were the first parents of all mankind after the Deluge. This is a remarkable testimony from the early records of a people that had afterwards inculcated, even among themselves, a tribal diversity of Caste, as coeval with the creation. That such a diversity did not exist in the beginning, that Arians and non-Arians, Brahmanas and Sudras, Hindus and Mlecchas, were all of the same stock, is thus acknowledged in the Veda itself. The same was the teaching of the Mahâbhârat in a later age, and that, as the solution of a doubt propounded by an interlocuter. Bhrigu had said that "the colour (varna) of the Brahmans was white: that of the Kshettriyas red; that of the Vasyas yellow, and that of the Súdras black. Bharadwaja here rejoins: 'If the caste (*varna*) of the four classes is distinguished by their colour (*varna*), then a confusion of all the castes is observable. Desire, anger, fear, cupidity, grief, apprehension, hunger, fatigue, prevail over us all: by what then is caste discriminated? Sweat, excrement, phlegm, bile, and blood (are common to all): the bodies of all decay: by what then is caste discriminated?' Bhrigu replies: "There is no difference of castes: this world, having been at first created by Brahmá entirely Brahmanic, became (afterwards) separated into castes in consequence of works. Those Brahmans (*lit.* twiceborn men), who were fond of sensual pleasure, fiery, irascible, prone to violence, who had forsaken their duty, and were red-limbed, fell into the condition of Kshettriyas. Those Brahmans, who derived their livelihood from kine, who were yellow, who subsisted by agriculture, and who neglected to practice their duties, entered into the state of Vaisyas. Those Brahmans who were addicted to mischief and falsehood, who were covetous, who lived by all kinds of work, who were black and had fallen from purity, sank into the condition of Súdras. Being separated from each other by these works, the Brahmans became divided into different castes."[18]

The teaching of the Mahábhárat on the subject of caste is not consistent throughout. It will not be

---

[18] Muir's Texts, pp. 140, 141. The original passage is as follows:

ब्राह्मणानां सितो वर्णः क्षत्रियाणां च लोहितः ।
वैश्यानां पीतको वर्णः शूद्राणामसितस्तथा ॥
भरद्वाज उवाच । चातुर्वर्ण्यस्य वर्णेन यदि वर्णो विभिद्यते ।
सर्वेषां खलु वर्णानां दृश्यते वर्णसंकरः ॥
कामः क्रोधो भयं लोभः शोकश्चिन्ता क्षुधा श्रमः ।
सर्वेषां नः प्रभवति कस्माद्वर्णो विभज्यते ॥
स्वेदमूत्रपुरीषाणि श्लेष्मा पित्तं सशोणितं ।
तनुः क्षरति सर्वेषां कस्माद्वर्णो विभज्यते ॥
जंगमानामसंख्येयाः स्थावराणां च जातयः ।
तेषां विविधवर्णानां कुतो वर्णविनिश्चयः ॥
भृगुरुवाच । न विशेषोऽस्ति वर्णानां सर्वं ब्राह्ममिदं जगत् ।
ब्रह्मणा पूर्वसृष्टं हि कर्मभिर्वर्णतां गतं ॥
कामभोगप्रियास्तीक्ष्णाः क्रोधनाः प्रियसाहसाः ।
त्यक्तस्वधर्मा रक्ताङ्गास्ते द्विजाः क्षत्रतां गताः ॥
गोभ्यो वृत्तिं समास्थाय पीताः कृष्युपजीविनः ।
स्वधर्मान्नानुतिष्ठन्ति ते द्विजा वैश्यतां गताः ॥
हिंसानृतप्रिया लुब्धाः सर्वकर्मोपजीविनः ।
कृष्णाः शौचपरिभ्रष्टास्ते द्विजा शूद्रतां गताः ॥
इत्येतैः कर्मभिर्व्यस्ता द्विजा वर्णान्तरं गताः । इति शान्तिपर्वणि ।

difficult to find out passages inculcating doctrines essentially different from the above. But it can be easily shown that the tenets continued in the verses, just cited, have the sanction of the Vedas and are supported by numerous facts. The origin of the whole human race in the post-diluvian world from the same father, be his name Manu, Anu, or Noah, cannot be consistent with any other view of Caste.

The very etymology of the word "Brahmana," will show that the above representation of the Mahábhárat is correct in its main ideal. "Brahmana" comes from "Brahma," the primitive meaning of which was a mantra or prayer of the Veda, or its chants and their accompanying oblations. It stood also for food as the result of sacrifices, and for the priest who performed them, as in Rig Veda I. 10, 4, "O Indra, establisher of our home, do thou augment our food and sacrifice," or, as Sayana paraphrases it, "augmenting our sacrifice increase also its fruit, food."[19]

The word is used in the following verses[20] in the sense of *prayers*, *hymns*, *oblations*, or sacrificial accompaniments. i. 3. 5. "Receive the *prayers* (Brahmáni) of the sacrificer." i. 24, 11. "Beseeching thee with *prayers*, (Brahmaná) I ask it of thee." i. 34, 18. "O

---

[19] R. V. i. 10, 4 ब्रह्म च नो वसो सचेंद्र यज्ञं च वर्धय । on which Sáyana says: यज्ञं वर्धयित्वा तत्फलमन्नं च प्रवृद्धं कुरु ।

[20] R. V. i. 3, 5 उप ब्रह्माणि वाघतः । i. 24, 11 तत्त्वा यामि ब्रह्मणा वंदमानः । i. 31. 18 एतेनाग्ने ब्रह्मणा वावृधस्व । i. 15, 5. ब्राह्मणादिंद्र राधसः पिबा सोममृतूँरनु । i. 52, 7 ह्रदं न हि त्वा न्यृषंत्यूर्मयो ब्रह्माणींद्र तव यानि वर्धना । i. 61, 1 अस्मा इदु प्र तवसे तुराय प्रयो न हर्मि स्तोमं माहिनाय । i. 84, 3 युक्ता ते ब्रह्मणा हरी ।

Agni by means of this *prayer*, (brahmaná) do thou thrive." i. 15, 5. "From this *sacrificial vessel*, (bráhmanát), "O Indra, drink the Soma." i. 52, 7. "O Indra, like waves into a lake, the *hymns* (brahmáni) magnifying thy glory reach unto thee." i. 61, 1. "Unto Indra, powerful, quick,...I offer *oblations* (brahmáni) liberally supplied." i. 84, 3 "Thy horses are harnessed with *prayers* (brahmaná)."

These primitive significations of Brahma are not lost sight of even in post-Vedic Sanscrit. Kalidasa, as a representative of the age of Vikramaditya, uses the word in the sense of the *Veda*.

यद्ब्रह्म सम्यगाम्नातं यदग्नौ विधिना हुतं ।
यच्च तप्तं तपस्तस्य विपक्वं फलमद्य नः ॥ *Kum. Sambh.* vi. 16.

"That Veda (Brahma) which we have studied according to rule, those oblations we have made to fire, and the austere devotions we have practised have this day ripened into fruit."

Amara Sinha who lived in the same age gives the signification of "Brahma," thus:

वेदस्तत्त्वं तपो ब्रह्म ब्रह्मा विप्रः प्रजापतिः ।

"Brahma stands for Veda, true knowledge and austere devotion. Brahmá, (masculine) for Bráhmana and Prajapati (the god Brahmá, as distinct from the Supreme spirit)."

The Mediní defines the same word thus:

ब्रह्मतत्त्वंतपो वेदे न द्वयोः पुंसि वेधसि ।

"Brahma, when not in the first two genders, signifies true knowledge, austere devotion, and Veda. In the masculine gender it stands for the god Brahmá, &c."

It is a remarkable fact that both of the two popular lexicons here referred to, give precedence to the primitive signification of the word. The *Sribhágavata* introduces the word in its very first verse in the sense of the Veda

तेने ब्रह्म हृदा य आदिकवये

"Who imparted the Veda (Brahma) to the first poet or scholar through his heart."

The etymology of the word, as given in the Unadi Sutras (4.145) also ignores its Vedantic signification of *the Supreme Spirit.* Deriving it from बृंहि they recognize the meanings in the same order as the two lexicons already cited.

बृंहेर्नोच्च १४५ । नकारस्याकारः । ब्रह्मतत्त्वन्तपो वेदो, ब्रह्मा विप्रः प्रजापतिः ।

We may therefore safely conclude that the primitive meaning of "Brahma" was generally in the sense of *accompaniments of sacrifices*—standing variously for the *mantras* that were chanted, the oblations that were offered, the food that was expected as the result of the sacrifice, and certain ceremonial instruments used on the occasion.

The term "Brahma," thus used for sacrifices and their accompaniments, was easily transferred to their recognized *celebrants*, when a class of men were so appointed. Originally there were no such recognized celebrants. Every householder performed sacrifices for himself and family. He was in the proper sense of the term himself the यजमान, which literally signified a *sacrificer*.

That there was no separate order of priests, but that

all had the same privilege of celebrating a sacrifice, is apparent from the gradual creation of castes as given in the *Brihad Aranyaka Upanishad.* ब्रह्म वा इदमग्र आसीदेकमेव तदेकं सन्न व्यभवत्। तच्छ्रेयोरूप मत्यसृजत् क्षत्रं &c.

The leading word "Brahma" is thus explained by Sankaracharya—

ब्रह्म वा इदमग्र आसीद्यदग्निं सृष्ट्वाग्निरूपापन्नं ब्रह्म, ब्राह्मणजात्याभिमानाद्ब्रह्मेत्यभिधीयते।

The passage from the Upanishad then means that in the beginning there was but one order—the Brahmanical. (The Creator) was not satisfied with this one order. He successively created the Kshatriya and other orders.

Construing this passage of the Upanishad about the creation of Kshatriyas and others by the light of the above citation from the Mahábhárata, we are driven to the inference that as the celebration of sacrifices required the correct chanting of mantras which could not be done without some learning, and as incorrect chanting is often noticed with censure as दुष्टुतं it was found necessary for the due performance of sacrificial ceremonies to institute an order of priests to which the privilege of the altar service was restricted, all others being restrained from its exercise. These priests were also exclusively entitled to the appellation of "Bráhmanas," from "Brahma," the sacrificial accompaniments they dealt with. The distinction, at first intended to be *personal,* afterwards became hereditary.

We need not go further into the question of Indian caste and its interminable ramifications. What we have already cited will be ample evidence for holding that the ancient Indo-Arian records fully sustain the Biblical doctrine of the Unity of the human race. We cannot, however, omit mention of a mantra of the Rig Veda which apparently confirms the four-fold division of Caste.

In Rig Veda X. 90. 11, 12 we have the following mystical description: "When they divided Purusha, into how many parts did they turn him? his mouth, what was it? What the two arms? what were his thighs and feet called? His mouth was the Brahmin, the Kshatriya was made his arms, his thighs were the same as the Vaisia, of his two feet the Sudra was made (lit. became)."[21] These verses do not indicate the creation of diverse castes from the beginning. They only show that at the time they were composed, a fourfold distinction of offices or grades was already recognized in Indian society. There are three verbs used in the 12th mantra, viz. "ásit" *was*, "*kritah*" *was made, (factus)*, "ajayata," exactly the Greek *egeneto*, "was made," as the A. E. version in John i. 14. The Brahmin is therefore said to have existed from before, (say, *from the beginning*, if you like, since the Indo-Arian records expressly declare that all were alike Brahmins, *i. e. sacrificers* at first) as his mouth, but the Kshatriya or warrior had no existence from the beginning, but was at a certain definite time *made*, or

---

[21] यत् पुरुषं व्यदधुः कतिधा व्यकल्पयन्। मुखं किमस्य कौ बाहू का ऊरू पादा उच्येते॥ ब्राह्मणोऽस्य मुखमासीद्बाहू राजन्यः कृतः। ऊरू तदस्य यद्वैश्यः पद्भ्यां शूद्रो अजायत॥

turned into his arms. The "vis" is also recognized in the Vedas as existing from the beginning in the sense of the *people*, *hoi polloi*, those who, although entitled to the privilege of *celebrating* sacrificial ceremonies, yet either from lack of knowledge and learning, or being already represented, as junior members of a family, by the *householder*, or from any other *accidental* disability, could not perform the priestly office of the Brahmin, but yet served the community as workers in the field. The above mantra accordingly does not say that the "vis" or "vaisia" *was made* the two thighs of the Purusha, but the thighs were only identified as the Vaisia—"were the same as the Vaisia." The most remarkable passage, however, is that which describes the production of the Sudra. The hymnist does not say that the Sudra *was* the feet of the Purusha, or that he *was made* his feet, as the Kshatriya "was made" his arms. Here a different verb is used, "jan," and it is connected with "padbhiam," or *feet* in the ablative case. Now it is a well known rule in Sanscrit that *when the verb "jan" appears in connection with an ablative, the latter is held to be the material cause of the thing which is the subject of the former.*[22] The grammatical meaning of the mantra is that *the Sudra was made of the Purusha's feet*, or that on the cutting up of his body in the Sacrifice his feet turned into the Sudra.

We need not stop here to speculate about the mystical meaning of the passage. Suffice it to say, that

---

[22] Panini I. 4, 30 जनिकर्तुः प्रकृतिः ।

these verses do not contradict the implied dictum of the *Satapatha*, and the express declaration of the *Mahábhárata*, that there was no distinction of caste or colour in the beginning. The hymn last cited does indeed recognize a state of society which is generally ignored in the Rig Veda. That hymn does of course so far appear to be the composition of a later age than the great bulk of that Veda, and it contains nothing in its diction peculiar to the Vedic age. This consideration only shows that the whole of the Rig Veda cannot claim the antiquity which is usually assigned to it. But this is a question foreign to the present chapter. We shall for the present only refer the reader to Dr. Muir's Sanscrit Texts, Vol. I. pp. 9—15 where the question is fully discussed.

Unity of race involves unity of language, for some time at least. "And the whole earth was of one language, and of one speech. * * * And they said, Go to, let us build us a city and tower, whose top may reach unto heaven ; and let us make us a name, lest we be scattered abroad upon the face of the whole earth." But by divine interposition their devices were frustrated, and the site of their vain attempt was called Babel *(confusion)* "because the Lord did there confound the language of all the earth : and from thence did the Lord scatter them abroad upon the face of all the earth.[23]

Thus the unity of language did not continue long. Berosus the Chaldæan priest, whose historical credibi-

---

[23] Gen. xi. 1, 4, 9.

lity has been so remarkably established by the Cuneiform Inscriptions, bears curious testimony to the above facts. He says: The ancient race of men were so puffed up with their strength and tallness of stature that they ...laboured to erect that very lofty tower which is now called Babylon, intending thereby to scale heaven... the name of the ruin is still called Babel: because until this time all men had used the same speech, but now there was sent upon them a confusion of many and diverse tongues."[24]

The tradition thus recorded by Berosus is again confirmed by the discovery of a Cuneiform inscription which was deciphered by the eminent scholar Dr. Oppert. He says: "The Talmudists say that the true site of the Tower of Babel was at Borsip, the Greek Borsippa, the Birs Nimroud." "The Babylonian name of this locality is *Barsip* or *Barzipa* which we explain by *Tower of Tongues*, which was formerly a suburb of Babylon, when the old Babel was merely restricted to the Northern ruins, before the great extension of the city, which, according to ancient writers, was the greatest that the sun ever warmed with its beams." "This building, erected by Nebuchadnezzar, is the same that Herodotus describes as the Tower of Jupiter Belus."

And this probably was the same which, as we saw in the story of *Saramá and Panis*, was called *Valapur*, and qualified by the adjective *Vilu*, signifying "the lofty citadel of Vala" or Bel. We are encouraged

---

[24] *Pratt's Scripture and Science not at Variance*, p. 150.

the more to suggest this identification, because the Babylonian Barsip or "Barzipa" appears to be an Arian term, *bar* or *var* (from "vri *to cover*) signifying *an enclosure*, and "zipa" standing for our *jihva* contracted in the vernaculars into "jiv or jib" for *tongue*. The first word "var" with the *Unadi* affix ञंडन् becomes "varanda," a *portico*, a VERANDA.

In the inscription above alluded to, Nebuchadnezzar informs us: "We say for the other, that is, this edifice, the house of the Seven lights of the Earth, the most ancient monument of Borsippa: A former king built it (they reckon 42 ages), but he did not complete its head. *Since a remote time people had abandoned it, without order expressing their words.*"[25]

This confusion of tongues, this disordered utterance of words naturally led to the dispersion of mankind. From that time, probably, and in consequence of that event, it was, that disparity in language and articulation proved inevitably separating causes among mankind, just as unity of language and accent served as federative bonds. The Sanskrit "barvara" literally meant a person whose articulation and accents were incorrect and vulgar, and that was the sense in which all nations of any polish used the term *barbarian* as against strangers and aliens.

The events that occurred at Babel, confirmed as above by traditions preserved by Berosus and Nebuchadnezzar's Inscription, are further corroborated by history and philology. That Western Asia was the

[25] *Smith's Dictionary of the Bible*, p. 1553.

nursery of the Arian family we have already considered at large. The same may be said of all nations who have any records to exhibit. The pristine unity and subsequent confusion of languages are both proved by philology. Languages essentially different in their grammatical formations, and therefore mutually chargeable, *inter se*, with *disordered utterances*, such as the Arian and the Semitic, contain nevertheless many words which appear to have been common to them. In some cases they are identically the same, and in others their features are those of remote cousins. We shall give a few examples here.

1. *Hebrew* מֵחַ "meh" *fat* (sheep) and "moh" *marrow*. *Assyrian* "mahe" *fat* (sacrificial ox). *Sanscrit* मेष "mesha" *sheep*, and "medha" *sacrificial fat* or *marrow*.

2. *Heb.* מַיִם "maim" pl. of mai, *water*, *Assyr.* (and *Arabic*) "mie," *water*. *Sanscrit* अमू "amu" R. V. i. 23, 17.

3. *Assyr.* "agane" a *divine lady*. *Sans.* ग्ना "gna," a *divine lady*.

4. *Heb.* צָבָא "saba" an *army*, a *host*. *Assyr.* "zabi," *soldier*. *Sans.* शव and शवस् "sava," "savas," a *host*, *military force*, (R. V. i. 8, 5) *strength*.

5. *Assyr.* "Adis" I *trod down*, or devastated (Norris, p. 21) from Heb. and Chald. דוּשׁ "dush" (Arabic داس daus). *Sans.* दस "das" to *destroy*.

6. *Assyr.* "Pal," a *son*. Heb. and Chald. בַּר "bar," a *son*. *Sans.* बाल "bála" a *boy*.

7. *Assyr.* "quqquda," *head*. *Sans.* ककुद "kakuda" an Indian bull's *hump*, the highest point of his body.

8. *Assyr.* "satar" to *write.* *Sans.* चित्र "chitra," to *delineate*, to *draw*, *ch* in Indian languages is constantly pronounced like a sibilant.

9. *Heb.* סֵתֶר "sether" a *covering*. *Sans.* छत्र "chhatra," a *covering*, an umbrella.

10. *Heb.* אֲרִי "ari" a *lion*, and (in Isaiah xxix. 1, 2; Ezek. xliii. 15, 16) *an altar*. *Sans.* हरि "hari" *a lion*, अरि "ari" a *sacrificer* (R. V. i. 9, 10).

11. *Heb.* אָוֶן "awen" *evil*, *wickedness*. *Sans.* एनः "enah" *sin*.

12. *Heb.* עֹז "oz" *strength*. *Sans.* ओजः "ojah" *strength*.

13. *Heb.* עֵז "ez" *goat*. *Sans.* अजा "ajá" *goat*.

14. *Heb.* שָׁמַם "shamam" and דָּמָה "dama" to *destroy*, are like *Sans.* शम "s'ama" and दम "dama" to *subdue*, to *tame*, to *destroy*, and comparable with δαμάω and domo.

15. *Assyr.* "garbi" (Norris 4) *power*, *height*. *Heb.* גָּבַר "gabar" to be *strong*, *arrogant*. *Sans.* गर्व "garva" *arrogance*.

16. *Assyr.* "abir" (Norris 11) *strengthening*. *Heb.* אַבִּיר "abir" *strong*. *Sans.* वीर "vira" a *strong* man, *hero*.

17. *Assyr.* "abba" (Norris 7) *sea*. *Sans.* अब्धि "abdhi" *sea*, the essential word being "ap."

18. *Assyr.* "uddi" (Norris 28) *sea*. *Sans.* उदधि "udadhi" *sea*, the essential word being "ud."

19. *Assyr.* "Pal" *time*, *Sans.* पल "pala" *a measure of time*.

A list like this may be enlarged to any extent, but, as this is not a work on Comparative Philology, what we have already adduced will suffice to prove our point. Even in such diverse tongues as the Arian and the Semitic, we find unmistakeable relics of pristine *unity* in the midst of existing *variety*.

But it is in the languages of such illiterate people as are neither Arian nor Semitic that the *confusion* of tongues is found to be most remarkably consistent with the idea of pristine unity. We shall give a few instances from the languages spoken by the Santal and Khassia tribes of Bengal. These denizens of our hills have no letters, no literature of their own. Learned missionaries have introduced among them (in a few cases the Bengali alphabet, but generally) the Roman character, and published Scriptural translations and tracts in their languages as they collected them from their living speech. To some extent the Reverend gentlemen may have possibly, and in fact unavoidably, introduced terms from other languages, but such importations are easily detected, and they are not found to any appreciable extent. There is internal evidence of the new books and tracts representing the actual language of the people. The jargon found therein is itself the representative of the *Confusion of Tongues*, but in the midst of that confusion is found a lot of particles and vocables which prominently appear like the ruins of an old edifice of uniform structure, of which the varying Arian and Semitic elements once formed harmonious parts. Let the reader judge for himself from the following examples:

I. The Santali language, though neither Arian nor Semitic, in its structure and in the great bulk of its vocables, appears nevertheless so curiously interwoven, more or less, with the rudiments of both those linguistic families, that they cannot possibly be held as later superadditions by contact or intercourse with their living representatives.

The Arian element is found more abundantly in the vocables, than the Semitic, though the latter appears curiously prominent in its grammatical structure. We have "disom" for *country*, "páp" for *sin*, "ján" for *fortune-teller* from "jna" to *know*, "jánga" the *leg*, "parakrit" (Prakriti) for *nature*, disposition, "bahu" *wife*, "parámesat" *counsel*, and an interminable lot of similar words. The most remarkable phenomenon here is the currency of Sanscrit words or roots that had long become obsolete among the Brahmins themselves, and are only found in very ancient records, such as the word "pánáhi" (Sans. upánáh) for *shoes*, and "jum" the ordinary word for *food* and the act of *eating*. The Sanscrit "jam" is existent among the *Radices*, but it is scarcely found in book literature. The English word "chum" probably somehow owes its origin to it, and, along with the "jum" of the Santals, Coles and other hill tribes, continues a living witness of its quondam prevalence among Arians.

The Semitic element, though more sparse than the Arian in vocables, is, however, still more curious. The prohibitive particle is "álo" *don't*, like the Hebrew "lo." But the Santali is declinable in number and person, which the Hebrew is not. The historical negative is "bang" which is comparable with the Hebrew "bál."

Santali nouns, when they refer to genitive personal pronouns, are, like the Hebrew, subject to terminal variations according to the number and person of the pronoun to which they refer, but they take the Arian model when they refer to genitive substantives. Thus, "Galilee of the Gentiles" is in Santali *the Gentiles' Galilee,* but "*my* father" is *apu-ing* from "apa" father and "ing" the affix indicative of the first person, and making allowances for the final *nasal* for which the Santali appears to have a peculiar predilection, the word for "my father" is virtually "api," which is almost identical with the Hebrew "abi" *my father.* Here we have one of the first terms which a child learns to lisp, and a rule of Syntax peculiar to Semitic, still prevailing among the Santals, though they belong to a class different both from Arian and Semitic. Their word for *bathing* is "topon," which, allowing for the confusion between *l* and a *nasal*, is similar to the Hebrew "tábál," and their "river" is "nái," not very dissimilar to the Semitic "nahar," and, strange to say, they call the sacred stream of the Hindoos (Ganges) not by an Indian term but by "topon-nái, *the bath-river.* Their word for song or hymn is "sereng," which, relieved of the nasal termination, is substantially the Heb. "shir."

But leaving instances of single words which can be easily multiplied, we must notice two peculiarities in the conjugations of Santali verbs which have a curious resemblance with the rules of Semitic Syntax. The object of a transitive verb, if it be pronominal, is in

Semitic languages, indicated in the verb itself by an affix corresponding to the gender, number and person of the object. Thus in Gen. ii. 15 "And He put him into the garden of Eden"—for "He put him" we have but one word in Hebrew, connected with the conjunction "and," viz. "va-ianniche-hu" and, in verse 22, for "and He brought her" we have similarly only one word again "va-iebie-ha." The Santali verbs indicate their pronominal objects in a similar way. They have another peculiarity in the use of a particle or auxiliary in the conjugation of the *present* and *imperfect*, when the sense implies, *is* or *was doing* something. That auxiliary is "káná," it is used as a particle but is not otherwise known in Santali as a substantive verb at all. Káná, however, is the Arabic verb substantive, signifying *to be*, and is frequently used as an auxiliary in the same way as the Santali particle. Thus: the Santali vocable "me-tápe-káná-ing," though but one compound word, means *I am saying unto you.* The first expression "me" indicates the act of *saying*, the second "tápe" means *to you*, "káná" (the Arabic verb) is for "am," and "ing" indicates the person of the subject—*i. e. I.* This one compound expression shows conspicuously the analogy of the Santali syntax with the Semitic. It is not a servile imitation of either Hebrew or Arabic, though remarkably similar to both. The objective affix in Hebrew is placed at the end of the verb, and *after* the subjective indication. We have here the objective affix *before* the subjective. In the Arabic, again, "káná" is not blended with the verb in one compound, but stands separate preceding it. The Santali blends it with the verb, and then declines it according to the number and person of the subject. Here then we have a curious uniformity of grammatical rule with a remarkable variety in its application. There could have been so servile imitation in such a case. There must have been a quondam Unity disturbed by a subsequent Confusion.

Before we pass from the Santali to the Khassia, we shall refer to one more Santali word which seems to ferret out an old Sanscrit term in a striking way. The Santali word for *heaven* is "serma." This might at first sight appear to be a corruption of the Heb. "shâma" or the Arabic "sáma," the letter *r* being a liquid, which unlettered, and even civilized, people are often found to insert or omit by whim or sheer accident. But the Santals can here refer to high authority. There is an old Sanscrit word "sarma" in the sense of *the sky*, the *visible heaven* (see Wilson's and Williams' Dictionaries), the very meaning of the Semitic "sámá," and the Santali "serma." The Unadi Sutras refer it to the root "Sri,"[26] and impart to the word the signification of *motion*, of which the heavens were supposed to be the site. It now becomes a question, which probably will be difficult to decide, whether in the original word for *sky* or *heaven*, ("sama" or "sarma") the *r* was fitfully omitted by the Semitics or interpolated by the Arians. The long disuse of the word in Sanscrit shows that it was not *natural* to it. But leaving this question to be decided by learned critics, we have only to declare again that this curious vocable

[26] *Unadi* 1-137.

in the living speech of the Santals is a further confirmation of the *facts* of Unity and Confusion of Tongues.

The Khassia has but few words referable to Arian or Semitic rudiments. It has nevertheless some remarkable expressions which are readily traceable to one or the other of those great linguistic families. The word for the Deity is "Ble" or with the article "U Ble" ὁ θεος. Now "Ble" is easily traceable to Bel or Baal. "Byneng" *heaven* appears to have for its rudiment "Vyoman" (Sans.) *sky*, the termination being adjusted according to the peculiar nasals of the Khassia. "Pop" *sin* is from the Sanscrit *Pápa*. "Ktin" *word* from Sans. *ukti*. "Hok" *justice* from Heb. *hoq*. "Um" *water* may be referable to either Arian or Semitic. "Kylai" *kidneys*, from Heb. *kelaioth*. "Aiom" *time* from Heb. "Yom" *day*, *time*. "Bishar" to *judge*, Sans. "vichar." "Jor," *origin*, Heb. "zera" *seed*. "Maian" *mystery*, Sans. "maya." "Niam" *religious practice*, Sans. "niyama." "Pyrthei" *earth*, *world*, Sans. "Prithvi, the *earth*. The Assyrian "qatu" and "kup" for *hand* (Norris, pp. 203, 204) curiously correspond with the Khassia "kta" for *hand* and "khup" for *palm*. The latter, again, is traceable to the Hebrew "kaph."

We do not pretend to any scholarship in the languages of the Santals and the Khassias. We have only plodded over portions of translations and tracts with the help of the Introductions, Grammars, and Dictionaries of the Rev. Messrs. Phillips, Pryse, and Roberts.

We omit such words, whether of Arian or Semitic origin, as the hilly people may have collected from markets, and from intercourse with their neighbours on the plains, *e. g.* "dhud" for *milk*, "dawa," *claim*, "ruti" *bread*, "sisa" *zinc*, "musla" *spices*, "patok" *prison*, "jáwa" *grains*, &c.

We believe we may fairly conclude this chapter by declaring that the items of Sacred history mentioned here are abundantly confirmed by Arian records. The scientific aspect of the facts is foreign to the scope of this work. We can only say for ourselves that the late Archdeacon Pratt considered them thoroughly in his *Scripture and Science not at variance*, and, in our humble opinion, conclusively proved the point indicated by the title of his great work.

CHAPTER VII.

On the Institution and Doctrine of Sacrifices.

In our *Introduction* we gave a brief summary of the Scriptural account of the institution of Sacrifices and the doctrine therein involved. We need not repeat that the cardinal teaching of Christianity is connected therewith. Our business now is to show the extent to which the Arian records testify to the *fact* of the institution and approximate to the doctrine typified by it.

The practice of sacrifices, as a mode of propitiating the gods or supernatural powers, has indeed existed among all nations. We do not, however, know of any nation which manifested such an intelligible view of the underlying doctrines as the primitive Arians did in their early writings. Nor have we seen, outside the limits of Jewry wherein "God was known," such an approximation to the Scriptural teaching on the subject as is found in ancient Arian records.

The institution as a fact existed according to Arian records from time immemorial; and, as to this post-diluvian age, it is dated as early as the descent of the surviving man from the ship whereby he escaped the catastrophe of the Flood. The first act of Manu was, as we have seen, to sacrifice with the *páka* offering as he was *toiling in religious austerity.*

The institution was carefully maintained both by Iranians and Indo-Arians. In an early portion of the Zend Avesta, "Fire, the beresma, the cup, the Haoma, and the mortar," are described as the necessary furniture of "the habitations in this corporeal world," and as a sort of preservative from "the deadly serpent, the two-footed, who is very hurtful and impure."[1]

Now the fire, the beresma, the cup, the Haoma, the mortar, and, as another passage adds it, "the flesh,"[2] were the necessary implements for the celebration of sacrifices. The fire was for the consumption of the animal victim or any other oblation, the cup was for the drinking of the "Haoma" or consecrated Soma juice, the "mortar" was for the expression of that juice, and the flesh was the substance of the victim. Fire worship was held in such estimation because of the necessity of that element in the celebration of the sacrifices. Fire was accordingly honoured as "the son of Ahura Mazda," and "the Navel of the kings."[3]

The Indo-Arians cherished the institution of sacrifices still more fondly. In the antediluvian world they date it as prior to the creation. "The Lord of creatures initiated the Sacrifice." "The Lord of

---

[1] Bleeck. i. 44.

[2] Yasna xxv. 5. Bleeck. ii. 77.

[3] Bleeck. iii. 146.

creatures was in the beginning but one. He uttered the Nivid (a sacrificial formula) All things were created after it."[4]

The "nivids" in the primitive rituals appear to have been similar to the "Bodhana" of our modern Pujas. The "nivid" was so called because thereby the announcement of the ceremony was made.[5]

Again, "The Lord of creatures desired, "May I be produced, may I be multiplied. He practised austerity. Having practised austerities he saw this (sacrificial formula) Dwadasaha in his own limbs. From his own limbs he made it into twelve parts. He took it and sacrificed with it."[6]

Once more, "The Lord of creatures desired, May I be produced, may I be multiplied. He saw this Agni-stoma, (a Sacrificial rite,) he took it, and with it he created these creatures."[7]

Passages of this kind are numerous. It would severely try the reader's patience if we attempted to present a larger number of such citations. What we have cited show with sufficient clearness that in the conception of Indo-Arians, the institution of sacrifices

---

[4] प्रजापतिर्वा इदमेक एवाग्र आस ... तां निविदं व्याहरत्तां सर्वाणि भूतान्यन्वसृज्यन्त । *Aitareya Bráhmana*, p. 48.

[5] यदिभ्वा निविद्भिर्न्यवेदयंस्तन्निविदां निवित्त्वं । *Aitareya Brahmana*, iii. 9.

[6] प्रजापति र्यज्ञमसृजत *Taittiriya Sanhita*, vol. i. p. 204. प्रजापतिरकामयत प्रजायेय भूयान्त्स्यामिति स तपोऽतप्यत स तपस्तप्त्वेमं द्वादशाहमपश्यदात्मन एवाङ्गेषु च प्राणेषु च तमात्मन एवाङ्गेभ्यश्च द्वादशधा निरमिमीत तमाहरत्तेनायजत । *Ait. Br.* p. 101.

[7] प्रजापतिरकामयत बहुस्यां प्रजायेयेति स एतमग्निष्टोममपश्यत्तमाहरत्तेनेमाः प्रजा असृजत । *Tándia Mahá Bráhmana*, vol. i. p. 200.

was coeval with the creation,—curiously confirming the idea of "the Lamb slain from the foundation of the world."

The Vedas afford passages equally numerous on the institution of Sacrifices in the post-diluvian world by Manu, the man who survived the Flood, and from whom the present generation of mankind sprang. Agni, as the instrument and symbol of the Sacrifice, is, in the Rig Veda, said to have been placed or consecrated by Manu. "O Agni, adored by us, bring the gods in a most pleasant chariot. Thou art the Invoker, appointed by Manu." "O Agni, thou art the accomplisher of the burnt-offering, appointed by Manu."[8]

The same Agni is said to have "displayed the sky" to Manu, whose daughter Ila or Iḍa is again described as his "instructress."[9] The Ṭaittiriya Bráhmana, in like manner, calls Iḍa, the daughter of Manu, "the revealer" of Sacrifice;"[10] The lady's lessons to her father were on the *order* and the *direction* in which the sacred sacrificial Fire was to be placed. And both were to be the reverse of what the Asuras had done. There can be no doubt here as to the identity of the Asuras with the Assyrians, since "Sanda,"[11] their priest, is introduced as a hostile

---

[8] अग्ने सुखतमे रथे देवाँ ईळित आ वह असि होता मनुर्हित । R. V. i. 13, 4. त्वं होता मनुर्हितोऽग्ने । i. 14, 11.

[9] Rig Veda i. 31, 4, 11 त्वमग्ने मनवे द्यामवाशयः । इळामकृण्वन्मनुषस्य शासनीं ।

[10] इडा वै मानवी यज्ञानुकाशिन्यासीत् । vol. i. p. 9.

[11] निरस्तः शंडः । निरस्तो मर्कः । अपनुत्तौ शंडामर्कौ सहामुना । *Tait. Br.*

character in the very initiatory section of this Bráhmana. And as "Sanda" has already been identified with a divinity of the Assyrians, the "Asuras" could be no other than those people. The lecture of Iḍa appears to have also had a mystical reference to the subsequent movements of the Devas and Asuras, the former moving south-east from their original habitation and ultimately settling in India, represented as the way to "Heaven" which they, the Devas, ultimately *won*, the latter, the Assyrians, (including probably the Iranians too) keeping westward and in the west, and thus losing their good luck in the end. The Iranians were not, originally at least, repudiated by the Devas. Their guru Sukra"[12] identified as a

---

vol. i. p. 2 "Sanda is put out. Marka is put out." "Sanda and Marka are put out with that (cast out piece)." Sanda and Marka are sometimes considered as one name—Sanda-Marka. Possibly the Assyrian Sanda of Berosus was connected with "the city of Marqas," (Norris 409) and therefore called "Sanda Marka." See also p. 75 *supra*.

[12] Sukra was otherwise called Bhargava, and Usaná.

Strange to say, that while the preceptor of the Iranians is known in Hindoo astronomy by the name of Sukra as the bright morning and evening star, the Rig Veda identifies an aerial deity placed in the firmament as "Venas," the very name by which the brightest star in the sky is distinguished in the Latin world.

अयं वेनश्चोदयत् पृश्निगर्भा ज्योतिर्जरायू रजसो विमाने ।
इममपां संगमे सूर्यस्य शिशुं न विप्रा मतिभी रिहन्ति ॥ R. V. x. 123, 1.

The author of Hymns ix. 85 and x. 123 is called Vena Bhárgavah, that is to say, Sukra Venas. The meaning of the word is *lovely, agreeable, beautiful.* In i. 83. 5 Vena is represented as a second sun or Indra, born for the recovery of the lost cows, and helping him

planet is more favourably noticed, and "Brihaspati" the spiritual preceptor of the Devas is identified with the all-knowing Indra who is hailed as "the first" among "the gods," and the protector of the world, and also dignified with the title of "Viswakarmá," as the accomplisher of all manœuvres against the Asuras.[13]

The address of Iḍa to her father Manu was to the following effect. She had heard that the Asuras were placing the Fire. She went to see it. She found that they were placing first the *oblation* Fire, then the *household* fire, and thirdly the fire for cooking the sacrificial food. She said their Fortuna became adverse to them. Having prospered for a time, they would be overthrown. She then noticed the fire placed by the gods; 1st, the *food-cooking*, 2nd, the *household*, 3rd, the *oblation*. Their Fortuna tended eastward, they got to heaven, but had no offspring. Then Iḍa said to Manu, "I will so place thy fire that thou shalt first have offspring and cattle, prosper in the world, and ultimately obtain heaven." She accordingly placed *first* the household Fire, then that by which food was cooked, lastly the butter oblation Fire by which heaven is acquired. The mystical meaning seems to be that the Asuras having, after

---

together with Sukra, the Asura-guru, in "the taming" of the Asuras. यज्ञैरथर्वा प्रथमः पथस्तते ततः सूर्यो व्रतपा वेन आजनि । आगा आजदुशना काव्यः सचा यमस्य जातममृतं यजामहे ॥

[13] स (इंद्रः) प्रथमः सङ्कृति विश्वकर्मा । स प्रथमो मित्रो वरुणो अग्निः । स प्रथमो बृहस्पतिश्चिकित्वान् ।

placing the oblation Fire in the East, turned to the household Fire in the West, they lost their Fortuna which tended eastward, whereas the Arians having first served the *household* Fire and been blessed with offspring and cattle in the West, turned to the South for the food-cooking Fire and then by virtue of the oblation Fire obtained heaven in the East.[14]

Numerous passages in the Sanhitas and Brahmanas of the Vedas drive us to the conclusion that sacrifices and oblations were considered the most sacred ceremonies in the primitive ritual of the Indo-Arians. Sacrifice as well as Fire, its symbol of success, was called "the Navel of the world."[15] All the honors paid to Agni in the Rig Veda were because of his being the accomplisher of offerings and oblations, and Agni is well known as pervading that Veda from first to last. Indra who is equally conspicuous in the Vedic hymns with Agni was the most frequent at sacrificial ceremonies.

Those ceremonies are said to have existed prior to the institution of the Brahmanical order, and they were esteemed as a panacea for all evils, the one means for obtaining wished for objects, either here or the next world. This again was true both as to gods and men. We need not stop long to inquire elaborately *who the gods were.* Suffice it to say that the Veda itself constantly represents them as quondam

---

[14] *Tait. Brahmana*, vol. i. pp. 9 and 10.

[15] मूर्धा दिवो नाभिरग्निः पृथिव्या अथाभवदरती रोदस्योः । R. V. i. 59, 21.
इयं वेदिः परो अन्तः पृथिव्या अयं यज्ञो भुवनस्य नाभिः । R. V. i. 164. 35.

mortals, promoted to the dignity of immortals, and the enjoyment of heaven by virtue of sacrifices. Indra himself, according to the testimony of both Iranian and Indian tradition, was at one time a great chief who had slain Vritra, a common enemy of the two branches, and (as the Indian legends add) raised himself to the sovereignty of heaven by the hundred great sacrifices which he had completed.

"The gods were formerly mortals. As soon as they attained the Sanvatsara (which could only be done by the completion of a certain number of sacrifices for a certain number of days) they became immortals."[16]

Indra himself was described as a *man* and *the best of men*. "I again call our MAN, to come from the site of our ancient home to a multitude of sacrificers, whom, that is to say, thee, O Indra, I used formerly to call our father." "The showerer of desires, the best of men (Indra), the fierce worker, having by his arms struck his four-cornered weapon against the enemy, &c."[17] The birth of all the gods is also as we have seen recorded in the Rig Veda. But although they were human creatures like the rest of men, they attained to heaven by virtue of the sacrifices they had celebrated.

"The gods were formerly just like men. They

---

[16] मर्त्या ह वा अग्रे देवा आसुः । स यदैव ते संवत्सरमापुरथामृता आसुः । *Satapatha Br*. p. 828.

[17] अनु प्रत्नस्यौकसो हुवे तुविप्रतिं नरं यं ते पूर्वं पिता हुवे । R. V. i. 13, 9
वृषा वृषन्धिं चतुरश्रिमस्यन्नुग्रो बाहुभ्यां नृतमः शचीवान् । R. V. iv. 22, 2.

desired to overcome want, misery, death, and to go to the divine assembly. They saw, took, and sacrificed with, this Chaturvimsatiratra, and in consequence overcame want, misery, death, and reached the divine assembly."[18]

Hence the sacrificial ceremony is constantly represented as the path by which the gods attained to heaven—the very passport to the celestial regions—the secret by which they overcame the Asuras. All welfare for gods and men has its foundation in Sacrifice—it is the *summum bonum.* It abolishes death and redeems from sin, through the victim, which is the ransom thereof. It is the good boat or ark by which we escape sin and all perils of life—"and the Lord of creatures" had offered himself as a sacrifice with that view. Our object is not declamation but inquiry, and therefore we shall now see how far these statements can be supported by texts of the Vedas.

"To the regular performer of Sacrifices the breezes are sweet, and the rivers distil sweetness."[19]

"By means of the sacrifice gods got to heaven; by means of the sacrifice they turned out the Asuras; by means of the sacrifice enemies become friends. In

---

[18] Dr. Muir, who (Texts vol. i. p. 15) gives the following as the original passage from an unpublished manuscript at the India office. यथा वै मनुष्या एवं देवा अग्र आसन् तेऽकामयंतावर्त्तिं पाप्मानं मृत्युमपहत्य दैवीं संसदं गच्छेम इति ते एतां चतुर्विंशतिरात्रमपश्यंस्तमाहरंस्तेनायजन्त ततो वै तेऽवर्त्तिं पाप्मानं मृत्युमपहत्य दैवीं संसदमगच्छन् *Tait. Sanhita*, vii. 4. 2, 1.

[19] मधु वाता ऋतायते मधु क्षरंति सिंधवः । R. V. i. 90, 6.

sacrifice everything gets a firm footing, therefore, they say, sacrifice is the most excellent."[20]

"By this sacrificial hymn the gods had overpowered the Asuras. By the same does the sacrificer, whoever he be, still overpower the most wicked "cousin or foe" (or gets over the enemy which is sin, for the commentator reads भ्रातृव्यं as *synonymous* with शत्रुं) *Tandya Maha Brahmana*, vol. I. p. 105.[21]

"The gods were before called Sádhyas. They came to the heavenly world with the sacrifice and all its implements." *Tándya Mahá Bráhmana*, vol. 1, p. 491.[22]

"To them (the gods) the Lord of creatures gave himself. He became their Sacrifice. Sacrifice is food for the gods. He, having given himself to them, made a reflection of himself which is Sacrifice. Therefore they say, the Lord of creatures is a Sacrifice, for he made it a reflection of himself. By means of this Sacrifice he redeemed himself from them." *Satapatha Bráhmana*, p. 836.[23]

"The Lord of creatures offered himself a sacrifice for the gods." *Tandya Ma. Br.* p. 410.[24]

---

[20] यज्ञेन हि देवा दिवङ्गता यज्ञेनासुरानपनुदन्त यज्ञेन द्विषन्तो मित्रा भवन्ति यज्ञे सर्वं प्रतिष्ठितं तस्माद्यज्ञं परमं वदन्ति। *Taittiriya Brahmana*, p. 891. यज्ञेन वै देवाः सुवर्गं लोकमायन्। *Tait. Sanhita*, vi. 3. 4.

[21] एतया वै देवा असुरानत्यक्रामन्नति पाप्मानं भ्रातृव्यं क्रामति य एतया स्तुते।

[22] साध्या वै नाम देवा आसंस्ते सर्व्वेण यज्ञेन सह स्वर्गं लोकमायन्।

[23] तेभ्यः प्रजापतिरात्मानं प्रददौ यज्ञो ह्येषामास यज्ञो हि देवानां अन्नं। स देवेभ्य आत्मानं प्रदाय, अथैतमात्मनः प्रतिमानमसृजत यद्यज्ञं तस्मादाहुः प्रजापतिर्यज्ञ इत्यात्मनो ह्येतं प्रतिमानमसृजत स एतेन यज्ञेन देवेभ्य आत्मानं निरक्रीणीत।

[24] प्रजापतिर्देवेभ्य आत्मानं यज्ञं कृत्वा प्रायच्छत्।

This idea of the "Lord of creatures" offering himself a sacrifice for the benefit of the Devas, who were then but mortals, is also found, but in a more complicated form, in the celebrated *Purusha Sukta*. It would not be easy to account for the genesis of such an idea except on the assumption of some primitive tradition of the "Lamb slain from the foundation of the world," who was "over all, God blessed for ever."

"When the gods celebrated a Sacrifice with Purusha as their oblation, the spring was its butter, summer its fuel, and autumn its (supplementary) oblation. When the gods, celebrating the sacrifice, bound Purusha as the victim, they immolated him, the Sacrifice, on the grass—even him, the Purusha, who was begotten in the beginning. With him as their offering, the gods, the Sádhyas and the Rishis also sacrificed." *Taittiriya Aranyaka*, pp. 331-333.[25]

This description of the sacrifice of Purusha has by some eminent scholars been accounted for by "the barbarous practice of human sacrifices." But there are two difficulties in that theory which could not be easily explained away. In the first place, "Purusha" is not synonymous with *manushya* or man. It simply means a person—without distinction of divine, human, or aerial, and here he is represented as coeval with the Creation, "begotten in the beginning." And in the second place, this immolation of Purusha does not

---

[25] यत् पुरुषेण हविषा । देवा यज्ञमतन्वत । वसन्तो अस्यासीदाज्यं ग्रीष्म इध्मः शरद्धविः । यद्यज्ञं तन्वानाः अबध्नन् पुरुषं पशुं । तं यज्ञं बर्हिषि प्रौक्षन् । पुरुषं जातमग्रतः । तेन देवा अयजन्त साध्या ऋषयश्च ये ।

seem altogether of a different character from the self-sacrifice of Prajapati or the Lord of creatures noticed before,—or from the following story of the *purusha-medha* of Narayana.

"The Purusha Narayan desired—I shall surpass all things, I shall become all this. He saw for five nights that 'purusha-medha' Sacrifice. He took it. He sacrificed with it. Having sacrificed with it he surpassed all things. He who, knowing this, sacrifices with the 'purusha medha,' becomes everything—whoever knows this." *Satapatha Brahmana*, p. 997.[26]

These mysterious descriptions cannot refer to any custom, prevalent at the time, of human sacrifices. Such practices were certainly not in vogue in the Vedic period. Indeed, they had never existed among the Indo-Arians as an institution, and where instances of such inhuman sacrifices are found in Indian history or tradition, they were in the worship of beings of much darker hue than the ancient gods of Brahminism. It was almost unexceptionally in the worship of *Sakti*, as wife of Siva, in her blackest form, that such murderous oblations have ever been heard of. The name of Narayan has never been connected with such sacrifices. And it would be as great a violence to truth to construe the above *purusha* sacrifice into human slaughter, as was indeed the vulgar idea, in

---

[26] पुरुषो ह नारायणोऽकामयत । अतितिष्ठेयं सर्व्वाणि भूतान्यहमेवेदं सर्व्वं स्यामिति स एतं पुरुषमेधं पञ्चरात्रं यज्ञक्रतुमपश्यत्तमाहरत्तेनायजत तेनेष्ट्वात्यतिष्ठत् सर्वाणि भूतानि । इदं सर्वं भवति य एवं विद्वान् पुरुषमेधेन यजते यो वै तदेवं वेद ।

the early days of the Christian religion, deduced from the sacrament of the Lord's Supper and from the wording of the Liturgy, that the followers of Jesus sacrificed human beings and feasted on their flesh! A less revolting account is due of the sacrifices noticed in the Veda, which were probably indicative of some mysterious doctrine, originated from traditional recollections of the teaching of the *first Sacrificer* in the post-diluvian world. Noah's sacrifice met with divine acceptance, and Noah must have had some insight into the mystery of "the Lamb slain from the foundation of the world."

As to the efficacy of sacrifices in human concerns, we find these prominent ideas in the Vedas, viz.—(1) The mystical identification of the sacrificer with the victim, which is the ransom for sin; (2) Sacrifice the great remedy for the ills of life—the ship or ark by which we escape sin and all worldly perils. (3) Sacrifice the instrument by which Sin and Death are annulled and abolished.

"By the quintuple sacrificer, the animal victim is brought. The quintuple sacrifice is for heaven. The sacrificer is himself the victim.—It takes the very sacrificer himself to heaven." *Taittiriya Brahmana*, p. 202.[27]

The commentator expounds this passage thus:

"The oblation of the Agni-Shamiya animal (or victim) is the sacrificing fire. It is brought to the

---

[27] पञ्चहोता पशुमुपसादयति। सुवर्गो वै पञ्च होता। यजमानः पशुः यजमानमेव सुवर्गं लोकं गमयति।

altar by this quintuple sacrificial mantra. Its own mantra being a means of attaining to heaven, and the animal being for the redemption of the sacrificer, it leads the sacrificer himself to heaven." *Taittiriya Brahmana*, p. 448.[28]

"Because he presents the Agni-Shomiya animal, the sacrificer redeems himself from all gods ...... Even by this the sacrificer redeems himself." *Aitareya Brahmana*, p. 27.[29]

Dr. Haug cites a passage from the Kausitaki Brahmana to the same effect, viz. अग्निषोमयोर्वा एष आस्यमापद्यते यो दीक्षते तद्यदुपवसथे अग्निषोमीयं पशुमालभत आत्मनिष्क्रयणो हैवास्यैष तेन आत्मानं निष्क्रीय अनृणो भूत्वाथ यजते तस्माद् तस्य नाश्नीयात्।

He himself translates the passage thus: "He who is initiated into the sacrificial mysteries falls into the very mouth of Agni Soma (to be their food). That is the reason that the Sacrificer kills on the day previous to the Soma festival an animal being devoted to Agni-Soma, thus redeeming himself (from the obligation of being himself sacrificed). He then brings his (soma) sacrifice after having thus redeemed himself and become free from debts. Thence the sacrificer ought not to eat of the flesh of this (animal)."

2. Sacrifice is described as a ship, boat, or ark, pretty much in the same way as "the Church" in the

---

[28] अग्निषोमीयपशोर्यजुर्विस्तदग्निर्होतेत्यनेन पञ्चहोतृमन्त्रेण वेद्यामुपसादयेत्। तस्य स्वमन्त्रस्य स्वर्गसाधनत्वात् पशोश्च यजमाननिष्क्रयणार्थत्वात् यजमानमेव स्वर्गं प्रापयति।

[29] स यदग्नीषोमीयं पशुमालभते सर्व्वाभ्य एव देवताभ्यो यजमान आत्मानं निष्क्रीणीत। ... यजमानो ह्येतेनात्मानं निष्क्रीणीते।

Baptismal service,—"that they being delivered from Thy wrath may be received into the *Ark of Christ's Church*, and may *so pass the waves* of this troublesome world that they may finally come to the land of ever-lasting life, &c." In Rig Veda x. 113. 10 there is a mantra to this effect: "Give us, O Indra, multitudes of good horses with which we may offer our oblations by the repetition of the proper sentences—by the prospering of which we may escape all sins. Do thou now accept our service with much regard." "Do thou lead us safe through all sins by the way of Sacrifice." And we have in viii. 42. 3 "O illustrious Varuna, do thou quicken our understanding—we that are prac-tising this ceremony, that we may embark on the good ferrying boat by which we may escape all sins."[30] On this the Aitareya Brahmana remarks: "Sacrifice is the good ferrying boat. The black skin is the good ferrying boat. The Word is the good ferrying boat. Having embarked on the word, one crosses over to the heavenly world." *Aitareya Brahmana*, p. 10.[31]

The commentator of the *Taittiriya Sanhitá* remarks thus on the same passage: "May we also embark on

---

[30] त्वं पुरूण्याभर स्वश्व्या येभिर्मंसै निवचनानि शंसन्।
सुगेभिर्विश्वा दुरिता तरेम विदो षु ण उर्विया गाधमद्य॥
ऋतस्य नः पथा नयाति विश्वानि दुरिता R. V. x. 133. 6.
इमां धियं शिक्षमाणस्य देव क्रतुं दक्षं वरुण संशिशाधि।
ययाति विश्वा दुरिता तरेम सुतर्माणमधि नावं रुहेम॥

This is also found in the *Tándia Mahá Brahmana*, p. 294 and the *Taittiriya Sanhita*, vol. i. p. 290.

[31] यज्ञो वै सुतर्मा नौः कृष्णाजिनं वै सुतर्मा नौर्वाग्वै सुतर्मा नौः वाचमेव तदा-रुह्य तया स्वर्गं लोकमभिसन्तरति।

that safe and good ferrying boat of black skin by which we may at once get over all sins that beset us."[32] It was not unusual in those days for ferry boats to be made of leather.

The "black skin" and "the Word" above mentioned are explained in the *Satapatha Brahmana*, where "Sacrifice" is represented as retreating from the gods in a *black* form. They found it and took off its skin, and thence was produced the threefold knowledge (Veda) which, as a product of the Sacrifice, is identified with "the good ferrying boat."

"Sacrifice was retreating from the gods. It was going about in a black form. The gods having found it tore off its skin and took it. The same is the threefold knowledge, Sacrifice." *Satapatha Brahmana* p. 8.[33]

This accounts for the "boat" being assimilated with "the black skin" and "the word"—the latter two being inseparable from the "Sacrifice," which is also here declared "The threefold knowledge," otherwise called the Veda or its "word."

Another reason for assimilating the saving boat with "the word" is, that there was actually a hymn which was called *plava* "raft" or "boat," and it was to be used daily.

"The *plava* is used daily. Those who complete the

---

[32] वयमपि पारं गंतुं सर्वाणि विघ्नरूपदुरितानि यया नावा अत्यन्तं तरेम तां सुखेन तरणे समर्थामिमां कृष्णाजिनरूपां नावमधिरुहेम । p. 299.

[33] यज्ञो ह देवेभ्यो अपचक्राम स कृष्णो भूत्वा चचार तस्य देवा अनुविद्य त्वचमेवावच्छायाजह्रुः ।..सैषा त्रयी विद्या यज्ञः ।

Sanvatsara sacrifice have to dip in the Sea [so called from the "excessive depth" of the Sacrifice, according to the commentator] He who dips in the sea without a *plava* or raft never gets out of it. Where there is the *plava*, it leads to the attainment of the celestial world." *Tandia Maha Brahmana*, p. 293.[34]

3. Sacrifice has accordingly been held in all Vedic treatises as the great remedy for sins and trespasses. It is at the same time both a satisfaction for heinous and moral offences, and an atonement for trivial mistakes and transgressions. Katyayana says that Sacrifice procures heaven, and "heaven" is a word which stands for the highest happiness. The commentator of the *Taittiriya Sanhitá* tells us that it is Nirriti or the Sin-deity that is a disturber of Sacrifices.[35]

That sacrifice was held as the great means for procuring remission or annulment of sins of every description is declared in numerous passages—not only by the figures of saving boats or rafts, but literally in express terms. Witness the following formula in which, after slaughtering and cutting up the victim, the sacrificer says, as each limb is offered to the fire:

"(O thou animal limb now being consigned to the fire!) Thou art the annulment of sins committed by gods. Thou art the annulment of sins committed by the (departed) fathers. Thou art the annulment of

---

[34] प्लवो वक्ष्यं भवति। समुद्रं वा एते प्रस्नान्ति ये संवत्सरमुपयन्ति यो वा अप्लवः समुद्रं प्रस्नाति न स ततः उदेति यत् प्लवो भवति स्वर्गस्य लोकस्य समष्ट्यै।

[35] स्वर्गमन्वस्य सर्व्वात्कृष्टे सुखे रूढः—स्वर्गादिकं याथादेः फलं। निर्ऋतिं यज्ञविघातिम। *Tait. San.* p. 713.

sins committed by men. Thou art the annulment of sins committed by ourselves. Whatever sins we have committed by day or by night, thou art the annulment thereof. Whatever sins we have committed sleeping or awake, thou art the annulment thereof. Whatever sins we have committed, knowing or unknowing, thou art the annulment thereof. Thou art the annulment of sin,—of sin."[36]

The same is also the teaching of the Taittiriya Sanhita. "The animal he presents to the *Agni-soma* is his own ransom." On which the commentator says: "The presenting of the animal on the part of the Sacrificer is his own ransom. Having given the animal as a price to *Agni-soma*, he thereby redeems his own soul which had become subject to them."[37]

The Vedic argument appears to presume that "whosoever is *dikshita* or initiated in divine service, virtually devotes his soul to all the gods."[38] He can be redeemed only by a price, and the person so devoted, redeems his soul by presenting an animal as a sacrifice for himself.

But "it is not possible that the blood of bulls and of goats should take away sins." Our ancestors could

---

[36] (ये अग्नौ प्रक्षिप्यमाण मन्त्र) देवकृतस्यैनसो अवयजनमसि। पितृकृतस्यैनसो अवयजनमसि। मनुष्यकृतस्यैनसो अवयजनमसि। अस्मत्कृतस्यैनसो अवयजनमसि। यद्दिवा च नक्तंचैनश्चकृम तस्यावयजनमसि यत् स्वपन्तश्च जाग्रतश्चैनश्चकृम तस्यावयजनमसि यद्विद्वांसश्चाविद्वांसश्चैनश्चकृम तस्यावयजनमस्येनस एनसो अवयजनमसि। *Tandya Maha Brahmana*, p. 55.

[37] यदग्नीषोमीयं पशुमालभत आत्मनिष्क्रयण एवास्य सः। अथ यजमानस्य पश्वालम्भ आत्मनिष्क्रयणः। पशुं मूल्यत्वेनाग्नीषोमाभ्यां दत्वा तेन तयोः स्वभूतमात्मानं निष्क्रीणाति। vol. I. p. 369.

[38] सर्वाभ्य वा एष देवताभ्य आत्मानमालभते यो दीक्षितः।

not be entirely unconscious of that. And notwithstanding their hazy conceptions of *the scape-goat*, and of the self-sacrifice of the Lord of creatures, they felt a difficulty. The sacrificial ritual was more easily perpetuated than its meaning or purport understood, or communicated. It was difficult for recollections of the unwritten theology, on which it may have been originally founded, to be preserved in their purity from generation to generation. The ritual was held an *opus operatum.* There would be little difficulty for children to keep it up exactly as they saw their fathers perform it. The underlying doctrine in the absence of written records could not be so easily transmitted by tradition. The correct learning and correct transmission of *doctrine* always requires closer attention, and greater intellectual effort on the part both of preceptor and pupil, than the minute observation and imitation of external ceremonies. The ritual itself may have had "a shadow of good things to come, but could not with those sacrifices offered year by year make the comers thereunto perfect."

To what extent the Indo-Arians had correctly comprehended the doctrine on which sacrificial ceremonies were founded, we cannot easily guess. But we find they considered it a *mystery*, as in the following passage:—

"O death! the thousand myriads of thy bands for the destruction of mortals, we annul them all by the *maya* or mysterious power of sacrifice."[39]

---

39 ये ते सहस्रमयुतं पाशा मृत्यो मर्त्याय हन्तवे तान् यज्ञस्य मायया सर्व्वानवयजामहे। *Taittiriya Aranyaka, p.* 918.

The doctrine involved, whether the Indo-Arians rightly understood it or not, is doubtless a "mystery." Many things connected with the inscrutable will of the Almighty *must* be mysteries. The finite cannot grasp the Infinite. Whether there be any event in the history of the world's religions, capable of throwing light on Prajapati, or the Lord of creatures, *offering himself a sacrifice* for others, is a question we shall take up in the next chapter. It is manifest that the sacrificial ritual did not tranquillize the Brahmanical mind. It still brooded over theories of many kinds—it betook itself to philosophy, and even submitted to accept lessons from its hated rival Buddhism, but without any tranquillizing result. They seem to have had an idea that there must be a *really saving Sacrifice*, and that their own ritual was but its distant *reflection.*[40] We repeat an expression we have already cited above that "Prajapati, or the Lord of creatures, is Sacrifice, for he made it a reflection *(pratimá)* of himself." And he is further called "átmadá" or *giver of self*, "whose shadow, whose death, is immortality (to us)."[41]

---

[40] यज्ञो वा भवति तस्य सा छाया क्रियते । *Tandya Maha Brahmana*, Vol. i. p. 332.

[41] आत्मदा बलदाः ... यस्य छायामृतं यस्य मृत्युः Rig Veda x. 121, 2. The above refers to Hiraniagarbha, whom Sáyana identifies with Prajapati, citing the following from the Taittiriya प्रजापतिर्वै हिरण्यगर्भः । This identification is found in all later Sanscrit literature.

CHAPTER VIII.

Nature of the Vedic sacrifices,—their degeneration—Buddhism—Schools of Philosophy—Sects—Krishna-cultus.

The Vedic sacrifices, as reviewed in the last chapter, were doubtless curious and peculiar in themselves. They were not intended merely for the gratification of particular gods or supernatural powers having a relish for the fumes of fat burnt-offerings. They seem to have had a higher object in view. The limb of the victim as it was thrown into the Fire was accosted *as the annulment of sin*—not only the sacrificer's own sins, but the sins of all gods and men—that is to say, of the whole world. And along with this, we have the self-sacrifice of Prajapati, the Lord of creatures, the Purusha, begotten in the beginning of the world, out of whose limbs, as the body was cut up, sprang the different orders of men of which Indian society was composed.

Legends such as these naturally suggest the question of the origin of such conceptions in the Arian mind. Doubtless we recognize in them a hazy representation, a distorted view, of the great mystery of Christianity, *the Lamb slain from the foundation of the world*, and of the church, which was *his body*, the household of God, the spiritual society comprehending all believers. But how came the Arians to have got any insight into such a mystery so early as the age of the Vedas?

Abel's and Noah's sacrifices were accepted—the former having been so, by reason of *the sacrificer's faith*, and of the latter it is recorded that *the Lord smelt a sweet savour*. The last words are parallel to the concluding expressions in Eph. v. 2 "As Christ also hath loved us, and hath given himself for us, an offering and a sacrifice to God for A SWEET SMELLING SAVOUR." It is inconceivable that Abel's and Noah's sacrifices should be described as we find them to be, unless they were typical of the great Sacrifice mentioned in the text just cited, and unless both sacrificers were cognizant, to some extent at least, of the mystery of *the Lamb slain from the foundation of the world*. And there is no reason to suppose that either of them would put his candle under a bushel. Whatever they may have learnt by divine revelation on the subject would be naturally communicated to their children and contemporaries, and thus the teaching might somehow be transmitted to the Indo-Arian family—subject of course to such errors and distortions as were unavoidable under the circumstances. The stream of Truth is always liable to be tainted and coloured as it flows over the soil of human tradition.

Instead therefore of attributing the self-sacrifice and the immolation of the Purusha, to the *barbarous custom* of human sacrifices, of which there was hardly any trace among the Arians at so early an age, and which could not in any case account for all that is said on the subject, a better and more generous, as well as a more complete and consistent course it would be, to refer them to traditions of such divine disclosures as we have already mentioned.

Those traditions have no doubt been overlaid in India with many puerile additions, and tinctured with many arbitrary speculations, betraying a morbid fancy and a predilection for indecent and even obscene figures and images, by which their truthfulness and purity have been seriously affected.

The gold has become dim by the alloy which has been mixed up by unholy and impure hands. As far, however, as the original Vedas refer to the self-devotion of the "Lord of creatures," "begotten in the beginning," and to the primeval institution of sacrificial ceremonies as a typical "reflection" thereof, in which the sacrificer was himself the victim, they may be held, apart from subsequent concretions, to be evidences of ideas, originally pure, but afterwards debased under the corrupt suggestions of a wild imagination, in the absence of corrective influences. There are words and phrases among the citations made in the last chapter which cannot be accounted for, except as indications of something which underlay all sacrifices, such as those which Noah and Job had acceptably offered—something which related to Him *who gave His life a ransom for many*, and who was Himself the victim and Himself the priest. And so far the original legends of the Indo-Arians are in their pristine purity strongly confirmatory of a fundamental principle of Christian doctrine.

The overlaid impurities are doubtless as gross as they are numerous, but that only proves that the writers of the Vedas failed to place their traditional doctrine on the right foundation. That "other foundation can no man lay than that is laid, which is Jesus Christ,"[1] is not the dictum of an exclusive enthusiast. It is replete with most important lessons to mankind. A sound structure requires a sound foundation. *The mystery of the faith must be held in a pure conscience.*[2] The best of doctrines will fail in the hands of bad characters. True principle requires a true personality as its basis. The doctrine of the Lord of creatures' self-devotion,—of the sacrifice of Purusha "begotten in the beginning," could not be safe where the Lord of creatures and the Purusha were identified with false personalities. Purity cannot subsist with impurity. The Brahmins have not dared to attribute to Brahmá, or any other god, with whom they afterwards identified Prajápati, the self devotion and the primeval sacrifice recorded in the Vedas. Brahmá lost his credit in the Hindu pantheon for an attempt at incest, and the original teaching of the primeval sacrifice was forgotten. Like the sacred initial of the name of king Ahaz,[3] when he fell into idolatry, it was perhaps abandoned under an intuitive feeling of reverential awe. This is a suggestive warning to all who *concoct* religions. We have often heard of men

[1] 1 Cor. iii. 11. [2] 1 Tim. iii. 9. [3] See p. 96, *supra*.

instituting a religion, or forming a religious party—a society claiming to be the household of God. No such fabrication can have the sanction of Truth. It is as impossible for man to *fabricate* a household of God, as to *make* a god himself. The one is as gross idolatry as the other.

The sacrificial ceremonies of the Vedas when their original principle was placed on a wrong foundation soon became languid. They dwindled within a short time into mere mummeries. The life, which they may have possessed in the beginning, became extinct under the deleterious influences of polytheism and idolatry. The pantheon itself showed the instability of the whole system. Agni lost his position, as the doctrine of sacrifices became debased. Indra and Varuna, the great divinities of the Vedas, were superseded by other upstart gods, and the Vedas were neglected, as later compositions, written in language more popular, rose in Brahminical estimation. The Brahmins became the arbiters of society. New Sastras were concocted to enhance their dignity. Their aspirations after worldly power naturally led to contests between kings and priests. The former trusted to their bow and arrow, the latter to supernatural powers which, in that ignorant age, even royalty admitted and quailed under. The Brahminical hierarchy relying on the popular dread of maledictions uttered by priestly lips, hurled defiance against the sovereignty of princes, whenever the latter proved disobedient and refractory. The anathema of Brahmins would haunt the priest-ridden minds of Khettriyas by day and by night, if ever they incurred sacerdotal wrath. The legend of Haris Chandra who had consented to sell his queen and his only son, the heir-apparent of his throne, and had also submitted his own self to the vilest of servitudes, merely to avert the consequences of a priest's resentment, bears conclusive evidence of the extent to which Brahminical ascendancy had risen.

But, to borrow an idea from our indigenous poets, there is always a limit to rise and fall in all worldly affairs, as *in the motion of a chariot wheel.* As a spoke or a point in the tire ascends by that motion, it can only attain a certain height, and then it must tend downwards. The moon herself verifies this maxim by her phases. She wanes after waxing to her fulness. The Brahminical ascendancy was no exception to this rule. In the very royal line to which Haris Chandra had himself belonged, a prince at length arose, determined to dissolve the spell by which the popular mind was bound in servitude to the Brahmins. "S'ákya Muni imposed on himself the task of reforming the religion of his country. He cared not, like Vis'wámitra, for promotion to the Brahminical College—nor, like Janaka, for occasional participation in their exclusive privileges—nor yet for inflicting such temporary humiliation on the priestly order, as was implied in Rámachandra's triumph over Parusa'ráma. Disgusted, when young, with the evils of disease and death, he renounced the pleasures of dignity and royalty, and went about preaching every where on the necessity of seeking for Nirváṇa, or release from transmigrations, as the only remedy for the evils of life. He pronounced the rites and ceremonies of the Veda to be idle sports, and the exclusive privileges arrogated by the Brahmins, to be empty pretensions. He assailed the authority of the very books on which those pretensions were founded. He declared that the division of castes was a mere human invention, and invited all ranks to assemble under his banners on a footing of equality. The Brahmins add that he also denied the immortality of the soul, and pronounced the expectation of a future world to be a vain reverie.[4] Whether Buddhism was really liable to the charge of materialism preferred against it by the Brahmins, or not, it certainly had no divine revelation to plead for its support, nor could it appeal to any tradition in its favour. It could only stand on its *rational* pretensions. The study of philosophy and metaphysics was therefore absolutely needed for its very existence. So long as men believed in the infallibility of the Veda, they could appeal to its texts for the decision of controversies and the solution of doubts. But when revelation was ignored, disputes could only be settled by the verdict of *reason*. The necessities of Buddhism rendered the cultivation of logic and metaphysics absolutely indispensable, and thus were the first attempts at philosophy called forth in India. Hence it was that the terms *Haituka* and

---

[*] न स्वर्गो नापवर्गो वा नैवात्मा पारलौकिकः। नैव वर्णाश्रमादीनां क्रियाश्च फलदायिकाः। अग्निहोत्रं त्रयो वेदास्त्रिदण्डं भस्मगुण्ठनम्। *Sarvadars'ana Sangraha.*

Hetu-S'ástra were applied to heretical systems." (*From the author's Dialogues on the Hindu Philosophy*, p. 47.)

Buddhism was, however, a mere *negative* system. Its strong weapons were those of opposition to Brahminical tenets which had fallen into disrepute. It inveighed against the purposeless doctrine of sacrifices, as it then presented itself in the forgetfulness of its original principles. It condemned the wanton destruction of animal life which the ceremonies involved without any redeeming feature in their objects. Its declamation against caste found an echo in the hearts of men, whose aspirations after social progress and personal advancement had been checked by it. Buddhism prospered for a time owing to the rebound of the popular mind against Brahminical ascendancy.

The Brahmins, however, by timely concessions on some points, and opposing logic to logic in other points, managed adroitly to regain their ascendancy, and by stigmatizing their adversaries as unprincipled infidels and atheists who only fomented disaffection, but had nothing new to inculcate in their teaching, succeeded in ridding the country of their formidable rivals. Their consummate policy in complimenting the founder of Buddhism as an incarnation of Vishnu, destined for the inculcation of heresy among the Daitias, or open opponents of the gods, succeeded in quietly banishing the enemy from Indian territory to regions where they cared not to pursue him. But Buddhism, though expelled from India, left unmistakeable traces of its anti-vedic rationalism on the field it abandoned. It had so successfully infected the Brahminical mind itself, that the work of destruction it had initiated was, after its overthrow, briskly carried on by champions of orthodoxy themselves. The seed it had sown, broad cast, had fallen largely in the Brahmin's own camp, and were bearing the fruits which S'ákya Muni had himself desiderated. Brahmins were indeed still respected, because they took pains to maintain their personal credit, but their teaching was inspired, not by allegiance to the Veda, but by a spirit of treason against its ritual—far more dangerous than Buddhism itself, because decidedly more insidious. Reverence there was but little for the Sastra, while its ceremonies were denounced as fruitless shams, and the enemy's own dogma of "Nirvána," or the *summum bonum*, was openly propounded as the highest object of sentient beings. The only difference was that the Brahmins taught absorption into Brahma, whereas the Buddhists had inculcated absorption into Buddha.

The bulk of the *twice born* classes, however, could not comprehend the transcendental logic by which "Nirvána," or annihilation, as they understood the term, was argued out as the chief end of human nature. They had been long accustomed to a theology, which with all its imperfections, had at least clearly laid down the practical duties expected from its followers. They could not therefore now rest satisfied with the dogmas of a Philosophy which demolished everything, but taught nothing, and only amused the fancy with hair-splitting subtleties leading to no intelligible results. And in reality they saw no appreciable difference between Buddhism and the

Brahminical schools of philosophy. Both were accordingly stigmatized as "Haituka" or *rational* Sastras, teeming with pernicious heresy.[5]

The rationalistic tactics which Buddhism itself had taught the Brahmins, and which had served effective instruments in their hands as against that hated system, did not, however, avail much to their credit with their own followers. The unsophisticated mind of Indian society became as discontented with the objectless Philosophy which had overturned Buddhism, as it had been with the pointless ceremonies which had provoked the rebellion of S'ákya Singha. And it was under the influence of these complications that Indian theology began to present a new phase, and brought on a new epoch which we shall designate *the epoch of Faith.*

---

[5] Siva, the god of destruction, is represented as acknowledging to his wife that he had himself, in the disguise of a Brahmin, inculcated, for the destruction of the world, the different systems of Hindu philosophy, which were all undilulated Buddhism under a false garb. These were wholly intended to promote atheism and the abolition of sacrificial rites and ceremonies. Thus:

शृणु देवि प्रवक्ष्यामि तामसानि यथाक्रमम्। येषां श्रवणमात्रेण पातित्यं ज्ञानिनामपि॥ प्रथमं हि मयैवोक्तं शैवं पाशुपतादिकं। मच्छक्त्यावेशितैर्विप्रैः सम्प्रोक्तानि ततः परम्॥ कणादेन तु सम्प्रोक्तं शास्त्रं वैशेषिकं महत्। गौतमेन तथा न्यायं सांख्यं तु कापिलेन वै॥ द्विजन्मना जैमिनिना पूर्वं वेदमयार्थतः। निरीश्वरेण वादेन कृतं शास्त्रं महत्तरम्॥ धिषणेन तथा प्रोक्तं चार्वाकमतिगर्हितम्। दैत्यानां नाशनार्थाय विष्णुना बुद्धरूपिणा॥ बौद्धशास्त्रमसत् प्रोक्तं नग्ननीलपटादिकम्। मायावादमसच्छास्त्रं प्रच्छन्नं बौद्धमेव च॥ मयैव कथितं देवि कलौ ब्राह्मणरूपिणा। अपार्थं श्रुतिवाक्यानां दर्शयल्लोकगर्हितम्॥ कर्मस्वरूपत्याज्यत्वमत्र च प्रतिपाद्यते। सर्वकर्मपरिभ्रंशान्नैष्कर्म्यं तत्र चोच्यते॥ परात्मजीवयोरैक्यं मयात्र प्रतिपाद्यते।" ब्रह्मणोऽस्य परं रूपं निर्गुणं दर्शितं मया॥ सर्वस्य जगतोऽप्यस्य नाशनार्थं कलौ युगे। वेदार्थवन्महाशास्त्रं मायावादमवैदिकम्॥ मयैव कथितं देवि जगतां नाशकारणात्। *Padma Purána.*

The new phase which Indian theology presented was that *of a personal divine objectivity*. The ritualistic phase was that of ceremonies gone through according to prescribed forms with or without reference to any personal object. The presence of a god could not be necessary for ceremonies which were declared to have been instituted before the generation of Devas. Prajápati initiated the Sacrifice prior to the Creation, and Creation was itself anterior to the production of gods. Those ceremonies, again, were practised by Rishís who openly denied or doubted the very existence of a Supreme Being.

This ritualistic blank was by no means remedied by the aphorisms of the Schools of Philosophy which depreciated all ceremonies in the lump, as inferior means of grace, and directed attention to transcendental notions, but ill adapted to the hopes and wants of human nature. The disappearance of Buddhism from the plains of Hindustan did not therefore tranquillize the Indian mind at all. It rather produced fresh groanings for the satisfaction of mental cravings, fresh aspirations, for something better than "sushka tarka," or pointless logic and dry speculation. This was attempted to be supplied by the founders and leaders of separate religious Sects among the followers of Brahminism.

Spiritual cravings had even reached the Sudras or the servant class. The Brahmins had debarred them from all religious privileges, and had gone the length of questioning the propriety of their attending to any other duty than the service of the three other classes, and of denying their fitness for religious exercises of any kind. That this was not a mere speculative theory, is proved by the sad case of Sambuca, a Sudra who was engaged in certain devotional performances, on the bank of a river, in the reign of Rama, after his return from Lanka. It is said that the whole kingdom was placed under the bann of divine displeasure, because of a serf's audacious attempt to get admission to the society of the gods. Untimely deaths began to take place even among the children of Brahmins, for which the king himself was held officially responsible. The son of Dasaratha could not gainsay the ethical logic of the age by which the head of the State was held answerable for national calamities, supposed to proceed from national sins, known or unknown. He went out, sword in hand, to explore the cause of the public calamity. He soon found it in the religious exercises performed by Sambuca in the open air, and in vindication of the law to which society was subject, and as an expiation of the national offence involved in the transgression of that law by the offending Sudra, struck off his head by a single blow.

But Buddhism had laid upon all classes the obligation of religious duties, and consequently accorded to the Sudras their much coveted liberty of engaging in religious exercises. This was a franchise which the servant class was now unwilling to surrender. The religious franchise virtually involved secular freedom. The founders of religious sects, under Brahminical auspices, accordingly received all men indiscriminately as members of their *spiritual guilds.* These were principally devoted to Vishnu, Siva or Sakti. The most popular guild was that of Vishnu.[6]

These religious *guilds* proclaimed faith and devotion to their respective deities as the all-absorbing duties of mankind—the shortest, if not the only, path to eternal salvation. It was the guild of Vishnu that attracted the greatest notice, and it was Krishna-cultus that mustered the largest number of devotees. So that the original ceremonies of the Vedas led, step by step, to the worship of Krishna as the consummation of Arian ideals.

The personal character of the presiding god of the Vaishnava guild, however, was not such as an educated and intelligent community may be proud of. In fact with men of position and social distinction, however devoted they may externally appear to Krishna, the policy generally is, *less said about his character, the better.*

Foreigners have not, however, been so prudent. They have boldly rushed into grounds which devout Hindus have trembled to tread. A divine exaltation has daringly been argued for Krishna, such as his intelligent votaries have not themselves attempted, nor any native scholar that cares for the reputation of an

---

[6] The Brahmins, without surrendering their own dignity or entirely rescinding the caste obligations of Sudras, absolved those who might attach themselves to the Vaishnava guild. त्यक्त्वा स्वधर्मं चरणाम्बुजं हरेर्भजन्नपक्वोऽथ पतेत्ततो यदि । यत्र क्व वाभद्रमभूदमुष्य किं को वार्थ आप्तो भजतां स्वधर्मतः ॥ *Sri Bhagavata.*

educated man of the nineteenth century. A French writer[7] has actually maintained that the Bible was but a piracy of the Hindu Sastras, and Christ a caricature of Krishna. Had such ideas been broached under the responsibility of a Hindu author of any literary reputation, it would have been incumbent on us to discuss the question in detail. But we are unwilling to take up a French gauntlet, and wade through the mire of *Bal*-Krishna's feats as described in works like the Sribhágavata and Jayadeva's songs. Such a task might bring us under the penalty of the law for the conservation of public decency, and it would amount to a gross unprovoked assault on Vaishnava feeling itself. We cannot acknowledge M. Jacollet as the plenipotentiary of the *guild* of Vishnu, unless he can produce his credentials. We proceed, however, to remark generally on the sects or guilds of especial divinities, and to trace the origin of *Krishna-cultus*, according to the representations of the Hindu records themselves. Without going into the merits of M. Jacollet's speculations, we shall simply put forth a *plea in bar*, by attempting to show that those speculations are *historically* inadmissible.

The sects established by the followers of special deities, and, in particular, by those who maintained the worship of Krishna, bear curious testimony to the Christian doctrine of *faith* as opposed to ceremonial works. But this testimony is somewhat different in its features from the confirmatory evidence of the

---

[7] M. Jacollet.

Vedas to facts in Sacred history and to the primitive institution of Sacrifices—indicative of *the Lamb slain from the foundation of the world.* These are independent Arian testimonies to facts disclosed by a primeval revelation, the heritage of all mankind alike. Such facts were preserved in the traditions of the nation itself, without borrowing them from without. We cannot say that when Rishis laid such stress on the performance of sacrifices as THE *great duty*, क्रिया यज्ञः they owed the idea to Mosaic. instruction. There is no evidence for holding that the Brahmins had ever gone to Palestine for religious tuition, or that Jews had travelled to disseminate their doctrines in Ariana. The Brahmins knew of it, like the pre-Mosaic fathers named in the Bible, as a relic of unwritten primitive Revelation. They had received it as a national heritage, having heard of the doctrine traditionally—and therefore was it that they used the word "Sruti," or *hearing*, as a general term for such primitive unwritten Revelation. The four Vedas into which the Sruti was afterwards classified, and written down, became the recognized Scriptures of the country. We have no reason to doubt that parts of those Scriptures were the correct *Smriti*, or recollections, of the original *Sruti* or traditional report of a real primitive Revelation—the common inheritance of all mankind, faintly disclosing the future dispensations of the Divine Ruler of the Universe.

But the Hindu testimonies to the doctrine of faith are of another kind. The dispensation of ceremonial works was revealed from the beginning, and although glimpses of the dispensation of Faith were doubtless also shared in by those who had got a conception of the god-man Saviour, to appear in due time and dwell among men for the destruction of the devil and his works, yet the doctrine of Faith in an *ishta-devatá* is one of later development, according to the confession of the Sastras themselves. Long had our forefathers patiently kept up the primitive institution of sacrifices and other ceremonies. But those practices had not satisfied their spiritual longings. Buddha arose, and, by persistently decrying those ceremonies, did much to impair their credit. But the doctrines and precepts which he inculcated were simple negations, and the result was the promotion of a subtle spirit of metaphysical discussion which could impart to the mind no more of relief or tranquillity than the effete sacrifices themselves. Some fresh impetus, some fresh movement must have taken place in order to produce results which shall now speak for themselves as apparent from the Hindu Scriptures.

The first point to which we are desirous of directing attention is an anecdote or adventure of the divine sage, Nárada, the son of Brahmá, who figures prominently in all later Hindu Sastras. The anecdote is found in the *Mahábhárata*, introduced by a question which Yudishthira puts to Bhishma: "Tell me, revered father, what gods must a person serve who wishes to attain perfection of bliss—whether he be a householder, or a student, an eremite, or a mendicant? ......Who is the god of gods and the father of fathers? Who again is superior to HIM—(*i. e.* supreme above all)? Bhishma replies, "You ask me a question concerning a mystery which cannot be unravelled by argument or logic, even if discussed for hundreds of years, nor without the comprehension of knowledge through divine grace can this deep mystery be unfolded to you."[8] Bhishma then refers to a dialogue between the incarnate Nárâyana and Nárada, in which the latter had inquisitively remarked, "We do not know what god or father YOU worship."[9]

Nárâyana then speaks of the supreme Spirit, ineffable and incomprehensible, adding that those who contemplate Him with fixed minds as the ONE object of meditation become unified with Him. Nárada, under divine direction, goes to Mount Meru for a vision of that supreme Spirit. "Looking to the north-west of that mountain he obtained that wonderful vision. To the north of the ocean of milk, at a distance, as poets make out, of more than 4,56,000 miles from Meru, there was a large continent, by the name of "White."... There lived white people without sensuousness, without food, without twinkling, being themselves of well-perfuming savour, and freed from all sin, whose very sight takes away the eyes of sinful

---

[8] युधिष्ठिर उवाच। गृहस्थो ब्रह्मचारी वा वानप्रस्थोऽथ भिक्षुकः। य इच्छेत् सिद्धिमास्थातुं देवता का यजेत सः॥ ... देवतानां च को देवः पितॄणां च पिता तथा। तस्मात् परतो यश्च तन्मे ब्रूहि पितामह॥ भीष्म उवाच। गूढं मां प्रश्नवित् प्रश्नं पृच्छसे त्वमिहानघ। न ह्येतत्तर्कया शक्यं वक्तुं वर्षशतैरपि॥ ऋते देवप्रसादाद्वा राजन् ज्ञानागमेन वा। गहनं ह्येतदाख्यानं व्याख्यातव्यं तवारिहन्॥ *Mahábhárata, Santiparva, chap.* 336.

[9] कं त्वद्य यजसे देव पितरं कं न विद्महे। *Ibid.*

men (by their dazzling brightness)."[10] It is repeated in an address from the same god to other Rishis: "You, full of devotion, desire to know where you may get a sight of the Lord? North of the ocean of milk is a continent called "White." The men of that place, resplendent as the moon, are votaries of Nárâyana. Single-minded, they are devoted to the most Excellent Purusha (person). Those men, inhabitants of the White continent, are called Ekantins, (or monotheists). Go there, ye Rishis—there is our spirit manifested."[11]

The "Excellent purusha" was no other than Krishna. He is in this very anecdote identified with the son of Vasudeva. We do not, however, pretend to such familiarity with geography as might enable us to identify the locality of the *White continent* at the alleged distance from Mount Meru. We leave it to learned *savants* to fix its situation on the globe, and to determine the number of ciphers in the given distance to be carried to the account of *poetic license.* As for Mount Meru itself, we may make bold to say, that the geography and topography of no place are at this moment more familiar to the foreign offices of both

---

[10] आलोकयन्नुत्तरपश्चिमेन ददर्श चाप्यद्भुतमुक्तरूपं। क्षीरोदधेरुत्तरतो हि द्वीपः। श्वेतः स नाम्ना प्रथितो विशालः॥ मेरोः सहस्रैः स हि योजनानां द्वात्रिंशतोर्द्ध्वं कविभिर्निरुक्तं। अतीन्द्रियाश्चानशनाश्च तत्र निष्पन्दहीनाः सुसुगन्धिनश्च। श्वेताः पुमांसो गतसर्वपापाश्चक्षुर्मुषः पापकृतां नराणां॥ *Ibid, chap.* 337.

[11] यूयं जिज्ञासवो भक्ता कथं द्रक्ष्यथ तं विभुं। क्षीरोदधेरुत्तरतः श्वेतद्वीपो महाप्रभः॥ तत्र नारायणपरा मानवाश्चन्द्रवर्चसः। एकान्तभावोपगतास्ते भक्ताः पुरुषोत्तमं॥ एकान्तिनस्ते पुरुषाः श्वेतद्वीपनिवासिनः। गच्छध्वं तत्र मुनयस्तत्रात्मा मे प्रकाशितः॥ *Ibid, chap.* 338.

European and Asiatic states, than those of *Merv*. But our business is with Nárada and the glorious vision of the Supreme Being of which he had a glimpse from the heights of Meru. We therefore turn now to his interview with the author of the Puranas and Vedant philosophy, presumably after his return from Meru.

In the Sribhagavat, which according to Professor Wilson, was written in the 12th century of the Christian era, its author is introduced sitting, pensively, in the shade of a noble peepul tree, on the bank of a river, one lovely morning, when the delicate breeze and the beauteous scenery were regaling every heart but his. There the divine sage Nárada, in whose ken had *swam* the fair land of the "White continent," encountered the author of the eighteen Puranas and of the Brahma Sutras, in a sad disconsolate posture, at a time when everything else was gay and cheerful. He inquired affectionately after the cause of his pensiveness: "Your wonderful researches have all succeeded. You have composed the Mahábhárata, replete with great objects of investigation. You have studied and inquired of the eternal Brahma. And yet, O Lord, you are grieving your soul as if you had failed in your pursuits!"[12]

Vyasa accepts the compliment, appreciates the kindness of the inquiry, confesses his uneasiness,

---

12 जिज्ञासितं सुसम्पन्नमपि ते महदद्भुतं ।
कृतवान् भारतं यस्त्वं सर्व्वार्थपरिबृंहितं ॥
जिज्ञासितमधीतञ्च ब्रह्म यत्तत्सनातनं ।
तथापि शोचस्यात्मानमकृतार्थ इव प्रभो ॥

protests his ignorance of the cause, and asks if Nárada could give the diagnosis of his melancholy.[13]

Nárada replies: "You have almost ignored the unspotted glory of the Lord. That Darsana or philosophy, which is not grateful to Him, I count for nothing. You have not celebrated the glory of the son of Vasudeva in the same manner as you have described Dharma or ritualistic ceremonies."[14]

If human language have any meaning, the foregoing statement is an admission that down to the 12th century of our era (certainly not earlier than the 8th century) the glory of Krishna, the son of Vasudeva, had not been duly celebrated, nor the doctrine of faith as opposed to ceremonial observances introduced. Nárada, who had been vouchsafed a vision of the Lord in the Fair land *of the Whites*, at a considerable distance north-west of Mount Meru, now warns the founder of the Vedant School, and the author of the Brahma Sutras, of the futility of philosophical speculations, which are not grateful to the Lord, the Saviour of the world, and moves him to recount His acts which accordingly he did in the Sríbhagavata.

Again in a work of great authority called after that very sage, the "Nárada Pancharátra," written, perhaps, about 800 years after Christ, the same Vyasa

---

[13] अस्त्येव मे सर्व्वमिदं त्वयोक्तं तथापि नात्मा परितुष्यते मे।
तन्मूलमव्यक्तमगाधबोधं पृच्छामहे त्वात्मभवात्मभूतं॥

[14] भवतानुदितप्रायं यशो भगवतोऽमलं।
येनैवासौ न तुष्येत मन्ये तद्दर्शनं खिलं॥
यथा धर्म्मादयश्चार्थो मुनिवर्य्यानुकीर्त्तिताः।
न तथा वासुदेवस्य महिमा ह्यनुवर्णितः॥

is introduced telling his son Suka-Deva that Nárada was on one occasion practising some austere devotion, when suddenly he heard a voice from heaven:

"If Hari (Krishna) is worshipped, what is the use of austerities? If Hari is not worshipped, what is the use of austerities? If Hari is within and without, what is the use of austerities? If Hari is not within and without, what is the use of austerities? Stop, stop, O Brahmin! Why do you engage in austerities? Go, O Brahmin! do go quickly to Siva the ocean of knowledge. Get, oh get, matured faith in Hari, as described by the guild of Vishnu, the splitter and snapper of the fetters of the world."[15]

We are thus led to the very genesis of the doctrine of faith in Hinduism. It was admittedly not an excogitation of the Brahminical mind itself. Nárada had brought it from the land of Whites where he got an insight into Vishnu, the Saviour, (identified with Krishna) which was not attainable elsewhere. He then persuaded the author of the Sribhágavata to recount the Lord's acts, and that work we actually find to be conspicuous for its history of Krishna, and enforcement of faith in his divinity—and we have again a voice

---

15 आराधितो यदि हरिस्तपसा ततः किं।
नाराधितो यदि हरिस्तपसा ततः किं॥
अन्तर्वहिर्यदि हरिस्तपसा ततः किं।
नान्तर्वहिर्यदि हरिस्तपसा ततः किं॥
विरम विरम ब्रह्मन् किं तपस्यासु वत्स।
व्रज व्रज द्विज शीघ्रं शङ्करं ज्ञानसिन्धुं॥
लभ लभ हरिभक्तिं वैष्णवोक्तां सुपक्वां।
भवनिगडनिबन्धच्छेदनीं कर्त्तनीं च॥

from heaven, directing Nárada to give up all ceremonial works, and betake himself to the Faith as it is in Hari—which means *the taker away of sins*. Change the name, and it is almost prime Christian doctrine.

Few will impugn the inference that, however small the element of *historical* veritableness may have been in the story of the "Ekantins," north-west of Mount Meru, it certainly appears to have had *some modicum* of truth for its basis. Fewer still will deny that the religion of that people was a form of Christianity which might be called "Ekantin," without reference to the strict orthodoxy of the form. And thus we have the Hindu Sastras themselves teaching the reverse of their Gallic champion's position. Not that the Bible was a piracy of the Indian Scriptures, but that the Vaishnava sastras by their own acknowledgement have accepted light from Christian sources, and used the same in brightening the colour imparted to their personation of Krishna as some compensation for the dark hue of his *Braja-lila*.

This inference is further confirmed by the ascertained fact that the first Vaishnava sect arose in the South of India, under the leadership of Rámánuja, who had his seat at Conjeveram, (or "Kanchipur" as we of Northern India call it), and that in the very South of India, Christianity was introduced at an early period, probably by some pious ecclesiastics of Syria.

We do not say, we have no right to say, that the Syrian Christians in the South, now certainly in a very degenerate condition, have ever produced any influence on their Hindu neighbours. But human experience will concur with the Scriptural adage, that "the wind bloweth where it listeth, and thou hearest the sound thereof, but canst not tell whence it cometh, and whither it goeth: so is every one that is born of the Spirit." We can only observe and mark results. We have seen (1) that the vision of "Purushottam," identified with Krishna, and still the prevailing designation in Orissa of "Jagarnatha," appeared in a land of *white people*, a glimpse of it being vouchsafed to Nárada on the heights of Meru, (2) that Vyása had not sung Krishna's praises until long after the beginning of the Christian era, and then only on the expostulation of Nárada, (3) that the doctrine of *Faith*, as opposed to ceremonial works, was equally unknown in India, until, according to a Vaishnava Sastra of high repute, it was communicated, at a much later period than the rise of Christianity, by a voice from heaven addressed to Nárada, (4) that the first sect adopting Krishna-cultus and the same doctrine of faith appeared at a still later period in the South of India, and (5) that it was in the South of India itself that Christianity was in an early age introduced by Syrian ecclesiastics. These are facts. We do not prescribe any deduction from these facts. We only chronicle the facts. We leave the deduction in the hands of the reader.

THE END.